Parallel Lines

Parallel Lines

POST-9/11 AMERICAN CINEMA

GUY WESTWELL

WALLFLOWER PRESS
LONDON & NEW YORK

A Wallflower Press Book
Published by
Columbia University Press
Publishers Since 1893
New York • Chichester, West Sussex
cup.columbia.edu

A complete CIP record is available from the Library of Congress

ISBN 978-0-231-17202-8 (cloth : alk. paper)
ISBN 978-0-231-17203-5 (pbk. : alk. paper)
ISBN 978-0-231-85072-8 (e-book)

Cover image: *Zero Dark Thirty* (2012) © Annapurna Pictures
Cover design: Elsa Mathern

Columbia University Press books are printed on permanent
and durable acid-free paper.
This book is printed on paper with recycled content.
Printed in the United States of America

c 10 9 8 7 6 5 4 3 2 1
p 10 9 8 7 6 5 4 3 2 1

Contents

Acknowledgements

Federico, this book is for you and describes some of the things that happened in the decade before you arrived.

I am extremely grateful to Yoram Allon, Neil Calloway, Vinet Campbell, Dr Jack Holland, Sebastian Horn, Nadia Khan, Athena Mandis, Daniel Robson, Salvatore Salafia, Dr Rick Saull, Dr Rachele Tardi, Maren Thom, Joe Ursell, Professor Cynthia Weber, the staff of the Humanities Two reading room in the British Library, my wonderful colleagues at Queen Mary and the MA Film Studies classes of 2008–09 and 2013–14. Professor Annette Kuhn and Dr Nick Jones offered editing support that was above and beyond the call of duty. Of course, any errors of substance or presentation remain my own.

As always, I extend my most heartfelt gratitude and love to Debora Marletta.

Introduction

On 11 September 2001, terrorists hijacked four passenger planes and used them as weapons against civilian targets in the US. Two of the planes were flown into each of the Twin Towers of the World Trade Center in New York, another was flown into the Pentagon in Washington, DC, and the fourth crashed in Pennsylvania. A total of 2,948 people were killed as a result of the attacks, including over 400 police officers and firefighters.[1] The attacks produced a series of spectacular and shocking images – the planes flying into the buildings, people jumping to their deaths, lower Manhattan disappearing into an apocalyptic cloud of ash and dust – and prompted an outpouring of uncertainty, anger, patriotism and grief that shaped the first decade of the twenty-first century in US culture and politics. In the days following the attacks political leaders walked the rubble of Ground Zero, rallying rescue and construction workers and building a consensus in support of war. By early October, Afghanistan, a nation accused of harbouring members of al-Qaida ('The Base'), the terrorist organisation responsible for the attacks, was bombed and invaded, heralding the beginning of over a decade of continuous war. Within weeks, wide-ranging legislation was introduced in the US that dramatically expanded federal government power and endorsed widespread surveillance measures at home and abroad. The legacy of these events, or simply '9/11', as the attacks and the events that followed quickly became known, has been considerable. David Simpson claims that 9/11 has 'both reproduced and refigured culture' (2006: 18), and Richard Gray considers the events 'a defining element in our contemporary structure of feeling' (2009: 129). Thirteen years after the attacks, and with a particular focus on US cinema, it is the aim of this book to examine the reproduction and refiguration of US popular culture post-9/11.[2]

Mark Redfield describes the use of the abbreviation '9/11' as 'a blank little scar around which nationalist energies could be marshalled' (2009: 1), and it is these 'nationalist energies' as they shape post-9/11 cinema that I wish to describe. In an age of globalisation, high immigration, rapid technological change and the fragmentation of political consensus, the concept of national identity is contested; but I will argue that it remains useful. The work of Benedict Anderson describes the synthetic and relatively recent 'invention' of the modern nation state and the ways in which national identity results not just from the establishment of territorial borders but also as a result of the cultivation of a history, tradition and culture based on shared attitudes, habits, feelings and assumptions (1983: 111). A key aspect of Anderson's argument is that modern communications (in his case the print media, in my case the cinema) are essential in creating this 'imagined community' among strangers from a disparate range of geographical, social and ethnic backgrounds (1983: 46). More prescriptively, David Miller offers five facets to any given national identity: first, a shared belief and mutual commitment; second, a sense of shared history; third, a particular territory; fourth, an active participation in the community; and fifth, a distinct public culture (1995: 21–47). Similarly, Stanley Allen Renshon claims that national identity is predicated on shared

> ways of seeing and understanding the world, the use of language and the cultural frames embedded in it, and the web of relationships and experiences that provide the internal skeleton upon which later external experience is built. (2005: 3)

As these different models show, the imagined community within a particular time and place is brought together through lived experience meshing with social practice. The cinema is a form of cultural production in which Miller's different facets can be seen to reinforce one another: films distributed over a national territory, audiences actively seeking out and participating in a distinct public culture, the regimens of genre and the cycles of entertainment responding to the audience's preferences and shared historical reference points, and so on. Mette Hjort and Scott MacKenzie write that

> individual films will often serve to represent the national to itself, as a nation. Inserted into the general framework of the cinematic

experience, such films will construct imaginary bonds which work to hold the peoples of a nation together as a community by dramatising their current fears, anxieties, pleasures and aspirations [and as a result those in a given society are] thus invited to recognise themselves as a singular body with a common culture. (2000: 6)

Conceptualised this way, individual characters act as ciphers for different ideological positions, with narratives seeking resolution for conflict and contradiction within the story of the nation, and with viewers offered specific points of view and modes of identification that shape and steer them to interpret events according to the wider national narrative. The findings of a Harris poll commissioned by the Bradley Project on America's National Identity in 2007 showed that 84 per cent of those surveyed believed that there is a unique US national identity based on shared beliefs and values, and 76 per cent of respondents reported that despite the great ethnic diversity in the US there is still a uniquely American culture. My argument in this book is that this strong investment in the idea of the nation can be related to the events of 9/11 and a number of films that evidence a making, unmaking and remaking of US national identity in the decade following the terrorist attacks.

The 'imagined community' being described in this book is that of the US, which since the struggle for independence from British colonial rule in the eighteenth century has established a raft of shared attitudes, habits, feelings and assumptions. Describing this 'imagined community' in just a few paragraphs is a challenge, but one way to approach this challenge is to consider US national identity as predicated on three interrelated realms of experience, with each realm having its own specific history and complex set of relations with the other realms. First, many early settlers who travelled to North America in the seventeenth and eighteenth centuries did so to escape religious persecution and as a result maintained a firm commitment to a particular faith – primarily Protestantism, but also Catholicism and Judaism – and to the freedom to express their religious beliefs. Many of these early settlers were also driven by a strong providential sensibility that imagined America as a promised land and placed them, as a religiously distinct group *and* as nascent Americans, in the role of God's chosen people. With time, these two facets of US national identity, grounded in religious belief and historical experience, shaped political institutions, popular culture and social practices in the form of a strong commitment to faith and to freedom (of religion, of speech, and in a more general idealistic sense). Second, alongside these religiously rooted sensibilities, the revolutionary struggle for independence from British colonial rule in the eighteenth century resulted in the drafting of a framework for national self-determination using the political and philosophical principles of the Enlightenment, especially those of universal rights, egalitarianism and liberalism (as well as fear of executive power). With time, this struggle resulted in the establishment of political institutions founded on democratic principles and republican federalism. From a different point of origin to that of religious persecution and providence, these experiences further compounded a commitment to freedom in a political sense, as well as a commitment to a series of checks and balances across the political system. Together, carried by settlers and lawmakers, these impulses shaped the further settlement of the North American continent, thus grounding the idea of American exceptionalism and Manifest Destiny in the historical narrative of the nation and fostering a rich, culturally specific mythology. Third, throughout the history of discovery, settlement, colonisation, the struggle for independence and the move west, capitalism has provided the primary mode of economic and industrial organisation. In different forms, from colonial mercantilism and slavery in the early period, through monopoly capitalism in the early twentieth century, to neoliberal variants in the late twentieth century, capitalism has formed a structural base for a society that endorses the market and rewards risk-taking, competition, speculation, entrepreneurialism, innovation and the pursuit of profit in ways that underpin and inflect the previous two realms.

Writing in 1917, and attempting to somehow capture the spirit of a distinct US national identity resulting from these three realms of experience, William Tyler Page published the American's Creed – a ubiquitous feature of US civic life that is still used as part of the naturalisation and citizenship ceremonies undertaken by those wishing to become US citizens. The Creed reads:

> I believe in the USA as a Government of the people, by the people, for the people, whose just powers are derived from the consent of the governed; a democracy in a republic; a sovereign Nation of many sovereign states; a perfect union, one and inseparable; established upon those principles of freedom, equality, justice, and humanity for which American patriots sacrificed their lives and fortunes. I therefore believe it is my duty to my country to love it; to support its Constitution; to obey its laws; to respect its flag; and to defend it against all enemies. (Quoted in Renshon 2005: 60)

Introduction

Renshon observes that Page's Creed is predicated on political principles but also implicitly acknowledges historical process and the necessity of strong emotional – even existential – attachment, and that this evinces how the US 'imagined community' is bound by a combination of abstract ideas, the memory of violent historical struggle and lived experience.

It is, of course, necessary to question this rather too neat and tidy account, but first I wish to explore how this conventional sense of national identity played a role in the initial response to 9/11: indeed, how 9/11 might be said to have brought fully into focus – to literally have 'made' – this version of national identity (after a lengthy period of contestation). For example, during the reporting of the terrorist attacks the caption on the US television news channel CNN read simply 'America under attack': a clear indication of how the attacks were presented as something that threatened the nation, collectively and without differentiation. Similarly, the pronouncements of shared feelings of national shock made by news presenters – often utilising the collective identifiers 'we' and 'us' – indicated how viewers were asked to imagine themselves as belonging to a unified national community threatened by external forces. The US flag, known colloquially as the Stars and Stripes, was the most visible symbol of this spirit of national togetherness. Wal-Mart reportedly sold 116,000 flags on 9/11 and 250,000 the following day (see Huntington 2004: 3), and the flag appeared as television logos, on tie pins worn by news presenters, and flew over public buildings, private businesses and private homes: the flag's ubiquity signalled the widespread activation of a deep-seated patriotism.

On 12 September 2001 a photograph taken by Thomas E. Franklin, and subsequently labelled *Ground Zero Spirit*, was published in *The Bergen Record* and then syndicated to newspapers and broadcast on national television. The photograph, also published on the cover of *Newsweek* on 24 September, shows three firefighters raising the Stars and Stripes amidst the ruins of the World Trade Center, thereby offering its viewers an image of heroism, bravery and, considering the deaths of a large number of rescue workers, self-sacrifice. The sentiment of Page's American's Creed, in which 'American patriots sacrifice their lives and fortunes' in defence of their country, is in plain view. The photograph self-consciously recalls an earlier propaganda photograph called *Flag-Raising on Iwo Jima*, which shows a hard-won US military victory in the Pacific during World War II (see Westwell 2008). In US cultural memory, World War II is remembered as a collective and moral national endeavour in which ordinary Americans, so-called 'citizen soldiers', sacrificed their lives in pursuit of patriotic and idealistic goals. This sense of

World War II is imbricated with the photograph of Ground Zero – a profoundly unstable location on 12 September in both a literal and a symbolic sense – and this imbrication allows 9/11 to be placed within a redemptive national narrative familiar to all. This utilisation of the cultural memory of World War II, and the logic that attends it, was reinforced in newspaper reports and television coverage that linked 9/11 with the Japanese attack on the US fleet at Pearl Harbor in December 1941. In these reports the sense of innocence violated and the need for military retaliation (indeed revenge) associated with this earlier event were quickly appropriated as a suitable model for responding to 9/11 (see Landy 2004: 86–7).

This combination of a jingoistic sense of national identity and a desire for retribution pervaded official discourse. In a defining speech made on 20 September 2001, President George W. Bush used a combination of nationalist and religious rhetoric to argue for the need to go to war. John M. Murphy notes how Bush self-consciously echoed the famous 'four freedoms' speech made by Franklin Delano Roosevelt during World War II and placed 9/11 'in a biblical context through quotation of the opening of the 23rd psalm, [thereby] shaping the meaning of 9/11 as a passage through the valley of the shadow of death yet simultaneously assuring [his listeners] that the Lord was with [them]' (2003: 609).

To take another example, between 2001 and 2002, the toy manufacturer Hasbro reported a 46 per cent increase in sales of GI Joe action figures: a neat demonstration of how a tried and tested signifier of national identity was used to anchor and direct imaginative play for the next generation of Americans during a moment of crisis (see Martin and Steuter 2010: 70). Similarly, Hallmark, a major US greetings card retailer, circulated a memo on 17 September to managers in its retail stores advising how they might reposition 75 existing products, including cards showing the Stars and Stripes and the 'Everyday Heroes' range, in order to capitalise on post-9/11 patriotic sentiment (see Jackson 2005: 20). By 24 September the company had launched the 'Together We Stand' series, which gave prominence to clear iconic symbols of US national identity such as the US flag, the American bald eagle and the Statue of Liberty. Notwithstanding the threat of anthrax spores placed in the post between September and October 2001 in 'the eleven months following September 11, consumers purchased nearly 6.5 million patriotic cards, with Hallmark sales up 75% on the previous year' (ibid.). The purchasing, giving and receiving of cards in the wake of the attacks signifies myriad ways of expressing kinship, condolences, gratitude, and so on, but it also serves as a clear example of how national identity is constituted through and by cultural artefacts and social practices. Evelyn Alsultany notes that

> In the weeks after 9/11, patriotic advertising campaigns flooded high-way billboards, radio, magazines, newspapers, and television. Some corporations used the tragedy directly or indirectly to market and sell their product. General Motors launched a campaign, 'Keep America Rolling,' offering zero percent financing deals on new cars and trucks. The New York Sports Club encouraged New Yorkers to 'Keep America Strong' by joining the gym on September 25. Some corporations, such as AOL/Time Warner, MSNBC, Ralph Lauren, Sears, and Morgan Stanley advertised that they would not be advertising, instead buying advertising space on billboards, magazines, and television to express their condolences, solidarity, and an inspirational message. (2007: 593)

These examples show how 9/11 was made to serve the construction of national identity as a feature of the thick social relations of family and community.

Michael Billig observes that this outpouring of nationalist sentiment belies a national identity that is usually unspoken and taken for granted (1995: 5–6). For Billig this nationalist outpouring is only possible as a result of what he calls 'banal nationalism': a form of (largely disavowed) nationalism that keeps national identity in a state of constant readiness. Billig writes that 'the metonymic image of banal nationalism is not a flag which is being consciously waved with fervent passion; it is the flag hanging unnoticed on the public building' (1995: 8). And, as he notes, the everyday, or 'banal', nature of this form of nationalism should not lead one to underestimate the leverage it has, especially during times of crisis, where this nationalism 'primes' the charge to war (1995: 7). In public appearances Bush made it known that he carried the badge of a rescue worker called George Howard who had been killed on 9/11; this talismanic object – a powerful piece of nationalist *mise-en-scène* – sided him, and his statements, with the every-day lived experience of a federal employee and that employee's sacrifice. A symbol of 'banal nationalism' – the identification badge of a government employee – became richly significant and primed the nationalist and patriotic discourses that led the country to war.

The scant examples I have considered thus far – news photographs, children's toys, greetings cards – indicate that cultural production during and immediately after the terrorist attacks offered a strong, unified version of US national identity, including a particular view of a shared national history.

But what role did the cinema play? Did the cinema respond similarly to bolster and reiterate this prevailing view? Marilyn B. Young reports that in October 2001 forty Hollywood executives attended a two-hour discussion at the White House with Chris Henick, deputy assistant to the president, and Adam Goldman, associate director of the Office of Public Liaison; at this meeting, Leslie Moonves, president of CBS, is reported as saying, 'Tell us what to do. We don't fly jet planes, but there are skill sets that can be put to use here' (2003: 256). A second meeting, known as the Beverly Hills Summit, followed on 8 November, at which

> a smaller group of Hollywood executives, along with representatives of the television networks, labor unions, and Cineplex owners as well, responded to an invitation from Karl Rove, senior White House advisor, for a more focused and high-powered discussion of how Hollywood might help the war effort. (Ibid.)

This meeting was 'co-hosted by two stalwarts of Liberal Hollywood: Sherry Lansing, chair of the Paramount Pictures film division, and Jonathan Dolgen, head of Viacom's entertainment group' (Cooper 2001). While it is unusual for politicians to call upon filmmakers with the express aim of petitioning them to create a sympathetic cultural context for a specific policy agenda, it seems that this is exactly what Rove hoped to achieve. He asked Hollywood executives to enshrine in forthcoming films and television shows the seven-point message

> that the war is against terrorism, not Islam; that Americans must be called to national service; that Americans should support the troops; that this is a global war that needs a global response; that this is a war against evil; that American children have to be reassured; and that instead of propaganda, the war effort needs a narrative that should be told [...] with accuracy and honesty. (Ibid.)

Attendees at both meetings noted that the World War II propaganda films of Frank Capra might provide a model of 'the kind of patriotic, pro-America film and television production desired by the White House' (Prince 2009: 80). However, as Jean-Michel Valantin notes, care was also taken to avoid any direct request for the production of propaganda; indeed, it is reported that Rove 'implored Hollywood producers and directors not to dramatise the "war against terrorism onscreen"' (2005: 90).

Introduction

The release schedules of late 2001 and early 2002 suggest that Hollywood producers did indeed seek to manage the flow of cultural production in response to Rove's request. Their first step was the removal of anything that might be seen to have a direct reference to 9/11, or similar events: the Twin Towers were removed from *Serendipity* (2001), *People I Know* (2002) and *Men in Black II* (2002), as well as the promotional material for *Spider-Man* (2002) (see Schneider 2004: 30). Even a film that might be said to align with the dominant discourse, such as *Collateral Damage* (2002), an Arnold Schwarzenegger action film that tells the story of a firefighter who seeks revenge on terrorists responsible for the death of his family, had its publicity materials toned down and was held back from release until 10 February 2002 (see Pollard 2011: 8–9).

This amending and repositioning of already completed films which might be seen to have direct links with 9/11 served to head off accusations that Hollywood was behaving in an unduly political way or seeking to 'cash in' on the event. With these measures in place, as J. Hoberman observes, the production slate of late autumn 2001 and early 2002 was amended in such a way as to amplify the dominant discourse described earlier in this chapter. For Hoberman, war films such as *Behind Enemy Lines* (December 2001), *Black Hawk Down* (January 2002), *We Were Soldiers* (March 2002) and *Windtalkers* (June 2002) depicted the US as victim and showed the moral imperative of military intervention, thereby corroborating the wider call to war (2002: 45); with the exception of *We Were Soldiers*, these films received considerable assistance from the Pentagon in exchange for script changes to ensure favourable representation of the military, a clear indication of the political alignment of the films (2002: 46). *Black Hawk Down*'s release date was brought forward by ten weeks to 30 December 2001. Vice President Dick Cheney, Defense Secretary Donald H. Rumsfeld and Deputy Defense Secretary Paul Wolfowitz attended the film's premiere and endorsed the film, while Secretary of the Army Thomas E. White claimed that 'the values portrayed here are absolutely authentic. They represent the core Army ethic of courage and selfless service' (see Robb 2004: 59–66, 91, 181–2). *We Were Soldiers* also received a well-publicised White House screening, with Bush, Rumsfeld, Condoleezza Rice and Karl Rove expressing favourable opinions (see Kozaryn 2002), and a week after the film's release the cover of *Newsweek* borrowed the title to provide an elegiac frame for its story of US casualties in Afghanistan. This high-profile cycle of films (which show modern warfare as a moral imperative in defence of human rights and as a justified response to vicious and unprovoked attack) – along with the careful, tactical treatment of any direct address of the attacks – aligned neatly with Rove's directive and served to discursively amplify the dominant ideological response to 9/11: a nationalist call to arms.

The nationalist sentiment was further maintained through the decision to hold some films back. For example, *Buffalo Soldiers*, a warts-and-all satire of US military corruption in West Germany in the late 1980s, was completed in November 2000 and the film played at the Toronto International Film Festival on 8 September 2001. Here, the film's producers persuaded Miramax to handle distribution in the US in a deal clinched on 10 September 2001. Though contractually obliged to release the film within a year, Miramax delayed for fear of appearing anti-American and alienating potential viewers. Against this backdrop, the film was finally released in July 2003 with little by way of marketing, and hence virtually no critical or commercial traction. Similarly, *The Quiet American* was originally scheduled for release in the autumn of 2001, but was held back until 24 November 2002. Based on Graham Greene's anti-war novel exploring the CIA's clandestine role in Vietnam during the period of decolonisation following World War II, the film was shelved by Miramax because, according to co-chairman Harvey Weinstein, the studio felt it could not 'release this film now; it's unpatriotic. America has to be cohesive and band together. [Nobody has] the stomach for a movie about bad Americans anymore' (quoted in Thompson 2002).

As these examples indicate, pre-existing views (both pro-war and anti-war, and indicative of a range of opinions) were managed in order to segue with patriotic constructions of US national identity, and in particular a call to arms that led to war in Afghanistan and Iraq. Concerted self-censorship practised by studios like Miramax ensured that films that challenged or questioned this reality were pushed to the margins. As such, Hollywood played a significant role in the production and maintenance of a belligerent response to 9/11. Chapter two describes how this nationalist filmmaking – a form of entertainment in support of war – continued through 2002 and into 2003 (see also Kaplan 2005: 16).

Of course, given ethnic and racial difference, different and conflicting religious traditions, political radicalism, capitalist competition, and tension between regional and national allegiances, US national identity is intrinsically tenuous and fragile (see Gitlin 1995; Krakau 1997; Renshon 2005). Even a cursory glance at US history (the subjugation of Native Americans, slavery, the Civil War, the Great Depression, Vietnam) reminds us of this. The three realms of experience underpinning the US's 'imagined community' – Christian faith, Enlightenment political philosophy and capitalism

– have fostered significant contradictions and conflicts. Indeed, the US national motto – *E pluribus unum*: out of many, one – stresses unity and togetherness yet also points towards difference and a process of struggle. Todd Gitlin observes that historically speaking, 'the phrase "life, liberty and the pursuit of happiness" is at war with itself; as the abolitionists insisted, the liberty of the slave owner steals the happiness of the slave' (1995: 48). The novelist John Updike attempts to capture the same contradiction by describing America as a 'conservative country built upon radicalism' (quoted in Bigsby 2006: 27). Clearly, then, US society is shaped by powerful centrifugal forces that will threaten any attempt to foster a singular, shared 'imagined community'. In the early stages of the 2007/08 presidential campaign, Barack Obama chose not to wear a US flag tiepin, arguing that the flag had become a substitute for true patriotism, a symbol with powerful implicit meanings that were not being subjected to critical inquiry. His actions were controversial, but as his election to president demonstrates, his stance was appealing to many Americans and pointed to the way in which the bringing together of an imagined community is never straightforward.[3] Although *Buffalo Soldiers* and *The Quiet American* were marginalised, the existence of these films points to the presence in culture (and in society at large) of oppositional and critical perspectives. In chapter one I describe how the straightforward nationalist discourse that came to prominence in the immediate aftermath of the attacks was subjected to criticism and remains so. As such, any presumption of a straightforward top-down relationship where conventional forms of US national identity are reproduced and reinforced in popular culture is simply wrong. The processes at work are not simply those of iteration, reiteration and amplification, but more those of a constant making, unmaking and remaking. This book details numerous instances of the national identity made in the immediate aftermath of 9/11 being unmade and remade: documentary filmmaker Nina Davenport's iconoclastic road trip from West to East in *Parallel Lines* (2004), the raising of an inverted Stars and Stripes to signal national emergency in the closing sequence of *In the Valley of Elah* (2007) and the reflection of a troubled CIA agent's face in the glass of a framed US flag in *Zero Dark Thirty* (2012) (see cover image).

    Struggle, then, is central to any discussion of US national identity, and is a defining term for this book. In film studies, analysis that is driven by an explicit impulse to comment on political struggle is often referred to as ideological criticism. The term ideology is shorthand for the 'relatively well-systematised set of categories which provide a "frame" for the belief, perception and conduct of a body of individuals' within a particular time and place (Eagleton 1991: 43). Utilising this term, and the Marxist philosophy that frames it, the work of Theodor Adorno and others associated with the Frankfurt School in the 1920s and 1930s sought to question how processes of political struggle related to culture and how film served to legitimate (and in some cases critique) ideology.

In the late 1960s and 1970s, ideological criticism in film studies was underpinned by the ideas of French philosopher Louis Althusser. Drawing on Lacanian psychoanalysis and structuralism, Althusser attributed greater agency to culture than classical Marxist versions of ideology, and sought to explain how ideological apparatuses – such as education, the church and popular culture – shaped consciousness or subjectivity. Influenced by Althusser's ideology critique, the editors of the influential French film journal *Cahiers du cinéma* produced a typology for detailing the different relationships between film and ideology (see Editors 1972): 'category A' films reproduced the dominant ideology in unadulterated form, 'category B' films actively refused the dominant ideology, and so on. Acknowledging the fact that popular entertainment cinema often failed to clearly align with neatly demarcated political viewpoints, the 'category E' film was said to reproduce the dominant ideology but to do so in an ambiguous manner. As this typology sought to demonstrate, the determining of the relationship between films and any given political landscape is not straightforward.

A parallel though overlapping strand of ideological criticism is associated with the work of Italian Marxist Antonio Gramsci, who used the term 'hegemony' to describe how ideology is shaped by powerful (or hegemonic) groups seeking consent from less powerful groups for the widespread adoption of their view of the world. This consent is often refused or hard won, and consequently culture is evidence of, and bears the marks of, ideological struggle. Conceived of thus, ideological criticism sought to identify how struggle appears within film texts (a 'category E' film bears the marks of such struggle) and across cycles of films and genres. This Gramscian approach has inflected a number of works that examine post-9/11 cinema (see Birkenstein *et al.* 2010; Dixon 2004; Prince 2009), with the title of Douglas Kellner's *Cinema Wars* (2010) indicative of the general approach, and this book occupies similar territory.

Written between World War I and World War II, Gramsci's work adhered to the Marxist principle that society consists of groups that have political power and those that do not, with the latter oppressed by the former. According to Marxist orthodoxy the class that controls the means of production have the ability to instil, via culture, a worldview – or ideology – that is shared by all but which serves only their interests. The primary function of ideology, then, was to dupe those disadvantaged by the system into supporting it and granting it their consent. In contrast, Robert Bocock argues that Gramsci wished to demonstrate how

> the relationship between these two is not conceived of as being such that one, the material, the economic, determined the other, the realm of culture and ideologies. Rather Gramsci sees the relationship between the material, productive base, and the cultural sphere as being a complex, reciprocal one in which human beings mediate between the two zones. (1986: 79)

According to this line of reasoning, people's beliefs are not

> something manipulated by capitalists, or put into the minds of the masses by them, but rather they flow from the exigencies of everyday life under capitalism. The workers, and others, hold the values and political ideas that they do as a consequence of both trying to survive, and of attempting to enjoy themselves, within capitalism. (1986: 32)

According to Gramsci, then, ideology is not just the smokescreen that those with political power use to veil their vested interests (though it is this as well), but is the consensus view of things, the end result of a dynamic, complex interaction between individuals, social groups, institutions and power structures. Gramsci's account of ideology retains a Marxist commitment to culture being shaped differentially, with the powerful able to exert their will, but nuances this by drawing attention to the ways in which powerful groups will maintain their position by making concessions to, and accommodations of, competing groups and positions. Gramsci describes the position of power attained by the ruling class as hegemony, a dominant position underpinned by economic and political power but also hard won in the sphere of culture. In order for change to take place – whether it be incremental and within the system or revolutionary and with the intention of replacing the system – hegemony must be unsettled: there must be some form of counter-hegemonic struggle. For Gramsci, this struggle is not restricted to political conflict – the ballot box, the picket line, the barricades, and so on – but extends to the lived experience of everyday life, with popular culture an important arena in which counter-hegemony can take shape. The range of films discussed in this book – Hollywood blockbusters, semi-independent feature films and small-scale documentaries – reflects the diversity of views in any modern polity as well as the different roles they play in reproducing and challenging power through the shaping of the popular imagination.

As noted, much of the writing on 9/11 tends to adopt a 'quasi-Gramscian' approach in which right-wing films are contrasted with left-liberal films, and with struggle between the two posited as offering two competing ideologies, doing battle to establish hegemony (see Slocum 2011). Kellner, for example, argues that post-9/11 cinema agitates for the election of Barack Obama and that the Obama ascendency constitutes a left-liberal ideology replacing that of a neoconservatism under Bush. However, it is important to retain the kernel of political/structural analysis that shapes Gramsci's thinking. The Marxist bottom line has it that the system – in this case US liberal democracy and capitalism – will produce a self-serving ideology, and that, following Gramsci, this ideology will be flexible enough to allow change to take place without the status quo fundamentally altering, that is, hegemony will be brokered and concessions will be made in order to continuously maintain it. So, the question is not one of either this (neoconservative) ideology or that (left-liberal) one; more, the question is what kind of deal will be brokered to establish an equilibrium that will maintain things more or less as they are? In spite of a decade of politically partisan skirmishing across popular culture, hegemony holds; despite, or even because of, Obama's election, the status quo has been maintained. This book reveals how films and cycles of films that appear to lock horns and be irreconcilable with one another, politically speaking, partake in a process of making, unmaking and (most crucially) remaking US national identity in response to a moment of crisis. The early chapters indicate how individual films and cycles of films might be said to adopt an adversarial relation with clear-cut political positions, but as the book progresses it will be shown how post-9/11 cinema seeks mechanisms for reconciling political difference in service of hegemonic renewal, especially in the realm of mainstream feature film production. Here it is necessary to recall Richard Maltby's (1982) argument that Hollywood is a 'cinema of consensus' and that, although its films display a 'commercial aesthetic [that] is too opportunistic to prize coherence, organic unity, or even the absence of contradiction among its primary virtues' (Maltby 2003: 35), it will generally align with any given hegemony. As will be shown, this process is rarely straightforward: entertainment cinema amplifies, negotiates with, escapes from and imagines utopian alternatives to the status quo, but in the end it will err to the political centre.

Introduction

Karl Rove's attempt to gain the ideological advantage of having the world's most powerful entertainment industry work with the grain of a neoconservative policy agenda was an attempt to actively broker hegemony, if you will. And, on the face of it, it would appear that many of those involved in the production of popular culture readily shouldered this work. Yet, as I will demonstrate in chapter one and at a number of other points in this book, cultural production was already taking place in the immediate aftermath of the attacks that would lead to the production of films that addressed 9/11 in a critical way, prefiguring much of the challenge, critique and contestation that would come to define post-9/11 cinema. Structurally, and by way of orientation, this ideological struggle – a central focus of this book – can be considered by reading chapter one and chapter two in parallel; indeed, these two chapters serve to map the parallel lines – or two clearly politically differentiated responses to 9/11 – to which the book's title refers. In later chapters, although acknowledgement of political struggle will continue to be given, attention will shift to the ways in which post-9/11 cinema often seeks to bring together and accommodate both positions, to broker hegemony out of cultural/political conflict. Throughout, national identity is taken to be a central – though partial – element of ideology but one that might be said to be metonymic – that is, revealing of the wider operation of ideology in any given moment. As such, the following chapters offer an explanation of how, more than ten years after 9/11, the US reveals a sense of self via popular culture, and how this fraught revelation is a marker of wider political struggle.

I wish to guard against the danger that ideological criticism can create a misleading sense of polarisation, and I do not wish to present hegemonic and counter-hegemonic struggle in an overly neat way. Indeed, films such as *We Were Soldiers*, which seem to function as robust incarnations of a conservative and (in early 2002) prevalent construction of US identity, are, in fact, relatively thin on the ground and – with the exception of *Black Hawk Down* – were not particularly successful at the box office. Similarly, the critical viewpoint adopted in *The Quiet American* (and temporarily silenced in the immediate aftermath of 9/11) is hardly typical either. I have used films in the introduction – and as a structuring element of the book – to put the process of struggle in stark relief. However, films will usually fall somewhere in between, seeking to reconcile conflicts and contradictions replete in the events they depict in a dynamic (a Marxist might say dialectical) way. As such, although a marked separation between different, and competing, versions of US national identity can usually be identified, there are also significant points of convergence and contact, often resulting in conflict and incoherence, but also embodying compromise and consensus. US national identity, then, results from the drawing together of seemingly oppositional political viewpoints/tendencies in ways that reconcile and accommodate their differences in preference for a shared, common ground. This is what interests me most: as struggle subsides equilibrium returns.

Each chapter of this book addresses a key theme in post-9/11 US cinema: loss and uncertainty (and a feeling of unreality) in chapter one; unity films and revenge films in chapter two; conspiracy films in chapter three; the return to and direct representation of 9/11 in chapter four; visions of the end of the world and disaster in chapter five; the predominance of a discourse of trauma and therapeutic recovery in chapter six; the depiction of torture in chapter seven; the representation of the war in Iraq in chapter eight; the way in which the experience of 9/11 has shifted senses of history in chapter nine. This thematic approach is organised according to a loose chronology that indicates how films and cycles of films have mirrored wider cultural shifts and tendencies as the decade has unfolded. For example, the revenge films examined in chapter two, including *Collateral Damage* and *Man on Fire* (2004), are read as part of the initial hegemonic response to 9/11, and it is argued that this cycle of illiberal films activates patriotic and jingoistic senses of US national identity and advocates vengeful retribution, thereby corroborating the move to war in Afghanistan and Iraq. In contrast, the Iraq war films examined in chapter eight, including *Iraq in Fragments* (2006), appear late in the decade and can be read as counter-hegemonic and as more properly belonging to a period of rising anti-war sentiment and political realignment in late 2008, in anticipation of the election of Barack Obama. This chronological approach will necessarily give way at times to a more free-ranging discussion of key themes – of which revenge and war are good examples.

Taken together, the different chapters build a picture of how, in negotiating post-9/11 political and social realities, the US cinema has been multi-fold: on the one hand, producing countless films that serviced the dominant discourses associated with 9/11 and sought consent for a banal nationalism and support for an ever-expanding 'war on terror', and on the other, delivering many films that in their political engagement and aesthetic and generic variety are almost without precedent. Against this polarised filmmaking there are also numerous examples of a post-9/11 cinema that sought to pull discrete political positions together, to acknowledge historical complexity and yet also renew nationalist sentiment and re-establish and maintain the status quo. This book is an account of the relations between these different tendencies of the post-9/11 cinema.

Uncertainty

In the introduction I described a patriotic response to the events of 9/11 founded on a pre-existing 'banal nationalism'. This response cultivated a sense of crisis, cast 9/11 in reductive Manichean terms and recalled US history in a partial way, especially through a jingoistic view of World War II. This avowedly patriotic response could be found in the mass media, in the speeches made by politicians and policymakers and across significant realms of popular culture, including the film industry, which used self-censorship and the reconfiguration of the release dates of a number of films to align itself with the prevailing cultural mood. In contrast to many books that address popular cultural responses to 9/11 – and which trace these responses into film culture – I wish to begin by examining films that, even in the immediate aftermath of 9/11, can be said to take an opposing view. In chapter two I examine a cycle of what I call 'unity films', but for the moment I wish to draw attention to those responses that resisted the easy constructions of national identity found in the mainstream media immediately after the attacks. This cycle of films indicates how processes of contestation and resistance were active from the very moment of the attacks, and how these processes would – over the long arc of the next ten years or so – remain available and be returned to.

In *The Forever War*, Dexter Filkins, a foreign correspondent for the *New York Times*, describes being at Ground Zero when the attacks took place:

> Walking in, watching the flames shoot upward, the first thing I thought was that I was back in the Third World. My countrymen were going to

> think this was the worst thing that ever happened, the end of civiliza-
> tion. In the Third World, this sort of thing happened every day [...] I
> don't think I was the only person thinking this, who had a darker per-
> spective. All those street vendors who worked near the World Trade
> Center [...] When they heard the planes and watched the towers fall
> they must have thought the same as I did: that they'd come home.
> (2008: 44–5)

Here, Filkins distances himself from the predicted reaction – that the collapse of the Twin Towers would provoke a response of the kind already
described in the introduction to this book – and instead identifies with a
group of people with lived experience of the Third World for whom the violence would be in some way recognisable. Filkins's 'doubled' response points
to the way in which 9/11 propagated not only understandable reactions of
fear, anger and the desire for retribution, but also something more complex:
that is, reflection on the interconnectedness of the globalised economy, the
already established and often unequal relation between the US and other
nations and the ways in which the Third World is a part of the lived experience and social and cultural histories of a large number of Americans.
Filkins's response was not unique; journalist William Langewiesche
described how the scene he witnessed could be readily related to those he
had seen in failed states around the world (2003: 8–9). Similarly, E. Ann
Kaplan, in the introduction to *Trauma Culture*, describes walking through
Manhattan shortly after the attacks and experiencing, in sharp contrast to
the wider media discourse, 'the multiple, spontaneous activities [such as the
building of shrines, the adornment of war memorials with peace symbols,
graffiti calling for reflection] from multiple perspectives, genders, races,
and religions or nonreligions' (2005: 14). Noam Chomsky, speaking on
21 September 2001, sought to amplify this kind of response as an alternative to the dominant discourse, noting that 'even' the *New York Times* was
reporting that 'the drumbeat for war [...] is barely audible on the streets of
New York', and that calls for peace 'far outnumber demands for retribution'
(2011: 61). Another figure who adopted a critical and questioning stance was
Susan Sontag (2001), who wrote a short polemical column in the *New Yorker*,
published on 24 September, that suggested that the attacks might have been
a consequence of previous US actions, especially the ongoing bombing of
Iraq after the first Gulf War. Sontag's attempt to establish rational cause and
context and to figure the event as the result of some form of interrelation-
ship between the US, the perpetrators of the attack and the wider world

Uncertainty

was quickly censured, and she became the victim of vitriolic condemnation (see Faludi 2007: 28–30).[4] As later chapters of this book will demonstrate, these responses were prescient: it was precisely these themes that would give structure to much post-9/11 cinema, though the shift from the one response to the other would be fraught and take time. The prevailing cultural mood, however – seen clearly in George W. Bush's Manichean construct, 'Either you are with us, or you are with the terrorists' – ensured that any response to 9/11 that sought to resist the call for retribution and attempted to figure the attacks as, at least in part, the result of complex, dialectical relations between the US and the rest of the world was, in the wider public sphere at least, quickly subsumed by the dominant media discourse (see Bush 2001).

Faced with censure, those with critical views often loudly protested that they were adhering to principles central to US national identity in their will-ingness to talk truth to power and in their refusal to bow to the prevailing ideological viewpoint. Todd Gitlin identifies that this *disrespect* of authority, what he terms 'egalitarian irreverence', is a key characteristic of US national identity and, as we shall see, it was an attribute that was widely, and often vocally, upheld (1995: 43). Using a national Random Digital Dialing (RDD) telephone survey in late 2001, Darren Davis and Brian Silver discovered that '53 percent of Americans attributed responsibility to the US for the hatred that led to the attacks' and that 'even among political conservatives, 42 percent saw the US as at least somewhat responsible' (2004). The telephone survey indicates how, even under considerable pressure to conform to the mainstream media discourse, many Americans reserved the right to have their own opinions. Critical acts took a more coherent shape as the days and weeks passed: teachers at educational institutions staged teach-ins, con-sciously emulating the political consciousness-raising strategies of the 1960s and 1970s (see Anon. 2001). As Jacqueline Brady notes,

> At a time when dissenting voices and contesting ideas seemed to be absent from public discussion, we hoped these teach-ins would provide a forum for exploring the dense map of political, economic, historical, cultural, and personal coordinates connected to the terrorist attacks. (2004: 96)

A group formed by relatives of some of the victims of 9/11 called 'September 11 Families for Peaceful Tomorrows' stated that their mission was to 'seek effective nonviolent responses to terrorism' and 'to spare additional inno-cent families the suffering that we have already experienced – as well as to

19

break the endless cycle of violence and retaliation engendered by war' (see Lawrence 2005: 46). An anti-war bumper sticker read simply: 'Justice Not Vengeance'.

The popularity of the bestselling book *Why Do People Hate America?* (2002) suggests that many Americans sought to make the events of 9/11 intelligible by means other than the mainstream news discourse. The relationship figured by the book's title is phrased in adversarial terms – emphasising how a discourse using the strict binary oppositions of 'us' and 'them' was operative in popular culture – but authors Ziauddin Sardar and Merryl Wyn Davies offer an alternative to this binary reasoning, constructing instead a series of logical answers to the question posed (2002: 195–203). The book asks readers to consider how countries in the Middle East and Europe might view the US in critical terms, and most importantly, why this might be the case. Sardar and Davies argue that in place of hatred people should seek to make 'visible the nature, conditions and dimensions of the problem so that new debates, new constituencies of dissent that bridge the divide between America and the rest of the world, can be built' (2004: xii). In doing so, they claim, a patriotic nationalism, which constructs US national identity in a partial and insular way, might be resisted. ZNet, CNN, Comedy Central's *The Daily Show* and other middle-brow areas of popular culture also offered some limited space for discussion and debate, and within a year of the attacks a number of anthologies, including *September 11 and the US War: Beyond the Curtain of Smoke* (Burbach and Clarke 2002) and *September 11, 2001: American Writers Respond* (Heyen 2002) sought to understand the attacks via a series of alternative critical frameworks. It is in this context – one of critical questioning, egalitarian irreverence and the active refusal of the kind of dominant ideological response sketched in the introduction and profiled in more detail in the next chapter – that the first wave of film production that directly addresses the experience of 9/11 must be situated. The remainder of the present chapter examines a number of early 9/11 films as articulations of an unruly, democratic and questioning response that would consolidate and gain in confidence and coherence as the decade progressed.

One of the earliest documentary films to show the events of 9/11 was Etienne Suaret's *WTC – The First 24 Hours*.[5] Screened at the Sundance Film Festival in January 2002, Suaret's documentary is described by Stephen Prince as 'one of the essential films about 9/11' (2009: 126). The film is distinctive in a number of ways. First, the opening sequences feature 'locked off' shots of the second plane strike and the collapse of the North Tower;

these shots are denotative, objective, unflinching: seeming categorical statements of fact. The decision not to edit from one view of the event to another – and thereby establish some form of continuity – leaves the offscreen space resonant and encourages the viewer to search for a suitable framework other than that provided by the mainstream media. Second, the titles are followed by handheld shots taken by Suaret in the aftermath of the attacks (carefully selected parts of his footage also appear in *In Memoriam* (2002), discussed in chapter two). These shots are tentative, uncertain, thoughtful and quiet. There is no commentary, only the ambient sound recorded with the image. At regular intervals – almost as if offering a pause for thought – the sound drops out. This has the effect of aestheticising the image for a moment before, as the sound returns, the evidential nature of the footage once again comes to the fore.

These carefully considered aesthetic decisions are striking in part as a result of their marked distinction from the ways that the event was being depicted in the mainstream media and the heavily editorialised documentaries described in the next chapter. There is something forensic about the film's gaze and its eye for counter-monumental detail. Film of deserted shopping malls and fast food restaurants – the word 'evidence' painted on a wall – recall crime scene photographs. Ground Zero is here a place bereft, and in need of investigation. In stark contrast to *Ground Zero Spirit*, for example, the futility of the rescue operation is expressed through images of workers forming lines, their bodies tiny and their hard work ineffectual against the scale of the ruins. In its blend of handheld *vérité* footage, careful, quasi-structuralist presentation of iconic scenes and a self-reflexive use of sound, *WTC* seeks a materialist aesthetic with which to respond to 9/11, one that details what has happened but also seeks to question the act of representation, especially where this is too quick to attribute meaning to an event that demands further, detailed inquiry. In this, the film is a corollary to collections of photographs such as *Aftermath* (Meyerowitz 2006) and works of careful observational journalism such as *American Ground* (Langewiesche 2003) that similarly blend an iconoclastic eye for detail, a fascination with the quotidian and the posing of difficult questions.

Other responses, appearing within months of the attacks, sought to record the many voices and opinions in play. In the weeks following 9/11, San Francisco-based experimental filmmakers Jay Rosenblatt and Caveh Zahedi invited 150 independent filmmakers and artists to create a short film in response to the events and their aftermath. From the sixty works received, thirteen were selected to form the feature-length omnibus film *Underground*

Zero (2002), which was shown at film festivals in the US in early 2002. Gareth Evans claims that the film was intended to 'offset the monotone of political propaganda with a plurality of opinions' and that together the short films claim 'a degree of street-level access and democracy for the moving image, they make central the communal and private in the face of governmental blustering and manipulative patriotism' (2002: 5). Following this democratic principle, the documentary film *Seven Days in September*, directed by Steve Rosenbaum, brings together film footage of 9/11 shot by 27 different filmmakers. Screened in New York and Los Angeles in September 2002, each individual film, or series of film fragments, is edited in parallel in the chronological sequence in which the events unfolded. The film shows that on the day of attacks responses were very similar – shock, sympathy, bewilderment, anger. However, from the morning of 12 September, with some time for reflection, a range of views begins to appear. Filming from Sunset Park in Brooklyn, and reflecting on the now significant gap in the New York skyline, filmmaker Alan Roth admits that, although he is sympathetic to the plight of the people who have been killed, he 'never liked the World Trade Center': 'I always thought, from a political point of view, that these two buildings represented, you know, what I thought was evil about the economic system in terms of its relationship to poor people around the world.'

In plain words, Roth articulates something that emerges across all the films discussed in this chapter: namely, reflection on the ambiguous meaning of the World Trade Center as a symbol. As he cycles across the Brooklyn Bridge into lower Manhattan, Roth films a group of people praying for peace and inviting passers-by to join hands in a circle to sing 'Amazing Grace'.

Later that evening, and drawn to the crowds gathering in Union Square, King Mopalo, a filmmaker from South Africa, films a candlelit vigil he claims is driven by a desire to find some respite from the constant repetition of images of destruction on the television news. Stephen Prince notes that Mopalo's film shows

> one man in the vigil [who] decries the US treatment of Muslims, Palestinians and Arabs around the world and says that Americans have to reflect on this in connection with the attacks. Sensing that war could easily follow in the wake of the attacks, and expressing a wish to forestall it, the crowd begins singing 'Give Peace a Chance'. (2009: 142–3)

In another sequence filmed in Union Square on 13 September, chalk is given to people to write messages on the pavement. A black woman is

Fig. 1: Dissenting voices: *Seven Days in September* (2002)

shown writing 'the American flag propagates violence', leading a man to call for a dog to urinate on the message and a woman to attempt to wash the message away with a bottle of water. The crowd intervene and the documentary reports that an hour-long heated debate ensues, ranging across such topics as freedom of speech and the First Amendment, the necessity of war, the need to resist the call to war and God's role in the attacks. This sequence ends with the plea, 'Why don't we stop arguing and start reflecting', suggesting that there is also a desire to find some way of reconciling these opposing positions. Because of its inclusion of these difficult, often fraught, encounters, *Seven Days in September* can serve as a marker of the critical and challenging views that were quickly excised from the popular media. David Holloway celebrates this response as 'a decentralised republic of voices': a complex, inclusive, democratic holler (2008: 102). The film corroborates Chomsky's sense that the prevailing mood in New York was at odds with that of the mainstream media response and the complex reality on show foreshadows the wholesale questioning of the meaning of 9/11 that would shape popular culture through the following decade.

The omnibus film *11'09"01 September 11*, produced by Alain Brigand, brings together eleven directors from as many countries, each contributing a film lasting eleven minutes, nine seconds and one frame. The film was released in late 2002 in Europe, and early 2003 in the US, indicating that the filmmakers were writing, shooting and editing their work in the weeks and months immediately following 9/11. In keeping with this book's focus on US cinema, I examine here the contribution to the film made by actor/filmmaker Sean Penn. In Penn's film an elderly man (played by Ernest Borgnine) is shown living in a run-down but clean and orderly apartment in New York. The man has failed to get over the death of his wife and begins each day talking to her and choosing a dress for her to wear; the apartment is darkened by the shadow of the World Trade Center. On the windowsill a pot of roses has shrivelled and died, leading the man to observe that 'like him' the flowers 'need light to wake up'. The use of split screen and slow motion draws attention to the film's detailed *mise-en-scène*: the rusted patina on a faucet, streamers blowing in the draught of an air-conditioning unit. The viewer is encouraged to scrutinise the detail of Borgnine's craggy face, his stooped and scarred physique, and his vernacular, implicitly political speech – 'rich people! A bunch of crumbs bound together by dough'; 'they shouldn't have been there in the first place'. Photographs on a bedside table show the man's wife as a younger woman and a soldier in dress uniform. The soldier is possibly the man, or perhaps the couple's son: in either case, the photograph indicates that this is a family that has served. Unusual shots from above provide an objective vantage point looking in on the man's life. In this 'plan view' we see the apartment's careful order: the man's commitment to his chores, his carefully ironed clothes, his clean shoes. By these means the film skilfully conveys the life of an old man who has lived a tough existence replete with hard work and honest resolve, a man who is living in grief-stricken limbo.

On the morning of 11 September, as the South Tower of the World Trade Center collapses, the shadow cast over the man's apartment disappears and

Fig. 2: Lives in context: Sean Penn's contribution to *11'09"01 September 11*

the room is filled with brilliant sunlight. Woken by the light, but unaware of what has happened, the man is confused – slow-motion and dropped-focus shots of his bewilderment are composited with fast-motion shots of the roses on the windowsill blooming. This dreamlike reality comes slowly into focus and the man excitedly tells his wife that she will now be able to grow plants. But then, almost immediately, he realises that his wife is dead. The man breaks down and cries and the camera tracks out of the apartment window, leaving him isolated in his grief as the North Tower collapses.

Penn's simple and moving film – singled out for criticism by many reviewers – searches for a suitably complex response to the events of 9/11 in a number of ways: there is an acknowledgement that before the attacks all was not well (poverty and loneliness might well be the reward for a life of hard work and service; by way of contrast, high capitalism – symbolised by the Twin Towers – casts a long, unyielding shadow). As shown in later chapters, the signature colour of 9/11 is grey: both the colour of dust that subsumed lower Manhattan and a metaphorical colour – neither black nor white – that shades narratives of moral compromise. The shadowy greyness of the man's apartment – and the short film's fixation on the play of light and dark – puts Penn in the position of being a pioneer of this new colour array (subsequently picked up by a host of cinematographers across a range of post-9/11 films). For him the shadow, or greyness, is something that lifts on 9/11: the bright blue sky does not disappear in a grey dust cloud that immerses, engulfs, terrifies and disorientates. Instead, for the man, the collapse of the World Trade Center is illuminating. The attacks shed light on the man's imaginary half-lit fantasy world, forcing him into a difficult and painful process of remembering which requires the acknowledgement of his wife's death. Only via this painful process of truth being revealed and confronted in the moment of the Twin Towers' collapse might positive consequences flow (i.e. the man is now in a position to move on). The aspect of the film that reviewers seemed to object to – the overly simple sense that Penn wishes to say that 9/11 is not an ill wind for all – must be judged against these other aspects: for Penn, the consequences of the attacks are manifold and complex, and, crucially, differentiated and calibrated in relation to different social perspectives and positions.

On the one hand, then, the film situates 9/11 within an intensely personal – one might say myopic – realm. On the other, this is not the usual strategy of eschewing the political via a retreat into the personal that gives shape to the films discussed in chapters three, four and six. Here, the personal is a realm shaped, indeed determined, by the political: 9/11 is cataclysmic, refiguring personal relations in ways not fully knowable. The film ends with the man in abject despair, but it is not the hopeless, terrified and fearful state presented as the default reaction to 9/11 by the mainstream media. It is a state that admits possibility for reflection and for change. Penn's film offers a route out and away from the news footage of the attacks (which play in a very contained way on the man's aged television set, undifferentiated from old reruns of Jerry Springer) into the various fraught viewpoints in evidence on the streets of New York immediately after the attacks, and from there into the world at large. It is worth mentioning, in anticipation of further discussion later in this chapter, that Penn's film presents in cinematic form some of the controversies of the World Trade Center site – that the buildings were disliked by many Americans and were considered by many to be symbolic of the inequities of US capitalism.

Stef Craps argues that a key strength of *11'09"01 September 11* is the way it 'decentres' the events of 9/11 by bringing together a range of views from around the world, a decentring further indicated by the title's use of the date as it appears on a European calendar (2007: 195). As such, the film might be said to belong to the kind of response embodied by the reactions of Filkins, Kaplan and the diverse New Yorkers recorded in active, often heated, debate at the various memorial sites in *Seven Days in September*. Craps notes that the contribution by British director Ken Loach, for example, links '11 September 2001 with 11 September 1973, when Chilean president Salvador Allende was killed during a CIA-backed *coup d'état* that put dictator Augusto Pinochet in power', and that 'in the episode contributed by Egyptian director Youssef Chahine, the ghost of a US Marine is lectured on various international atrocities carried out in the name of American foreign policy' (ibid.). By these means the film contextualises the terrorist attacks within a broader geographical and historical landscape, insisting, as Holloway notes, that '9/11 and the war on terror would only become knowable events if knowledge about them was de-Americanised, or at least stripped of its American-centrism' (2008: 159). Predictably, the film's spirit of searching inquiry and desire to seek a broader set of reference points led to its denunciation by *Variety* as 'stridently anti-American' (Godard 2002), a fate that would befall myriad attempts to think beyond the dominant discourse in the months immediately following 9/11.

The first scene of Nina Davenport's personal documentary film *Parallel Lines* takes place at a lawn bowling club in San Diego, the affluent setting emphasised by the bright Californian sunshine. Here, Davenport asks an elderly Hispanic woman to reflect on the events of 9/11 and 'how these events have changed the way you see the world'; the woman struggles to contain her tears and speaking in Spanish laments the lack of love in the world. Davenport, a New Yorker, then explains that on 9/11 she was located in San Diego for work and that she grew frustrated watching the events from afar on television. In mid-November, desperate to return home but also seeking to understand what had happened, Davenport placed her camera and sound recording equipment in her car and embarked on a six-week road trip back to New York. *Parallel Lines* is a documentary film of her journey, and brings together digital video footage of the many conversations about 9/11 she had with the wide variety of people she met on the way with her recordings of her own thoughts and feelings in the form of a video diary.

As with the filmmakers who contributed to *Seven Days in September*, there is something genuinely brave about Davenport's commitment to seek out and interview a wide range of people at a time when trust among strangers was at the mercy of a prevailing culture of fear and paranoia. Her interviewees include, among others, a long-distance lorry driver (who did not hear of the attacks until 15 September because he was on the road), a conspiracy theorist (who claims he heard about the attacks five years before they happened), a pastor at a drive-through wedding chapel in Las Vegas, a park ranger, a mixed-race couple, a World War II veteran and beekeeper, a retired cowboy, a waitress, a black homeless man, a pair of teenagers, an ex-Marine and a group of cattle farmers. There are marked displays of patriotism: Davenport interviews a man who has put up a God Bless America sign on the road outside his diner and she joins marksmen shooting at images of Osama bin Laden at a shooting range. There are also accusations of government conspiracy and claims that 9/11 is a consequence of the US's past misdeeds: two waiters from Waco, Texas, describe the US as the 'land of the opportunist' and ask 'How can a country that has raped the Indians, the blacks, the Chinese, expect anything different than 9/11?' A teenager in Natchez, Mississippi, states that he hopes that Bin Laden is captured alive 'just to see how he thinks and how he views things, as opposed to how I see and view things'. Interestingly, as with *Seven Days in September*, and with only one exception, religion appears as a force for good, with religious faith providing a moral viewpoint that inclines people to resist the prevailing jingoistic nationalist response. What emerges across many of the testimonies is an intensely personal response whereby 9/11 is measured in relation to pressing everyday problems and losses. A woman working at a petrol station in Ludlow, California, is brought to tears as she talks about her grandparents who live in New York and who she hasn't seen in many years. In Pine

Springs, Texas, an American man and Costa Rican woman who have a baby discuss the difficulty of their relationship: the woman is homesick and cries when asked about 9/11 – she states that when she saw other families suffering it made her feel pain to be away from her own.

As with Sean Penn's film, 9/11 is here keyed into a complex web of personal experiences and relations, leading to reflection on the loss of family members to illness or personal difficulties, often within a context where poverty or the complexities of, say, immigration law have exacerbated difficult personal circumstances. As such, 9/11 meshes with a complex depiction of a US capable of treating 9/11 with disinterest, narcissism, empathy and generosity. It is through this collage of responses – some patriotic, some critical, some divisive and racist, many preposterous – that Davenport's film becomes distinctive; 9/11 loses its sacrosanct status and becomes part of a complex reality. The US flags that feature so heavily in the film's *mise-en-scène* mark the ways in which people reached for the flag in the aftermath of 9/11 but also the ways in which the flag takes on different connotations in relation to this range of perspectives. In an interview published on the BBC4 Storyville website Davenport stated:

> A lot of the stories I heard were quite sad. I'm still not sure if it was because I was sad or because everyone was sad about 9/11 or whether that sadness was pre-existing. I tend to think it's a combination – that 9/11 gave people a way to release their own private sadness onto this more national tragedy.

Davenport's presence in the film, and her video diaries, offer the viewer a distinctly left-liberal perspective; we listen to her reflections on the different testimonies she has gathered and also to her commentary at the end of each day's drive as she watches the television news and its description of the ongoing 'war on terror'. In these scenes, there is an imbrication of a mainstream news discourse, the views of the characters that Davenport meets, and Davenport's own thoughts, across which two discourses interact: one, a hegemonic mainstream response; the other, Davenport's doubts and questioning of this mainstream view in dialogue with the gathering of a wide range of alternate views. Here the film is something of a model of post-9/11 cinema more generally, and the film's title, which is said to refer not just to the Twin Towers and the dividing lines of the Interstate, but also to the individual storylines paralleling the nation's tragedy, has, for this reason, provided the title for this book, which, like her film, seeks to examine these different versions of US national identity as they respond to the shock of 9/11.

There is a further dimension to the film. Davenport's itinerary combines the serendipity of a series of chance encounters by the side of the road with the seemingly magnetic pull of sites richly imbricated in the US national imaginary. In her attempt to make sense of 9/11 she is drawn to, and intuits connections with, past events and the places in which they occurred. Her first stop is Las Vegas, Nevada, where she stays in a hotel that is a simulacrum of New York City: here there is a sense of unreality: of a doubling of, but separation from, the mediated event. From here she drives via the Grand Canyon to Monument Valley, Utah, the landscape redolent of John Ford's many westerns. Here, Davenport talks to a Navajo Native American who describes how as a child he was prevented from using his native language. The man implies that violent events like 9/11 have precedents in US history and will continue to occur. In Los Alamos, New Mexico, in a museum commemorating the first nuclear bomb tests and the dropping of the atomic bomb on Hiroshima and Nagasaki, Davenport meets an elderly couple who had been involved in the project; they reflect that the test explosion was more spectacular than 9/11 and that the bombing was necessary to save US soldiers' lives. Davenport's liberal bent is in evidence here: as she leaves Los Alamos she listens to an audio book and explains that some historians claim that the bombs need not have been dropped. She here prefigures later commentary on the way in which the use of the phrase 'Ground Zero' recalls these earlier events of World War II (a point discussed further in chapter four). In Marfa, Texas, which she visits on 7 December (the sixtieth anniversary of Pearl Harbor, as already noted a key reference point in relation to 9/11), Davenport meets a beekeeper and World War II veteran, a member of the 'greatest generation' who warns that 'you don't want to look back too much do you?' Indeed, in contrast to the way in which World War II was called upon by the mainstream media to celebrate US patriotism and consolidate the call to arms, the veterans of World War II, Korea and Vietnam who appear in Davenport's film are shown to have been deeply troubled by their experience of war and counsel against it. Davenport states, 'I wish I could feel wholeheartedly patriotic but instead I feel angry about all there is to be ashamed of in our history'. The symbolic locations she visits point to the way her journey might be understood as something of an unravelling or demythologising of the narrative of Manifest Destiny: an anti-road trip that seeks to encourage critical reflection on the 'grand narratives' that hold national identity in place.

Parallel Lines

Davenport's journey also includes sites related to more recent events. She stops at the memorial to the Oklahoma City bombing in 1995, a reminder that, in contrast to many accounts in the immediate aftermath of 9/11, terrorism had taken place on US soil in the recent past. In Somerset, Pennsylvania, Davenport visits the crash site of the fourth hijacked plane, and she spends time at the Pentagon in Washington, DC. At these sites she observes the informal work of commemoration as people quietly gather to reflect. The film ends on New Year's Day 2002 with Davenport visiting Ground Zero. She does not film the site directly, preferring to show people as they leave the viewing platform. She interviews a photographer who is eloquent about not looking at Ground Zero directly – 'you can't look at the sun directly; you can only look at it through something that is reflective' – and *Parallel Lines* closes with a poetic shot of Davenport's own shadow on the street in deference to the ways in which the voices that she has recorded and the places she has visited on her journey might speak more eloquently about the meaning of 9/11 than any image of the remains of the Twin Towers. This tactful and complex final image stands in marked contrast to photographs such as *Ground Zero Spirit* and the wider official discourse.

Parallel Lines took some time to secure the necessary funding for release, only appearing in film festivals in the US in June and July 2004. However, it has been included in the first chapter of this book because Davenport's journey and the voices of the people she interviewed were part of the immediate response to 9/11. Like *Underground Zero* and *Seven Days in September*, the film screened only at a number of minor film festivals, in independent cinemas and on television outside the US, with this slow and marginal release evidencing the way in which alternative voices and critical perspectives were, initially at least, curtailed.

The films described thus far run against the grain of the dominant nationalist response – that is, a patriotic clamour, the call to arms, the tightening of national security, and so on – and instead visualise a range of different responses, including the placing of the events of 9/11 into the context of the lived experience of an array of different Americans *and* a wider historical perspective in relation to both US history and the history of relations between the US and the rest of the world. The films also touch on the *possibility* of change of a different nature, that is, change for the better. In addition, these films indicate how the short film format – *Parallel Lines* might also be seen as a series of loosely connected vignettes – was found to be the most appropriate form for gathering, but not unifying, a range of responses to 9/11. Of course, these films – the work of independent and amateur video/

film artists, a collection of amateur film reportage, a European-funded portmanteau film and a low-budget, single-handed documentary – are marginal. However, the critical views they seek to articulate did also appear fleetingly in the multiplex via Spike Lee's *25th Hour* (2002), albeit as a result of a series of contingent circumstances.

25th Hour tells the story of New York drug dealer Monty Brogan (Edward Norton) and his last day of freedom before submitting to a lengthy jail term. The film was not initially intended as a 9/11 project. In fact, Lee brokered the deal to film David Benioff's turn-of-the-millennium novel (published in 2000) with Touchstone Pictures well before the attacks. Lee shot the film in 37 days during the early summer of 2001 on a modest budget of $15 million. After 9/11, and in contrast to the many film producers who had attended the Beverly Hills Summit (who were discussing how to digitally manipulate their prints to remove references to the attacks), Lee's production team discussed how they might create a post-9/11 mood around the existing script, one that would encourage a critical rather than a belligerent response (see Felperin 2003: 15).[6] The creative freedom to make these changes stemmed from a combination of Touchstone's hope that the film had the potential to win an Academy Award and a supportive A-list star (Norton was paid $9 million for *Red Dragon* (2002) but agreed to work on *25th Hour* for a nominal fee of $500,000).

25th Hour's dramatic opening sequence was one of the elements added to help create this post-9/11 mood. The sequence begins with abstract patterns of blue light framed by a cityscape at night. Long-time Lee collaborator Terence Blanchard provides the score – a classical rendition of Irish and Arabic folk music that lends a powerful cry of pain and suffering to the images. As the sequence unfolds, the cityscape is shown to be New York and the light is seen to be emanating from Ground Zero, where an installation of 88 searchlights was placed between 11 March and 14 April 2002 to create two vertical columns of light in remembrance of the attacks. This 'Tribute of Light' was a tangible desire to replace the loss, to fill the gap and to turn a negative, traumatic experience into a redemptive, affirmative experience; and yet, the lights are also ephemeral and fleeting, signalling both a desire to move on and the difficulty of doing so. Gustavo Bonevardi, one of the designers of the Tribute, stated,

> We set out to 'repair' and 'rebuild' the skyline – but not in a way that would attempt to undo or disguise the damage. Those buildings are gone now, and they will never be rebuilt. Instead we would create a link

between ourselves and what was lost. In so doing, we believed, we could also repair, in part, our city's identity and ourselves. (2002)

The final shot of the sequence shows lower Manhattan in long shot from the perspective of Brooklyn, the bridge providing a line of sight across and into the city. This latter shot is carefully chosen as it presents the viewer with a perspective found in a number of iconic photographs of the Twin Towers before and during 9/11, and of the skyline without the towers after the attacks. The film's opening sequence – a musical score of mixed ethnic provenance, the foregrounding of a solemn and reflective act of commemoration and a view of New York that offers some critical distance – conveys anger and loss, but also functions as something like a call to understand. There is no montage sequence of missing person posters and heroic firefighters, no detailed description of communal grieving and therapeutic healing, and no Stars and Stripes. Instead the film's opening credits seem to wish to prime the viewer to subject the characters and the events of its narrative, and their relation to 9/11, to critical scrutiny.

In keeping with this, the film's cinematography depicts the city through the understated use of a dark, steely grey colour palette. The reviewer at the *Economist* observed that the 'bleached colours suggest a city covered with ashes' (Anon. 2003), while Ryan Gilbey noted that 'Lee's use of space expertly evokes the general air of a city bereft (2003: 58). This style of cinematography to depict post-9/11 New York had become something of a cliché by mid-decade – *In the Cut* (2003), *Flightplan* (2004), *War of the Worlds* (2005), *The Interpreter* (2005) and *The Brave One* (2007) all adopt a similar colour palette. But, alongside Penn's contribution to *11'09"01 September 11* with its play of light and dark and *Parallel Lines* with its final shot of shadows on a darkened street, *25th Hour* is a pioneer of this way of using film form to key a searching account of identity and difference in relation to 9/11 and its aftermath.

The film explores the question of personal responsibility, with each of the main characters – Monty Brogan, Jacob Elinsky (Philip Seymour Hoffman) and Frank Slaughtery (Barry Pepper) – wrestling with alienation, regret and guilt. At key moments of hiatus in the narrative, the three characters are privileged with a shot in a mirror in which they contemplate their 'distorted or fractured reflection' in the light of their desire to change themselves and their acknowledgement of the difficulty of achieving this change (Gilbey 2003: 58). The characters' respective existential crises are in part driven by earlier life decisions and experiences, thus reinforcing the film's commitment to a thematic and narrative design set on interrogating the relationship between past and present.

The key sequence here is the scene in which Monty stares at his reflection in the toilet of his father's bar; the sequence is preceded by shots of photographs of eleven firefighters killed on 9/11, and to the right-hand side of the mirror a sticker shows the silhouette of the Twin Towers against the backdrop of a US flag. As Monty looks in the mirror, his reflection (an angry alter ego) subjects him to a misanthropic rant that attacks the homeless, Blacks, Jews, the NYPD, the Church, Jesus Christ, Chelsea homosexuals, Bensonhurst Italians, rich Upper East Side wives, Hasidic Jewish diamond traders, Russian mobsters, Korean grocers, Pakistani and Sikh taxi drivers, Wall Street brokers, Enron, Cheney and Bush, Puerto Ricans, Dominicans, his friends, his girlfriend, his father and Osama bin Laden.[7] Monty's alter ego's rage-fuelled invective – blaming others for anything and everything – is a tactic that enables him to avoid negotiating the unpalatable fact that he has 'been living high on other people's miseries' (O'Neill 2004: 6). It can also be read as an articulation of the violent, Manichean discourse prevalent in the aftermath of 9/11, whereby all others are subject to criticism and complaint and no self-reflection is undertaken.

However, as Monty vents his spleen, cutaways show the people who are the victims of his tirade, New Yorkers who look directly at the camera. In the early part of the sequence these New Yorkers appear to function as embodiments of Monty's alter ego's invective, but as the sequence progresses these caricatures give way to more objective, almost documentary-style portraits and then, finally, to images of neighbourhoods that give a sense of the city as the sum of its many parts. The sequence asks the viewer to reconcile Monty's alter ego's perspective with the presence of actual New Yorkers, encouraging an undoing of his reductive stereotyping, in what amounts to a complex acknowledgement of difference. The sequence draws to a close with Monty telling his alter ego in no uncertain terms that he himself is to blame – 'No, fuck you', he mutters calmly – and resolving to take responsibility for his own actions. In a theme that runs throughout the film, with people in positions of authority (a mid-level drug dealer, a city financier and a high-school teacher) shown taking advantage of those in less powerful positions than themselves, Monty acknowledges that he has behaved unethically.

This moral awakening is punctuated with flashbacks that show key moments of Monty's life, thereby creating a strong sense of before and after, of lost opportunities and of regret. As such, *25th Hour* indexes the need, in the immediate aftermath of 9/11, for self-reflection and the assumption of personal responsibility, especially with regard to how actions in the past lead to consequences in the present. Monty comes to recognise that his past behaviour has harmed others and that he must break the cycle by acknowledging this, atoning for his actions, and pledging to take a different course in the future. This structure – operating in the realm of the personal – lends itself to being read as something of an insistence that the events of 9/11 should also give cause for reflection about US history and can be read in relation to Chalmers Johnson's (2002) concept of 'blowback': namely, that the violent clandestine actions of the CIA and other government agencies may precipitate unanticipated and unpredictable events. While the dominant tendency was to efface the past, with 9/11 detached from any historical perspective, *25th Hour*, like Sean Penn's film (which points to the history of the World Trade Center) and *Parallel Lines* (which connects the events to the mistreatment of Native Americans, a qualified account of Pearl Harbor and the bombing of Hiroshima and Nagasaki), tells a story of how past events cannot be effaced or repressed, and how these events will both shape and determine future courses of action.

Having constructed this difficult reality, the film offers two possible endings to consider. On the day Monty is due to go to prison, one ending has him and his father driving west together – a road trip running counter to the one undertaken by Davenport in *Parallel Lines* – and we see him starting a new modest life and, in time, raising a family. This is the conventional Hollywood ending that would give the film uplift, activating as it does a deep-seated mythology of Manifest Destiny. Yet easy closure of this sort would simply continue the eschewal of personal responsibility that the film has shown to be the root cause of a wider social and cultural malaise, and, by extension, a causal factor in the terrorist attacks themselves. Monty must serve his time, the film's logic suggests, if he is ever to get back to those values and experiences that his criminal behaviour has led him to let drift. As such, the film ends with his father ignoring the road west and taking his son to prison, indicating how, if the US is to build a fair, egalitarian, socially democratic society, individual Americans must refuse the myths of self and nation proffered by the mainstream media in the period following 9/11, and instead take responsibility for themselves and their actions. Here the film's score deploys the Bruce Springsteen track 'The Fuse', taken from his seminal post-9/11 album *The Rising*, leading Jeffrey Melnick to note that

> the appearance of Springsteen's song acts as a final reminder ... that
> 9/11 is the explanation for the feelings of fragmentation and loss that

anchor the movie. 9/11 is the 24th hour implied by the title: the 25th
hour is what comes after, which Lee's film tells us looks a lot like
prison. (2009: 13)

Through the selection of this seemingly more pessimistic ending, Monty
is required to acknowledge how his own actions impinge on those around
him – strangers marked by racial and social difference – and to change his
behaviour in order to maintain the well-being of these people. At the film's
close, the New Yorkers who were subject to racial slurs in Monty's alter ego's
earlier rant reappear and wave to him as he leaves, the city's dispossessed
wishing him well. In their hailing of him – a young black boy writes his
name on the window of a bus and waves goodbye – they point to a reci-
procity and sense of community in marked contrast to a general anger and
suspicion based on their racial difference.

Crucially, the film does not offer redemption for those, like Monty,
whose actions are exploitative and violent: corrupt corporations (Enron,
Worldcom), capitalists (stockbrokers, diamond traders), politicians (Bush,
Cheney) and terrorists (Bin Laden). These people – and the historical forces
they signify – are identified as related to and responsible for 9/11. Here
25th Hour is more determined to address in a complex, or dialectical, way
something gestured towards in Penn's film and articulated with blunt rhetorical force in *Seven Days in September* and *Parallel Lines*: namely, that the
inequities and corruption at the heart of neoliberal capitalism had a role in
precipitating the events of 9/11.

Adopting a similarly iconoclastic position, a number of left-liberal commentators sought to counter the mass media's construction of Ground Zero
– via photographs such as *Ground Zero Spirit* – as consecrated ground (see
Grant 2005). Edwin G. Burrows describes the troubled history of Manhattan
from the colonial era onwards (this long history a counter-narrative to that of
Pearl Harbor) and concludes that 'the city has always been deeply implicated
in the world', and that 'this is not the first time its people have paid a heavy
price as a result' (2002: 32). Michael Sorkin and Sharon Zukin argue that
'however anonymous they appeared, the Twin Towers were never benign,
never just architecture' (2002: xi), and that

from the 1920 bombing of the Morgan Bank to the displacement of the
largely Arab community that once thrived on the Lower West Side, to
the destruction of an intimate architectural texture by megascale constructions, this part of the city has been contested space. (Ibid.)

Marshall Berman respectfully acknowledges the human losses on 9/11 – from stockbrokers to cleaners – but argues that this does not change the fact that the World Trade Center was an expression of 'an urbanism that disdained the city and its people' (2002: 6). Gabriel Kolko refers to the World Trade Center simply as 'Wall St', with the Twin Towers no more than synonyms for the US financial system in its entirety (2002: 11). These attempts to ground the experience of 9/11 in the material facts of the destroyed building's primary use were not part of the mainstream response. David Harvey observes that on 9/11 the BBC reported that the terrorists had attacked 'the main symbols of global US financial and military power' whereas the US media reported an attack on 'America', 'freedom', 'American values' and the 'American way of life' (2002: 57). Afterwards, as 'New Yorkers, faced with unspeakable tragedy, for the most part rallied around ideals of community, togetherness, solidarity, and altruism as opposed to beggar-thy-neighbor individualism' (2002: 61), the media (via a series of short obituaries in the *New York Times*)

> celebrated the lives and special qualities of those that died, making it impossible to raise a critical voice as to what role the bond traders and others might have had in the creation and perpetuation of social inequality either locally or world-wide. (2002: 59)

It is precisely this kind of stance in the mainstream media that the films described in this chapter, and *25th Hour* in particular, seek to challenge.

In another key sequence in *25th Hour* (also added to the film after 9/11 and shot on location at Ground Zero), Frank and Jacob have a conversation in an apartment overlooking the ruins of the World Trade Center. They discuss how real estate values will be damaged by the attacks and their own culpability in Monty's crimes. The music from the film's opening sequence returns here and combines with a zoom that takes us out of the window and allows us to gaze on the remains of the foundations of the Twin Towers. In contrast to the abstracted New York of the opening sequence, Ground Zero is shown here in documentary style, lit by the floodlights of the men working there (the scene is evocative of Joel Meyerowitz's photographs).[8] In stark contrast to *Ground Zero Spirit*, at the centre of the site an improvised American flag on a scaffold is dwarfed by the scale of the destruction. The combination of image and sound here suggests that Blanchard's score is not a call to arms – two value systems/musical styles in conflict – but rather a dialectical synthesis, a call for a forensic look at how things are interconnected in the eerie light and emptiness of Ground Zero. By activating a critique of the system (and its victims within the US and further afield, with New York standing in for globalisation and its negative effects), the film hints that the US requires a period of critical self-reflection in which it admits that its power and status comes at the expense of others.

In realigning and augmenting *25th Hour* in the immediate aftermath of the terrorist attacks, Lee sought to register and decipher the experience of 9/11 through the mechanism of a complex and challenging narrative of guilt, critical reflection and atonement. Monty's personal journey can be read allegorically: the US has pursued a bare-toothed capitalism (of which drug-dealers are metonymic), presided over by opportunist and self-interested politicians and corrupt corporations and financial institutions. The protection and maintenance of the system has required the condoning of clandestine, often terrorist, actions, as well as supporting repressive regimes in the Middle East and Latin America. Implicit here is the belief that activities in the past have played a role in shaping the circumstances of the present, that, in other words, 9/11 constitutes a return of the repressed. Monty's decision to face up to these difficult facts (rather than blaming others who have had little power or role in defining this reality) offers an alternative to the overtly patriotic nationalist sentiments at play in the immediate post-9/11 aftermath.

On its release in December 2002 and into early 2003, reviewers accused *25th Hour* of opportunism and insensitivity as well as heavy-handedness. Like those films with a more satirical or critical view of war, such as *Buffalo Soldiers* and *The Quiet American*, the film was discreetly sidelined, opening in only five theatres in New York and Los Angeles, and then left to languish without a suitable marketing budget, reaching 460 screens at its most visible (*Spider-Man*, by way of contrast, opened on 3,500 screens). More generally, the fate of the film illustrates the ways in which the dynamic, unruly reaction to 9/11 described in the present chapter struggled to gain purchase amidst mainstream offerings of escape and elision.

This chapter has demonstrated that one of the more remarkable consequences of 9/11 is the way in which the event precipitated not only an outpouring of anger, patriotic nationalism and a desire for revenge but also pleas for unity, altruism, forgiveness and love. In an attempt to capture how these different emotional states might form the basis for different possible futures, British novelist Martin Amis described the moment of the second plane strike as 'the worldflash of a coming future' (quoted in Randall 2010: 3). Amis's description here recalls one of Walter Benjamin's theses on the philosophy of history, that the past can be seized only as an image which flashes up at the instant when it can be recognised and is never seen again [...] To articulate the past historically does not mean to recognise it 'the way it really was' ... It means to seize hold of a memory as it flashes up at a moment of danger. (1969: 247)

The attacks and the contested struggle to make sense of them made visible what had previously been invisible. The questions – Who? How? Why? – led many, in resistance to the view offered by the mass media, to reflect on the rise of the US as the twentieth century's most significant superpower, on the limits and abuses of that power and on the unequal and unfair but thoroughly interdependent relationship between developed and developing countries. As well, an intensely personal form of reflection asked how the violence of the attacks also mirrors violence across the lives of those in the US who are also disadvantaged by the vagaries of capitalism. These aspects did indeed 'flash up', and as the films discussed here indicate, were recognised and seized upon. In this moment of crisis, two choices – parallel lines, if you will – became available: close down the uncertainty or embrace it. From the moment the terrorists struck, films were produced that sought to ask questions, challenge authority and protest against injustice. Journalists, teachers, screenwriters, bloggers, activists and filmmakers shouldered the task in different ways, but each sought to detail the complex nature of the genealogy of the attacks and the wider response to them. Even just a few days, weeks and months after the attacks, patriotic nationalism was being actively resisted. The films described here were certainly not the dominant response, but they were part of a spectrum of critical responses that, if followed, might have illuminated a path that avoided the quagmire of the 'war on terror' and Abu Ghraib. Indeed, the films discussed above have much in common with the more avowedly critical post-9/11 cinema that will be described in later chapters of this book. However, this critical sensibility notwithstanding, a hegemonic jingoistic nationalism did initially prevail, as the next chapter will demonstrate.

Unity

In a survey of the press coverage of the terrorist attacks and the language used in speeches by key politicians between 11 September and 13 September 2001, Martin Montgomery identifies a process of 'discursive amplification' whereby rhetoric was 'scaled up' in order to make sense of what had happened. He notes how the terrorists' murderous acts became evil acts, then barbaric acts and then acts of war, and how the attack on New York quickly became an attack on the US and that this subsequently became an attack on civilisation (2005: 155–6). Montgomery argues that this 'movement from concrete, verifiable entities to large abstractions serves in practice only to mystify the underlying event by immediately embedding it in larger discourses of patriotism, the homeland, and the imagined community of the nation' (2005: 158). Nicholas Thorburn observes the logic of this version of national identity at work in the speeches of George W. Bush, which

> included a hatred of the Other, an absolute and racialised division between good and evil, powerful emotive constructions of nation, forms of gendered masculine address, the impersonation of national-popular heroes, a wholesale absolution for consumerist ways of life, an insistence on working and shopping through all and any crisis, and an implied civilisational superiority associated with religion. (2007: 103)

Similarly, in a content analysis of the online version of the *Los Angeles Times* in the twelve weeks following 9/11, Christine M. Rodrigue noted how initial coverage (which included stories of the attacks and their investigation) was sidelined in favour of 'war stories of diplomacy, deployment, airstrikes, and the fall of the Taliban' (2003: 530). As a result, Rodrigue concludes, 'the context of the events of September 11th was poorly drawn out [with only] six stories appear[ing] on the front screen of the *Los Angeles Times* about the geopolitical background [to the attacks]' (2003: 550).

These studies evidence the dominant ideological response to 9/11 described in the introduction of this book: a response founded on a sense of patriotic nationalism, innocence violated, righteous anger and the demand for retaliation and war. Or, as Peter Knight describes it,

> a sense of urgent crisis and imminent threat to a specifically American way of life from an all-pervasive hidden enemy; the portrayal of America as an exceptional victim; the reassertion of traditional American values and a call to national unity in response; a Manichaean insistence on dividing the world into Them and Us; the demand that America lead an epic to-the-death fight against the plotters; the casting of all blame onto the enemy; and the portrayal of the enemy as completely alien, inhuman, all-powerful, and, above all, evil. (2008: 180)

According to this view, the attacks were unprecedented and unfounded (coming literally 'out of the blue' on a cloudless autumn day) and therefore discouraged reflection on how past events might have offered some insight into why the attacks had happened, with a mythologised view of World War II the primary reference point.

That this ideological dominant entered the lived experience of a great many Americans is revealed in the work of photographer Jonathan Hyman, who documented a representative sample of patriotic murals and tattoos after 9/11. Hyman observed that in 'several murals and tattoos, the towers are depicted as in heaven or in an apotheosis, ascending to heaven' and the Statue of Liberty was often shown wounded or damaged and receding into the background, with the Stars and Stripes and the more aggressive image of the bald eagle coming to the fore (2007: 183–92). Writ large across the mass media, on the front pages of newspapers, as murals adorning public spaces and inscribed in blue and green ink on people's bodies, the cultural response hardened a fragile neoconservative consensus. Douglas Kellner notes that the Bush presidency had not been popular before 9/11 – with the controversial election of 2000 offering anything but a clear mandate – but that with the terrorist attacks 'the bitter partisanship of the previous months disappeared and Bush was the beneficiary of [an] extraordinary outburst of patriotism' (2003: 39). A Gallup poll in November 2001 'showed that 87% of respondents rated [Bush] favourably, and the numbers were still high – 67% – when the Iraq War started in March 2003' (Prince 2009: 182). This consensus allowed for a joint resolution titled 'The Authorization for Use of Military Force' to be passed in the House of Representatives 420–1 and the Senate 98–0 on 14 September.[9] This legislation permitted the president to wage war against al-Qaida and its Taliban allies in Afghanistan, as well as in any other engagement deemed necessary to the 'war on terror'. Aerial bombardment of Afghanistan began on 7 October in a military operation code-named Operation Infinite Justice, with Bush declaring that 'this crusade, this war on terrorism, is going to take a while'. Bush's use of the word 'crusade' and the term 'infinite justice' – inflecting the war implicitly with a sense of religious providence – was heavily criticised, and as a result the operation was renamed Enduring Freedom.

It was noted in the introduction how the film industry altered release schedules to bring to the fore a cycle of patriotic war films that reinforced this jingoistic response and how films critical of US foreign policy such as *Buffalo Soldiers* and *The Quiet American* were delayed or sidelined. These critical films also fell victim to the accusation that they were somehow un-American, a term that was used regularly and with powerful censoring effect in the period immediately following the attacks. I also noted how in order to avoid drawing attention to 9/11 the producers of *Spider-Man* took the decision to remove a sequence showing the Twin Towers from advance promotional material for the film. However, by the time of the film's release in the summer of 2002, as Daniel Robson observes, the film's redrawn marketing posters showed 'a gilded New York skyline before a Manhattan sunset, convey[ed] an image of indestructibility and optimism, and utilis[ed] architectural icons to represent solidity and permanency' (2012: 52). Thus, Robson argues that *Spider-Man* activated and emphasised an 'indirect but overt patriotism' taking on 'an unanticipated political dimension due to its explosive aerial combat scenes set against a New York backdrop and a tagline – "with great power comes great responsibility" – that echoed pronouncements by policymakers' (ibid.). In a scene added after 9/11 a bystander shouts 'This is New York! If you mess with one of us you mess with all of us!' and this addition to the script shows the work undertaken to connect the film to the wider jingoistic discourse. Robson argues that the film's patriotic stance is encapsulated in the film's final shot, in which 'Spider-Man casts his protective eye over New York City from atop a flagpole flying the Stars and

Stripes', with the film's 'storyline and characters indirectly stand[ing] as a metaphor for political unity' (ibid.).

This chapter examines how a cycle of post-9/11 films, extending the ideological designs found in *Spider-Man*, repeats and reinforces the neo-conservative discourse. These films sought to silence the diverse voices and critical views found in films such as *Seven Days in September*, *Parallel Lines* and *25th Hour*, discussed in chapter one. These uncertain but politically searching films had sought ways to challenge Manichean constructions of 'us' and 'them', to question the presumption that war was the best course of action, to offer different historical models for the attack than World War II, and to entertain the notion that the World Trade Center and the Pentagon had been attacked because they were symbols of financial and military power. In contrast, a cycle of high-profile patriotic documentaries and a distinct post-9/11 revenge film cycle sought to relate 9/11 to the banal nationalism prevalent in the wider culture and in doing so consolidate the move to war.

The most widely viewed and critically lauded films to directly show the events of 9/11 appeared on television, where they were presented as discrete, almost cinematic, events. Upon broadcast these films were carefully demarcated as historic occasions, often with advertising respectfully suspended for the duration (as it had been during the rolling news reports on 9/11). The most high-profile and representative of these films is called simply *9/11*. Directed and produced by French filmmakers Gédéon and Jules Naudet in collaboration with New York firefighter James Hanlon, *9/11* was screened commercial-free on CBS on 10 March 2002. The film was 'hosted' by Robert De Niro, who appeared at three points during the documentary to offer counsel and direction. The DVD edition released by Paramount Pictures in 2002 under the title *9/11: The Filmmakers' Commemorative Edition* does not feature De Niro but contains an additional fifteen minutes in which a number of scenes are extended. The film was reshown on 10 September 2006 to mark the fifth anniversary of 9/11, and again on the tenth anniversary, with updates on the individual narratives shown therein.

In the weeks before the attacks the Naudet brothers had been making a film about Tony Benetatos, a probationary firefighter, or 'probie', as he joined a fire station and waited for the call that would allow him to gain his first professional experience. While investigating a gas leak at an intersection less than a mile north of the World Trade Center, Jules Naudet recorded the first plane hitting the North Tower (this now iconic footage appears in almost all 9/11 documentaries).[10] Jules then attended the rescue operation and filmed events from the vantage point of the command post in the lobby of the North Tower. He continued filming from this restricted position as the second plane struck the South Tower. Meanwhile, Gédéon Naudet filmed Benetatos and other firefighters responding to the attacks and recorded the second plane strike on the South Tower. Both filmmakers continued to film independently, and without knowledge of the other's fate, as the towers collapsed. The quality and quantity of highly detailed footage that the filmmakers recorded has made their work central to early attempts to document the event, with their footage appearing in a large number of different documentaries, including those described in chapter one. After 9/11 considerable resources were made available to turn their low-key film about a probationary firefighter into something more significant: a national television event that, when broadcast, would be viewed by 39 million viewers, the largest ever audience for a documentary.

By virtue of its subject matter – namely, the firefighters' response to the attacks – the film was able to bind strongly with the dominant patriotic discourse. This was, in part, fortuitous. By the evening of 11 September and in the days following, firefighters were lionised as symbols of strength, courage and self-sacrifice. Photographs such as *Ground Zero Spirit* cast the firefighters as heroic figures. One billboard poster showed a firefighter in full uniform and stated simply, 'When others ran out, he rushed in'. On 7 January 2002, 'Faces of Ground Zero', an exhibition of epic large-scale photographs of rescue workers by Joe McNally, opened at Grand Central Station.[11] Reflecting on the heroic behaviour of the firefighters one year after the attacks, the *Observer* journalist Peter Conrad wrote that the 'firemen obediently troop upstairs in the burning towers, and their dogged, tramping march becomes a kind of ascension; the rising itself is a kind of resurrection' (2002). Like the tattoos – many of which showed the World Trade Center ascending to heaven – the firefighters attained a near beatification and found themselves in the position of privileged gatekeepers to the meaning of 9/11. Susan Faludi notes that the Marvel Comics special edition comic book *The Call of Duty: The Brotherhood* (2002) depicted the firefighters as quasi-superheroes and describes how findings related to shortcomings in the emergency services' responses were held back by three years in an attempt to maintain this straightforwardly heroic version of events (2007: 72).

In this context, the Naudets' decision to adopt a *vérité*-style approach and to live and work alongside the firefighters meant that they experienced the attacks from an 'embedded' perspective that would by chance become one of the central ways in which 9/11 was recuperated by the mass media. As the film was already aligned with this perspective, it became relatively straight-forward in post-production to emphasise the heroic behaviour and sacrifice of the firefighters. In the opening sequence narrator James Hanlon observes that as a firefighter, 'You do your job, you risk your life to help people', and this is the film's credo as we witness the group respond to the attacks. The film places the viewer within the heart of the maelstrom: entering the lobby, climbing the stairs, travelling to the site when everyone else is fleeing. The film's hand-held style ensures that this experience is as an embodied one, with the heat, the sweat and the fear given a powerful immediacy. Crucially, the firefighters do not understand what is taking place and the film rein-forces this lack of comprehension by largely avoiding any reflection on the events from a position of hindsight. Instead, the film offers a claustrophobic and terrifying 'close-up' of the lived experience and bravery of those involved in the rescue operation. This sense of 9/11 contrasts sharply with the type of critical reflection sought by the films discussed in chapter one. Six months after the attacks, *9/11* reproduces and reinforces a fearful incomprehension girded with a sense of unquestioning civic duty and heroic self-sacrifice: a response that was understandable (and even laudable) on 9/11 but which lent itself readily to ideological appropriation in the aftermath of the events. As Stef Craps argues, this limited point of view places 9/11 'in a political and his-torical vacuum' that 'ends up echoing the official discourse' (2007: 195, 196).

9/11 nuances this blanket valorisation of the firefighter through its focus on the story of Benetatos. After initial teasers of spectacular action related

Fig. 3: 'If my country decides to send me to go kill, I'll do it now':
Firefighter Tony Benetatos in *9/11* (2002)

to 9/11, the documentary shows a number of vignettes of everyday life at the fire station, all filmed before 9/11, each of which is given a suspenseful inflection as Benetatos awaits his first fire. Early in the film, Hanlon declares, 'Soon they'd face the unthinkable. The question was: would Tony be ready?' This line of dialogue encapsulates the central dramatic structure: the rite of passage of a young man as he moves from innocence to experience. These early scenes are replete with an almost unbearable tension because we know that the defining event for Benetatos will be that of 9/11, and this tension is maintained by having Benetatos appear only in footage from before the attacks, thereby leading the viewer to fear that he may not have survived. A dramatic reveal late in the film shows Benetatos returning from Ground Zero, in the words of a veteran firefighter, 'like an urban cowboy, appearing alone from the cloudy, dust-covered horizon'. Having proved himself by travelling to Ground Zero, Benetatos's survival and the emotional reunion of the firefighters provides the uplift and release of tension more commonly associated with fiction filmmaking. Hanlon comments, 'It turns out Tony became a man in about nine hours, trying to help out on 9/11'. Craps notes that

> the viewer is led to interpret the probie's journey from innocence to experience as an allegory of the fate of the entire nation. The fire-fighters' community in general, and Benetatos in particular, metonymically and metaphorically represent the United States, a nation that sees itself as a force for good, the world's fireman. The probie's self-description as 'a person who tries to do good, just like every other person in the fire department' is entirely consistent with this benign national self-image. (2007: 193)

Reflecting on his experiences, Benetatos states, 'I know it's either this [the fire department] or the army now. And I like saving lives, I don't like taking them. But after what I saw, if my country decides to send me to go kill, I'll do it now.' In this statement, and the film's structural logic, the firefighter's commitment to self-sacrifice and civic duty segues with an unbridled patriotism and a desire to wage war. Or, as Craps puts it,

> the focus shifts from a disorienting and over-whelming sense of loss to comforting, ideologically charged notions of heroism and community that perpetuate an idealized national self-image and come to function as a moral justification for retaliation. (Craps 2007: 185)

The film consolidates Benetatos's reasoning by placing it among closing scenes of funerals of firefighters who died on 9/11. The way the film depicts the ritualised burial procedures of the fire service provides a concrete focal point for a collective outpouring of grief as well as a mechanism for closure and resolution. In addition, with the coffins draped in the US flag and funerals conducted in full uniform, the *mise-en-scène* here serves to emphasise how the move to war is underwritten with the blood of the fallen.

This resolute focus on the experience of the firefighter also fed the construction of 9/11 as an inclusive event – an attack not on symbols of US financial and military might but on 'America'. The deaths of financial traders and white-collar workers were subsumed into those of the firefighters (and to a lesser extent the police): honourable blue-collar workers on basic wages committed to public service, civic duty and political neutrality. The fact that the New York Fire Department was an overwhelmingly white, male group was negotiated through the layering in of the interrelated stories of the World Trade Center's ethnically diverse workforce: its cleaners, cooks and security guards.[12] This way of representing the events – riding roughshod over the specificity that gives shape to the films described in chapter one – served to sever the connection between the attacks and the high finance and capitalist speculation so central to the activities of the World Trade Center (activities acknowledged in *Seven Days in September* and *25th Hour*) and instead subject the events to what Susan Willis refers to as the 'federalisation of 9/11' (2005: 25). For many, the firefighters were beyond criticism, thereby validating the ideological position they were often (and often reluctantly on their part) used to reproduce. In this context, the design of the documentary in post-production, and the presentation of it upon broadcast – with Robert De Niro describing the professional role thus: 'Firemen live to help others live; it's that simple' – tied the raw, gripping film footage to this wider ideological discourse in ways that made criticism very difficult.

In the press, it was also reported that soldiers in Afghanistan were carrying debris from the World Trade Center with them as talismans to motivate their actions, and that at the launch of the USS New York, a US Navy warship made with steel salvaged from the World Trade Center, members of the New York Fire Department were given a prominent position in order to lend the ship (and the ongoing war) their official sanction. As Willis notes,

> The flag raised Iwo Jima-style over New York's Ground Zero was subsequently shipped to Afghanistan where it was raised over the Khandahar airport […] Indeed, in its power to evoke healing and perseverance over

Unity

New York and retribution over Kandahar this flag shows itself as an empty signifier, capable of designating a host of referents without being perceived as contradictory. (2005: 15–16)

Taken together, *9/11*'s combination of the intense scenes of the planes striking the towers and the firefighters' response, Benetatos's rite of passage and desire to wage war, and the funeral ritual as a form of patriotic closure all serve to amplify the wider cultural discourse described at the beginning of this chapter. The film feeds the iteration and reiteration of a belligerent nationalism, and this nationalism gives shape to military ritual and the production of the apparatus for waging war. In this case the Stars and Stripes is anything but an 'empty signifier'; indeed, its meaning remains stable as it is carried purposely forward from Ground Zero to the heart of military operations.

A similar logic gives structure to *In Memoriam – New York City, 9/11/01*, which was shown on HBO on 25 May 2002. The marketing for the film used the *Ground Zero Spirit* photograph, and the film begins with shots of the Twin Towers at sunset, golden and burnished. In voice-over, Rudy Giuliani – mayor of New York at the time of the attacks and voted *Time*'s Person of the Year in 2001 for his statesmanlike response – reflects on how much he loved the New York skyline, and especially the World Trade Center, which he considered a symbol of a particularly American type of 'freedom', defined here as the ability to succeed through individualism and hard work regardless of

Fig. 4: A hagiographic view of the World Trade Center: *In Memoriam – New York City, 9/11/01* (2002)

sex, creed or colour. Giuliani then counsels – by way of framing the film's unflinching depiction of the full horror of the event, including, controversially, images of people jumping from the buildings and a photograph of a body after the fall – that 9/11 must be looked at in all its awfulness so that it might fuel the resolve to defend the US (as imagined in his opening remarks).

Following this, the film consists of footage of 9/11 gathered from sixteen news organisations and 118 New Yorkers that has been subjected to considerable editorial work, through which a clear, chronological order is imposed. Thus, what David Bordwell terms 'intensified continuity' – that is, a loose, fast-paced continuity editing system usually reserved for high-budget commercial films – is used to make sense of the events of 9/11 (2002). The result is direct and gripping, signalling order and clarity rather than the tentative uncertainty that is the hallmark of the films described in chapter one. What is most significant is that although we see a number of different filmic points of view, there is a complete lack of differing ideological perspectives. Where *Seven Days in September* and *Underground Zero* accommodate a range of (often radical) political views, *In Memoriam*, through editorial manipulation, brings these diverse perspectives in line with the general tenor of the discourse circulating in the mass media. Here Giuliani's point of view is privileged (in one sequence a number of people react in horror to the people jumping from the towers, but it is Giuliani's response that is brought to the fore). This is further reinforced through a focus on the recollections of senior members of his administration, to which the filmmakers had 'unprecedented access'. As 9/11 draws to a close we learn that Giuliani returned home and read from the memoirs of Winston Churchill, and the film concludes with scenes of the Family Members Memorial service held at Ground Zero on 28 October. Giuliani addresses the service, stating that 'America will prevail'. Another unifying element is the musical underscoring, which is reminiscent of the vernacular classical style of US composer Aaron Copeland, whose work is evocative of both the modernist cityscape of New York and a sense of the sublime North American landscape, especially the west. This soundscape runs in counterpoint to the images of a broken and damaged US, but when taken together with Giuliani's (literal and structural) narration, the music recalls the epic history of Manifest Destiny; as such, 9/11 becomes a location in which American myths can be reclaimed and remade.

9/11 and *In Memoriam* share a normative perspective and a commitment to the celebration of the heroism and self-sacrifice of the firefighters. *In Memoriam* also celebrates the actions of resourceful, effective and headstrong politicians. The experiences of these two groups are tied to wider discourses of anger, desire for revenge and mourning. The films direct attention away from reasons for the attack and towards the rescue and clear-up operation, and this tight focus implicitly discourages any attempt to think through the event in relation to history, capitalism or the role of the US in the Middle East or elsewhere. They pull the event out of long and mid-shot into the closed-down space of the claustrophobic close-up. *9/11* was broadcast just one week after the cinema release of *We Were Soldiers*, while *In Memoriam* was screened as *Spider-Man* was breaking box-office records. Taken together, these 'unity films' are indicative of how a network of anchor points across the mass media, including film culture, tethered and made taut a certain patriotic nationalism. These films also offered a template for further representation. Seven years after the attack, the documentary *102 Minutes That Changed the World* (2008) screened on the History Channel. The film edits together footage shot by amateur filmmakers on the day, but it is modelled on *In Memoriam* more than *Seven Days in September*, and as such it indicates how mainstream documentary continued to depict 9/11 in ways that offered little or no attempt to contextualise or explain. Such close framing, maintained five to seven years after 9/11, may be regarded as an evasive strategy designed to discourage critical reflection and maintain a conservative view of the events.

In the context of a culture shaped by this patriotic discourse, a distinct Hollywood revenge film cycle can be identified. Revenge was implicit in many and myriad responses to 9/11 – and is voiced and acknowledged in all the documentary films described thus far in this chapter. Most obviously, the Japanese attack on Pearl Harbor was considered a comparable point of reference in much media coverage, thereby activating a chain of association that justified the US to respond with unrestrained military force. The most recent popular cultural recounting of that particular event, the war film *Pearl Harbor*, which grossed $450 million worldwide on its release in May 2001, was still playing in more than a hundred cinemas one month after 9/11. The film portrays the US as an undeserving victim and shows US military personnel responding to the attacks with tough, patriotic resolve (the US flag is ubiquitous and blood transfusions are improvised using Coke bottles), and ends with a depiction of the Doolittle raids, or 'payback' bombing, on Tokyo (see Landy 2004: 86–7). As already mentioned, *Collateral Damage*, an Arnold Schwarzenegger vehicle in production before 9/11 but held back due to its graphic depiction of terrorism, was eventually released in February 2002, and its revenge plot, in which a firefighter seeks out and kills the Colombian terrorists responsible for the death of his family, is a useful example of the cycle described below.

The remainder of this chapter focuses on *Man on Fire*, which I take to exemplify this revenge discourse. The film tells the story of retired counter-insurgency specialist, John Creasy (Denzel Washington), who is hired as a bodyguard to protect Pita (Dakota Fanning), the daughter of a rich Mexican industrialist married to a US citizen. Creasy strikes up an unlikely friendship with his ward, and when she is kidnapped and presumed raped and murdered he tracks down and kills all those involved. Although *Man on Fire* was released in the spring and summer of 2004, the average 18–24 month production period for a large-budget Hollywood film places the writing and shooting of the film in the context of the immediate aftermath of 9/11. As the bare bones of the plot indicate, *Man on Fire* is first and foremost a revenge film. John Kerrigan observes that questions of revenge and justice (and the relationship and balance between the two) have long been a feature of western culture:

> On a practical level, the human desire for retribution requires no elaborate philosophical rationalization. A victim wants to see an assailant punished not only for reasons of pragmatic deterrence but also as a means of repairing a damaged sense of civic order and personal identity. (1996: 9)

One could stop there, and certainly the mass media response to 9/11 would have it thus. But revenge plays out differently according to historical and cultural context, and here I want to examine how it takes on a specific form in the US context, with inflections that can be related to 9/11.[13] Here, the central argument made in Susan Faludi's *The Terror Dream*, an account of the popular cultural response to 9/11, is illuminating. She observes that 9/11 was quickly gendered; that is, the discourses circulating in response to the attacks were placed in a hierarchy using a patriarchal logic that was latent in the prevailing culture but which intensified in the immediate aftermath of the attacks. Analysis reveals that women's voices were marginalised in media coverage after 9/11 and that (especially) female journalists were pilloried for voicing critical views (2007: 29–38). Faludi argues that the media implicitly connected the attacks to the pervasive influence of feminism and political correctness on the wider culture, which had left it atrophied, emasculated and unready for war. The remedy was a process of remasculinisation, a process in which the films discussed earlier in the present chapter – with firefighters astride the rubble of Ground Zero, Rudy Giuliani and Robert De Niro offering leadership and consolation, and mothers grieving the dead – played their part. Faludi goes on to argue that responses to 9/11 (re)asserted a powerful mythology that can be traced back to what she calls the US's 'original war on terror', that is, the subjugation of Native Americans during the settling of the Great Plains. For Faludi, the response to the attacks shifted through a series of phases:

> Of those phases, the first was our peculiar urge to recast a martial attack as a domestic drama, attended by the disappearance and even demonization of independent female voices. The second framed our suddenly vulnerable state as a problem between the sexes, in which the American man and the nation's vigor were sapped by female influence – and solved that 'problem' with a media and political campaign that inflated male strength by artificially consigning women to a fearful and vulnerable position. A final phase would underscore and document that feminine vulnerability with the invention of a female rape-and-rescue drama, thereby reinstating 'the classic happy ending of a classic American captivity story.' (2007: 216)

It is Faludi's final phase – the use of 'a rape-and-rescue drama' or 'American captivity story' to figure 9/11 – that reveals the connections between *Man on Fire* and 9/11. She argues that at times of crisis US popular culture calls upon mythology to provide its disoriented citizens with a sense of order. She notes that the mythology called upon in the immediate aftermath of 9/11 was that of the Hollywood western, with countless examples of western imagery – from Bush's cowboy hat and his statement that the terrorist 'evildoers' were wanted 'dead or alive' and that al-Qaida would be 'smoked out' of their caves in Afghanistan to the statement by a firefighter in *9/11* that Benetatos is an 'urban cowboy' – shaping the wider discourse. This mythology relates to the ways in which US national identity is founded on the historical experience of colonial settlement and expansion and the struggle between white European settlers and Native Americans. A key aspect of this struggle was its mediation through popular cultural forms: folklore, dime novels, theatre plays, the cinema, and so on. Here the captivity narrative, in which a white American woman is abducted, terrorised and raped by Native Americans, necessitating both rescue and revenge, came to the fore and was reproduced and repeated again and again, in what Faludi calls 'an engineering feat of national mythology' (2007: 265). Described thus, white settlers were licensed to use considerable violence against the Native Americans who resisted them. Faludi tracks the development of this narrative from the chronicles of homesteaders in the seventeenth century (where it appears in more complex versions and with women granted greater agency) through to the historical novels of James Fenimore Cooper in the early nineteenth century and into the twentieth century in films such as *The Searchers* (1956) (2007: 212–14). Faludi describes how, post-9/11, this captivity narrative became central to media reporting of the 'rescue' of US soldier Private Jessica Lynch, who was seriously injured when her convoy was attacked during the Battle of Nasiriyah in Iraq in early 2003. The press coverage of her rescue (including footage of a Special Forces raid) and the release of a television film titled *Saving Jessica Lynch* (2003) conformed to the captivity narrative template described above (2007: 179–83).[14]

A further reference point might be added here. In relation to the cinema, the captivity narrative overlaps and intersects with the rape-revenge film, which, as Jacinda Read observes, is strongly associated with the work of D. W. Griffith. In films such as *Broken Blossoms* (1919), for example, Griffith's star actress, Lillian Gish, appears 'as an apogee of white womanhood threatened by black, mulatto or working-class rapists' (2000: 78). Richard Dyer describes how Griffith used lighting to emphasise Gish's whiteness, marking her as 'aesthetically and morally superior, [looking] on from a position of knowledge, of enlightenment – in short, if she is so much lit, she also appears to be the source of light' (1993: 23). Gish's luminosity exaggerated the symbolism of the characters she portrayed, and came to symbolise all that was threatened with defilement at the hands of Griffith's predatory rapist (transposed from Native American to predatory Chinese man but with similar ideological effect).

Man on Fire draws on these related narrative schemas, being both a captivity narrative and a rape-revenge film: Mexican criminals capture a white, American child, who is then (seemingly) raped and murdered, resulting in an American man seeking bloody revenge. Dakota Fanning's porcelain complexion, blue-veined skin and plucky gregarious attitude make Pita a symbol of an imperilled US in a dangerous and threatening world.[15] In the way she is filmed – in the tradition established by Griffith's work with Lillian Gish – Fanning represents a morally and aesthetically pure whiteness set against the backdrop of a noisy and corrupt Mexico City. Fanning reprises the same role in *War of the Worlds*, which is discussed in chapter five. In addition, as a pre-pubescent child, the transgressive nature of her abduction and rape is further emphasised and revenge is offered as the only valid, necessary and

Fig. 5: Dakota Fanning as symbol of an imperilled America: *Man on Fire* (2004)

desirable response, with Pita's mother imploring Creasy to 'kill them all'.

The casting of African-American actor Denzel Washington as Creasy (the role was purportedly offered to Robert De Niro, Tom Cruise and Bruce Willis) might be said to complicate the clearly demarcated realms of good (white) and evil (black) as they give shape to the captivity narrative. However, in an early scene we see Pita's mother decide to hire Creasy because 'he is an American', and in a later scene in which Creasy accompanies Pita to a swimming race, a teacher states that 'today you are her father'; hence a white child becomes the daughter of a black man.[16] That she becomes an extension of him in this way is emphasised in the second half of the film: as he tracks down and kills those responsible for her death, Pita appears in his peripheral vision, motivating and approving of his actions. This multi-ethnic construction of 'Americans all', even when placed in a raced binary with non-Americans, was a common feature of neoconservative discourse post-9/11: Rove invited filmmakers to produce propaganda in support of the 'war on terror' (a war to be waged in the Middle East) but counselled against direct depiction of Islamic terrorists in fictional scenarios; Bush promised a crusade (a term associated with holy war) against the perpetrators of the attacks but applauded the patriotism of Arab-Americans. As Christopher Sharrett observes, 'the new vigilante cycle is smart enough to provide various liberal patinas to conceal its agenda' (2009: 34). This patination can be read into the wider political response. Statements by politicians that all Americans

– even those with a Middle Eastern background or Muslim beliefs – would be given protection and that Islam was a religion of peace separable from the corrupt fundamentalist beliefs held by the terrorists belied the fact that, as Evelyn Alsultany notes, 'the government's anti-terror campaign involved interviewing nearly 200,000 Arabs and Muslims; detaining and deporting thousands of Arabs, Muslims, and South Asians; instituting special registration requirements for Arabs and Muslims; and shutting down Muslim charities and other organizations' (2007: 593–4). These actions marked these identities 'as suspect and therefore un-American' (2007: 594).

As a symbol of US innocence, Pita licenses Creasy's focused and unrestrained revenge. In one sequence he tortures a kidnapper by cutting off his fingers and cauterising the wounds with a dashboard cigarette lighter, leading the man to reveal information about the kidnapping plot and thereby establishing that torture is necessary and effective. The film can here be related to the ways in which policymakers made an argument for the legitimacy and efficacy of torture in the years immediately following 9/11. After killing three of the kidnappers at a nightclub, Creasy sets fire to the building, and in another scene he tortures and kills a corrupt cop by inserting plastic explosives up his rectum: fire is here a purging force. The preferred reading here is clear: as a result of the kidnappers' actions against Pita as signifier of US innocence and moral rectitude, the violent retribution appears justified. By these means the revenge discourse is legitimated, and although we are once removed from the events of 9/11, the structural workings of this way of recounting the captivity narrative/rape-revenge film in the context of a prevailing discourse of revenge/retribution affirm and reinforce the dominant discourse. Creasy's capacity for violence and unwavering resolve are characteristics that Faludi (2007) identifies as celebrated and endorsed in the mass media response to 9/11 precisely because they are held in place by wider frameworks of mythmaking.

There is another pertinent strand to the narrative: Creasy is an alcoholic haunted by his past, which the film intimates has involved extrajudicial killings in Thailand, Pakistan, Jordan, Angola and Lebanon; he is also scarred, as if he has been subjected to torture. So, alongside the US's manifest goodness (Pita's idealised moral whiteness) there is some acknowledgement here of the nation's misdeeds (Creasy's past). As the two characters grow to like one another, we see Creasy resurrected as a father/protector figure, thereby redeeming his past behaviour. The film here acknowledges illegal state-sanctioned murder, but the pressing demands of revenge and redemption soon lift the burden of these past mistakes. As with the commemoration of the firefighters, Creasy's actions are couched in religious and providential terms. At one point Creasy asks his ex-CIA pal Rayburn (Christopher Walken), 'Do you think God will forgive us for what we've done?' 'No', replies Rayburn. 'Me neither', says Creasy. This dialogue exchange recurs in a later sequence in which Creasy tries to commit suicide, saved only because the bullet fails to fire, something he takes to be a sign from God. The same bullet kills Pita's father, who has arranged for her to be kidnapped so he can profit from the ransom. Later, bleeding from wounds suffered during Pita's abduction, Creasy rests between the executions of those involved in her capture by float-ing in a swimming pool (the site of earlier scenes of friendship with Pita), and a plume of blood forms a halo around his body. In these sequences blood and fire are offered as purifying forces, cleansing and redemptive. Earlier Creasy has been shown reading the Bible and quoting scripture, describing himself in a conversation with a nun as 'the sheep that got lost'. In the film's final scene Creasy bleeds to death in the back of the kidnapper's car, thereby trading his life for Pita's and achieving a state of grace: his revenge is a form of ascent, an apotheosis, recalling the Twin Towers in the tattoos and murals photographed by Hyman.

Situating *Man on Fire* in relation to the past cycles of rape-revenge films confirms its political colour. In *Death Wish* (1974), Charles Bronson plays a New York architect who, though initially a pacifist, goes on a killing spree after his wife is murdered and daughter raped by a criminal gang. Michael Ryan and Douglas Kellner note that in *Death Wish* 'women are associated with whiteness, purity and religion' and it is 'this sepulchral femininity that motivates [the lead character's desire for revenge and] conversion to conser-vatism' (1990: 90). Similar constructions are apparent also in 1980s vigilante films such as *The Exterminator* (1980), *Death Wish 2* (1983) and *Sudden Impact* (1983). In their celebration of purifying, retributive violence, these films foreshadow *Man on Fire*, which reproduces the same logic in service of a post-9/11 neoconservatism. This congruence between the post-9/11 cycle of films and the films of an earlier period – one characterised by a backlash against feminism and a conservative agenda that privileged male authority – is part and parcel of the way in which discourses around 9/11 bolstered and sustained pre-existing attacks on feminism, liberalism and multicultural-ism (see Faludi 2007: 25–7). *Man on Fire* can be traced back to this cultural context by virtue of its 1981 source novel by Philip Nicholson (writing under the pseudonym A. J. Quinnell).

The conservative logic that gives shape to *Man on Fire* can be seen in a revenge cycle taking shape through the 2000s, which includes *The Punisher*

(2004), *Sin City* (2005), *Hostel* (2005), *The Brave One* (2007), *Death Sentence* (2007, based on a novel by *Death Wish* author Brian Garfield) and *Law Abiding Citizen* (2009).[17] The captivity narrative – with the threat of rape at its centre – can also be seen in a number of further post-9/11 films, including *Rambo* (2008), in which Sylvester Stallone's eponymous protagonist intervenes to prevent the rape and murder of an abducted US aid worker in Burma, and *Taken* (2008), in which Liam Neeson pursues the Romanian and Middle Eastern sex traffickers who have kidnapped his daughter. This cycle of post-9/11 revenge films formed part of a broader raft of cultural production that extended patriotic and nationalist discourses of rescue and redemption, and tied these discourses to feelings of anger, vengeance and the necessity of waging war. As Faludi notes, 'recovering from our wound and prevailing against our enemies required sagacity and hard realism; instead we dreamed ourselves into a penny-dreadful plot that had little to do with the actual world in which we must live' (2007: 14).

However, in keeping with the aim of this book to identify cultural struggle and track parallel lines through contemporary cultural experience, it is also possible to identify, even early in the decade, revenge films that challenge and question the illiberal variants of which *Man on Fire* is an example. Writing in the *Guardian*, B. Ruby Rich identifies a cycle of revenge films that appeared during the Thanksgiving period in 2003, including *Mystic River* and *21 Grams*. Rich notes that these films 'base their storylines and emotional resonance on a thirst for revenge, the very emotion that has been dictating US foreign policy for the past two years' (2003). And yet, the films, both of which explore the considerable cost of 'botched revenge', also require their viewers to reflect on how seeking revenge may have unintended consequences (ibid.). In the Clint Eastwood-directed *Mystic River* ex-convict Jimmy Markum (Sean Penn) murders his childhood friend Dave Boyle (Tim Robbins), whom he believes (erroneously) is responsible for the murder of his daughter. Adrian Wootton observes:

> Given that Eastwood was once synonymous with *Dirty Harry*, it's resonant that *Mystic River* is a demonstration of the destructiveness of vigilante justice and maverick violence. Jimmy achieves his revenge, but there's no redemption – he simply commits a wrongful act that renders another child fatherless. (2003: 14)

The fact that 'the murder of Jimmy's daughter was an act of violence gone wrong because of Jimmy's past actions brings the cycle of retribution and despair full circle' and indicates that the film is seeking to make the moral point that revenge is wrong (ibid.). Films such as *Mystic River*, then, draw on the centrality to almost all considered and mature incarnations of the revenge plot of an 'ethical exchange'; that is, as Kerrigan notes, 'the symmetry of revenge is inseparable from a dramatic irony which complicates the moral situation of the revenger' (1996: 6). The revenge film as a site of 'ethical exchange' can be seen in the aforementioned films as well as *In the Bedroom* (2001) and *Memento* (2001) (both produced and released before 9/11 but discussed after the attacks as possible points of origin for a more mature discussion of the nature of revenge) and *The Count of Monte Cristo* (2002), *Flightplan, V for Vendetta* (2005), *Munich* (2005) and *Sweeney Todd* (2007) (see Weber 2005). Eastwood returns to this theme in *Gran Torino* (2008), where his 'greatest generation' tough guy refuses to pull the trigger. These narrative feature films are the ideological kin, arguably, of those documentaries described in chapter one that sought to retain a sense of complexity and ambiguity in face of the prevailing culture's desire to simplify responses in a politically expedient way.[17]

The presence of two distinct cycles of revenge films is indicative of a dialectic in US society, and enables us to glimpse, with hindsight, that in the first twelve to eighteen months following 9/11 the ideological dominant was fragile; the neoconservative consensus founded on a patriotic nationalism was contradictory and contested: consent had not been fully attained. If one reads chapter one into chapter two, *Seven Days in September* against *9/11*, *25th Hour* against *Man on Fire*, it becomes clear that at a time when 9/11 was being presented as a conflict between the US and al-Qaida (and the Taliban, and Saddam Hussein), there were also a number of films that explored how 9/11 had precipitated division and conflict between Americans. Indeed, 9/11 created a series of parallel possibilities: a banal 'Americans all' patriotism but also the spectre of some engagement with questions of social class and ethnic diversity; an amplification of conservative versions of American exceptionalism but also some sense of the ways in which the US is already and irrecoverably entangled with other nations and peoples in an often unexceptional manner; a year zero approach to history and politics but also a sense of how the past informs the present in complex and contradictory ways; a celebration of freedom and the American way but also a sense of how US freedoms are often gained at the expense of freedom elsewhere; the use of revenge (and religious discourse) to justify a call to war but also the identification of revenge as necessitating discussion of 'ethical exchange'.

This schism was clear enough to see in the wider culture. In the wake of 9/11 high finance companies (and their staff) refused to follow the patriotic 'Americans all' script and proceeded with business as usual: dumping falling US stocks and shares and poaching staff from firms such as Cantor-Fitzgerald which had been decimated by the catastrophe. Coinciding as it did with scandals at Enron and Worldcom, this maintenance of bare-toothed capitalism points to the ways in which US national identity is composed of different and incompatible elements. Similarly, compensation paid to those killed in the attacks proved divisive, as insurance companies based their actuarial calculations on the projected 'lifetime earnings' of those who died; as David Harvey put it, 'in death, not all Americans were equal' (2002: 63). As a consequence of 9/11 it is estimated that around 100,000 jobs were lost in New York, with an attendant rise in homelessness, especially among illegal immigrants who were not entitled to assistance or compensation (see Harvey 2002: 62). In *American Ground*, an account of the clear-up operation at Ground Zero (referred to prosaically by those involved as 'the pile'), William Langewiesche uncovered evidence that firefighters had been looting from the World Trade Center as the attacks were happening and that (often physical) conflicts between construction crews, firefighters and police, especially over the preferential treatment of the remains of firefighters, were not uncommon (2003: 154–61). Much of this pointed to a complex and contradictory reality, but this more complex reality was hardly given breathing space in mainstream accounts. This disconnect between seemingly parallel realities played a key role in fostering the feeling that 9/11 was subject to a 'cover up', a feeling that resulted in the rise of the '9/11 truth movement' described in the next chapter.

Conspiracy

This chapter explores a range of films – including political documentaries, web-based conspiracy films and big-budget Hollywood thrillers – that seek to reveal a more complex reality to be found by resisting, refusing and digging through the officially endorsed accounts of 9/11 described in the last chapter. This response can be understood as an extension of the critical and questioning perspectives found in the films described in chapter one. The chapter also indicates how, when faced with no outlet or opening in the wider culture, such a response became inward looking, suspicious, browbeaten and paranoid. As always, cultural production is here understood to be part of wider processes of ideological struggle, with different groups, aligned with different political perspectives, striving to determine or contest reality. As with chapters one and two, which depicted parallel responses to 9/11 in the immediate aftermath of the attacks, ideological struggle from 2003 through to mid-decade is traced in relation to critical left-liberal documentaries and the unruly political consciousness-raising of the conspiracy films (chapter three) vying with and provoking a cinema of conservative reaction and reassurance (chapter four).

One the most profound and enduring responses to 9/11 has been the introduction of legislation on an almost unprecedented scale. Only a week after 9/11, George W. Bush was granted power by Congress to 'use all necessary and appropriate force against those nations, organizations or persons he determines planned, authorized, committed, or aided the terrorist attacks' (see Prince 2009: 174). Six weeks later, Congress passed the United and Strengthening America by Providing Appropriate Tools Required to Intercept and Obstruct Terrorism Act (or PATRIOT Act), which set up or re-engineered a number of federal organisations, tasking them to prevent future attacks. Further legislation followed in November 2002, with the passing of the Homeland Security Act and the founding of the Department of Homeland Security, an evocatively named umbrella organisation designed to gather federal agencies together, improve lines of communication between them, and extend their jurisdiction and power in order to 'protect our homeland and safeguard our rights' (see Etzioni 2004: 1). The act allowed government agencies such as the FBI to conduct electronic surveillance and detain suspects without charges or due process, as well as permitting the monitoring of credit card transactions, mobile phone calls and web activity. In January 2003, 'the White House described these changes as "the most significant transformation of the United States Government since 1947", the year the USA National Security Act created the CIA' (Kaplan 2008: 15). Supported by the majority of Americans, and with the war in Afghanistan dominating the front pages of newspapers, the clandestine, quasi-legal and far-reaching consequences of this legislation would remain unexamined until later in the decade.[18] Alongside this legislation, and extending the terrain in which the debate about security and civil rights would play out, in 2001 and 2002 the Justice Department drafted a series of memos – a 'legal shield' according to Prince (2009: 176) – that claimed that the US laws and the Geneva Conventions that banned the use of torture did not apply to the struggle with al-Qaida (see Greenberg and Dratel 2005). This is discussed in more detail in later chapters, but it is mentioned here to indicate how a certain reality began to cohere in the aftermath of the attacks, with licence given for the military and other government agencies to work at the edges of legality, and in transgression of a number of constitutionally protected rights.

Another profound response to 9/11 was the extension of the 'war on terror'. In early/mid-2002, a concerted effort was made to convince the American public that it was necessary to open another battlefront, this time in Iraq. As with Afghanistan, the mass media rallied around the flag; Stephen Prince notes that between August 2002 and March 2003 the *Washington Post* 'ran nearly 140 front-page articles on Iraq, and all but a handful made the administration's case for war' (2009: 179). The US invasion began in March 2003, and in May, in a gesture that consciously emulated scenes from the Hollywood film *Independence Day* (1996), Bush landed on the aircraft carrier USS Abraham Lincoln in a Lockheed S-3 Viking jet plane and wearing full flight gear, with a 'Mission Accomplished' banner hanging behind him as he congratulated the troops.

However, Bush's photo opportunity was generally agreed to 'have been misjudged and failed to persuade' (Sardar and Davies 2002: xi), with the media reporting that the ship was stationed off the coast of San Diego and that Bush could easily have travelled to it by helicopter, and this response indexed a widely held scepticism with regard to the war in Iraq. Even before the invasion, large-scale anti-war protests at home and abroad had signalled the strength of feeling against the use of military force. Conflicting views were rife: at a concert in London, Natalie Maines, lead singer of Texas band the Dixie Chicks, criticised Bush and quickly became embroiled in a war of words in which strong pro- and anti-war positions were articulated (the controversy is recorded in the documentary *Shut Up and Sing* (2006)). The investigative reporting of Seymour Hersh (2004b) – much of the research for which was undertaken during this period – was published as 26 stories in the *New Yorker* and drew attention to the intelligence failures leading up to 9/11, a lack of post-war planning in Afghanistan and Iraq, and the use of dubious intelligence related to purported Iraqi chemical and nuclear weapons, and, perhaps most significantly, described prisoner abuse at Abu Ghraib military prison. Hersh's work is indicative of a culture that had the will, wherewithal and eventually a public outlet for descriptions that moved beyond the 'unity' discourse.

On 6 October 2003 a *Time* magazine feature article described the difficulties faced by US troops on the ground in Iraq and pointed to the lack of preparation of any post-invasion nation-building strategy. The article was given the headline 'Mission Not Accomplished'. As these examples indicate, from 2003, and with the events of 9/11 extended to include massive security legislation and two stalemated wars, the wider culture, and by extension the cinema, began to be shaped more evidently by competing/parallel views of 9/11: one supportive of the wide-reaching legislation and extension of the 'war on terror', the other suspicious, resistant and increasingly paranoid. Two films usefully mark this stark separation: *DC 9/11: Time of Crisis* (2003) and *Fahrenheit 9/11* (2004).

The Showtime television film *DC 9/11: Time of Crisis* was shown on 7 September 2003. A minute-by-minute dramatic reconstruction of the attacks, and a blow-by-blow account of decision-making in the days following, the film focuses on 9/11 as experienced by George W. Bush (Timothy Bottoms), Donald Rumsfeld (John Cunningham), Dick Cheney (Lawrence Pressman), Condoleezza Rice (Penny Johnson Jerald) and Special Counsel to the President Karen Hughes (Carolyn Scott). The film provides a concise and straightforward account of the events of the day, with Bush depicted as a heroic leader, protective husband and devout Christian who effectively responds to the crisis and who reads the Bible and asks his colleagues to lead meetings with prayers. Upon hearing of the crash of United 93 Bush growls, 'We're going to kick the hell out of whoever did this', later stating, 'We're going to get the bastards'. The film's clarity in the way it depicts events and the ideologically sympathetic view of the president's response is something of a hallmark of screenwriter Lionel Chetwynd, a conservative Republican who attended the Beverly Hills Summit described in the introduction.[19] Tellingly, Chetwynd was given support from the White House for *DC 9/11*, including an interview with Bush.

As a preface to the film we see Rumsfeld addressing a meeting on the defence budget. He argues with congressmen for a bigger spend to combat the threat of North Korea and terrorism: 'there's no social security without national security', he growls, implying that al-Qaida were already the target of neoconservative policy in the period preceding 9/11 (with Congress applying the brakes and preventing them getting tough with terrorists). In a later scene, upon learning of the attack, Condoleezza Rice is shown reacting to the words 'al-Qaida?' with a stern nod, suggesting that the government was already in a state of preparedness. Further rhetorical flourishes – Bush states at one point that the response will be robust and bloody, stating 'no "slap on the wrist" game this time' – imply that the Clinton administration had been too soft on terrorism, a trope that would reappear later in *The Path to 9/11* (2006). The film also uses throwaway dialogue – 'we're very constrained when it comes to domestic intelligence', 'the whole system of immigration must be rethought' – to offer a post hoc argument for the necessity of a radical overhaul of domestic security.

In its revision of the popular view that Bush had failed to act in a suitably presidential way during 9/11, the film opens with him receiving the news of the attacks whilst reading to children on a school visit. In contrast to the way this scene is presented in *Fahrenheit 9/11*, Bush is shown processing the information and stoically continuing with the lesson, the implication being that he does not wish to upset the children. He then makes a series of decisive phone calls: grounding planes, ordering military jets to fire on unresponsive civilian aircraft, reassuring and directing key advisors. In these scenes Bush is presented as a strong man, often leading wavering and emotional women (with Laura Bush, Rice and Hughes all beneficiaries of his largesse and comfort). Here the film conforms to the masculinist designs identified in post-9/11 discourse by Susan Faludi (2007). By 2003, of course, the orderliness and timeliness of Bush's reaction to the attack had been subject to considerable scrutiny, with even the 9/11 Commission Report casting considerable doubt on the efficacy of his, and the wider federal government's, reaction to 9/11. Here we see the schism between official discourse and a more complicated version of reality that informs the web-based and Hollywood-produced conspiracy films discussed later in this chapter.

DC 9/11 has relatively high production values for a television film, with the budget allowing for CGI inserts of Air Force One, the mobilisation of military personnel and the hiring of mid-range character actors. Careful attention is given to the editing together of news footage of the attacks and the re-enactment of key events involving the main players. In the scenes following the attack on the Pentagon, for example, the sequence showing Rumsfeld helping survivors is an almost shot-by-shot reconstruction of news coverage. In the dramatic reconstruction of Bush's address of the commemoration service at the National Cathedral, Timothy Bottoms delivers Bush's speech but the cutaways are to archive film of George H. W. Bush, Jimmy Carter, Bill and Hillary Clinton and Al Gore. This combination of actual footage and dramatic reconstruction works in ways similar to that described in relation to *9/11* and *In Memoriam*, with the powerful and shocking news footage and amateur video subsumed within a narrative that embodies coherence, order and meaning. Here, the clear ideological direction of the film is layered into the film record of the event, turning the archival record to the task of maintaining support for the neo-conservative discourse of vengeance and war. The ideological design can be seen especially in the ending, which functions as a distillation of the logic of the unity films described in the previous chapter. Here, a dramatic reconstruction of Bush's address to Congress is cut into news footage of the address; cutaways include Lisa Beamer (widow of Todd Beamer, presumed to have led the passenger fight-back on United 93), the crowd and players at an ice hockey match which has been stopped so that they can watch the address (these ordinary sports fans functioning as a surrogate for the television viewer), images of flags, the labours of rescue workers and missing person posters. Aligned with this patriotic montage, Bush's comment 'either you are with us or you are with the terrorists' is emphasised with a standing ovation in Congress and at the ice hockey game. The final shot of the film is of actual news footage of Bush telling the story of how he carries the shield of Port Authority police officer George Howard, who was killed on 9/11, which he claims motivates and justifies his responses to the attacks. This sequence arguably exemplifies the imbrication of a closing down of alternative responses and a cementing of a neoconservative view of 9/11 and its aftermath. Through classical continuity editing techniques the potentially unsettling meanings of film and photographs of the event are constrained and a conventional narrative structure provides resolution that brings together collective grief, nationalist anger and wholesale support for (a further) war.

Placed alongside *DC 9/11: Time of Crisis*, Michael Moore's polemical documentary *Fahrenheit 9/11* is a reminder of the inflammatory and divided political climate that had developed in the three years after 9/11. Released theatrically to 869 screens in June 2004, the film grossed just short of $120 million at the US box office, took another $100 million worldwide and won the Palme d'Or for Best Picture at the Cannes Film Festival. The highest-grossing documentary film ever made, it was deemed by David Holloway 'the most important film of the era' (2008: 104). Thomas Doherty claims that *Fahrenheit 9/11* is 'less a motion picture documentary than a Molotov cocktail tossed at the Bush administration' (2007: 413) – a judgement Moore would no doubt endorse, with the director stating that his film sought to prevent the re-election of George W. Bush in late 2004. However, the film's journey to the screen was troubled: given the controversies invoked by its partisan and adversarial stance, Disney Corporation-owned Miramax refused to distribute the film, with Miramax co-founders Harvey and Bob Weinstein stepping in to buy the rights and market it under the tagline 'The film they did not want you to see' (see Weber 2006: 117).

Fahrenheit 9/11 suggests how the public sphere had been co-opted by a self-serving political elite and how seductive media images and spin had been used to exploit the events of 9/11 in order to embark on an imperialist war in the Middle East. For Moore, this political malaise could be traced back to the period preceding 9/11. Bush is presented in the film not as a heroic father figure who will protect the nation but as an incompetent self-interested politician serving a social and economic elite. Indeed, it is implied that Bush is a borderline sociopath, solemnly declaring to journalists that terrorism will be thwarted one moment and inviting them to check out his golf swing the next. The Bush family is shown mired in a web of vote rigging, oil industry and high finance cronyism and dubious connections to the Bin Laden family in Saudi Arabia (the country from which the majority of the 9/11 hijackers came). Moore's film clearly found a sympathetic audience, but nevertheless Bush was re-elected, the success of the film and the election result clearly marking the divide across US culture and politics.

Conspiracy

In contrast to the way in which *DC 9/11* begins its account of 9/11 on the morning of the attacks (with neoconservative politicians in a state of readiness), *Fahrenheit 9/11* opens with a preface that recounts the events surrounding the controversial election of Bush in 2000. Moore asks, 'Was it a dream or was it real?' It is a rhetorical question that points to an epistemological crisis – an uncertainty in the mechanism for producing knowledge related to 9/11 – that is displayed by the films described in the remainder of this chapter, all of which, in their different ways, seek to articulate a sense that the official version of events – as presented by politicians, the 9/11 Commission and the mass media – is untrustworthy, unreliable and unstable. For many, reality had slipped. *Fahrenheit 9/11* digs below mainstream discourse by showing footage from inside the House of Representatives that reveals mainly African-American congressmen and women being prevented from raising objections to the manipulation of the electoral roll in Florida because their objections lack a constitutionally necessary endorsement from the Senate. In a Kafkaesque detail typical of the ironic tone of the film as a whole, presidential candidate Al Gore is tasked with silencing the dissenting voices (thereby assuring he will lose the election). This sequence reminds the viewer that post-9/11 political realities have a significant prehistory. In its recounting of this legalistic procedure the sequence also depicts politics directly, and in the taking up of an angry and ironic position in relation to this procedure, makes clear its moral judgement that the system itself is self-interested and corrupt. This preface is followed by

Fig. 6: Secretary of State Colin Powell prepares for a media appearance: *Fahrenheit 9/11* **(2004)**

the film's opening credits, which are intercut with footage of politicians having make-up applied before appearing on television, a simple montage sequence that draws attention to the way in which media images are constructed, thereby presenting Moore's film as a debunking of this self-serving manipulation of reality.

In keeping with this iconoclasm, the film undertakes a concerted unravelling of the media realities surrounding post-9/11 military interventions: the invasion of Afghanistan is presented in a pastiche of *The Magnificent Seven* (1960); the build-up to the war in Iraq is detailed through rapid-fire montage sequences that encapsulate how the repetition of the claim that Saddam Hussein had nuclear weapons turned questionable intelligence into exploitable reality; footage of the 'shock and awe' phase of the Iraq War used by the mainstream media is contrasted with images of civilian casualties, as well as US troops speaking openly about indiscriminate killing sprees conducted to heavy metal soundtracks; Bush's 'Mission Accomplished' stunt is edited together in a montage sequence with US casualties resulting from a roadside bomb. There is a clear agenda here: the ideological work done to exploit 9/11 and gain consent for war is craven and opportunist, the film argues, and the underlying reality is bloody, messy and unsavoury. Moore implores: don't trust what you are told and don't believe what you see. This sentiment is carried across into the other films described in this chapter.

This suspicion of the image extends to the way the film shows the events of 9/11. In contrast to the repetition of the footage of the planes striking the Twin Towers in the initial media coverage and the documentary films described in earlier chapters, *Fahrenheit 9/11* avoids showing the attacks directly, preferring instead a black screen and the sound of the strikes followed by video of ordinary people's shocked reactions. A refusal to use the iconic images may well be the result of a feeling that these images had, by the time of the film's release, become overdetermined by the discourses described in chapter two. By turning to the reactions of ordinary people, Moore takes as his starting point a moment in which the human responses of shock, sympathy and fear had yet to be co-opted into a call to arms. The decision not to show here gives shape to the film as a whole, which contrasts mass media representation with the experiences of ordinary people: this was praised by a number of critics, including David Holloway, who commends how the film gives voice to

> the soldiers, families of soldiers, conscientious objectors, school kids, writers, pundits and analysts, FBI agents and policemen, politicians,

bereaved victims of 9/11, 'senior' and other concerned citizens [whose views form] a decentralized republic of voices arrayed against Bush. (2008: 102)

According to this reading (which requires that we overlook for the moment the domineering, often hectoring, presence of Moore himself), *Fahrenheit 9/11* can be placed alongside documentaries such as *Seven Days in September* and *Parallel Lines*.

The work of deconstructing the mythmaking of the mass media coalesces in the latter part of the film into a clear anti-war stance. Moore uses the rhetorical device of giving voice to ordinary Americans as they describe their experiences of the iniquities of post-9/11 policies. In relation to this the story of Lila Lipscomb forms a central thread: Lipscomb is the mother of a mixed-race family who live in Flint, Michigan (the location of Moore's earlier film *Roger and Me* (1989)). She works at an agency designed to get unemployed people back to work. While raising a US flag outside her house, she tells Moore that the military is a good way for poor people to escape poverty and that two of her children have served. In this early appearance Lipscomb's comments are part of an argument about how those in lower social-economic groups are exploited by military recruiters, with the poor fighting (and dying) to maintain the interests of the elite. Later in the film, we hear from Lipscomb again and learn that her son, Michael Pedersen, has been killed in Iraq (a cause he no longer believed in). Now, the anti-war Lipscomb (sharing Moore's view that the poor should not be exploited in this way) makes a journey to Washington to petition politicians to bring the war to an end. It is a significant moment in the film in emotional terms but is also revealing of the logic shaping left-liberal responses to 9/11: namely, that the system has been hijacked by a corrupt group who no longer respect the values of ordinary Americans. The solution: overthrow this corrupt group (by electing John Kerry?) and reassert a truer US national identity from below (measured here in relation to Lipscomb's multicultural family and their sense of honour and duty). The problem here is that the people Moore depicts as victims of capitalism are at the same time commended and celebrated for their patriotic and dutiful behaviour under capitalism, thereby forming a paradox: they proudly serve the system that exploits them; indeed, they embody the finer values of that system. Thus, the military can remain a driver of social change, but it is engaged in the wrong war. The film presents its critique from within the system, so to speak, in what might be called counter-patriotism. As Holloway puts it,

The film's representation of the Bush administration as freakish and aberrant, and its populist valorizing of existing institutions as the route back to a normative and equitable political culture, were typical of a lot of liberal war on terror commentary, in that the film fetishized the American political system, separating it off from the broader structures of capitalist power in which representative democracy is enmeshed. (2008: 104)

Similarly sceptical, but more specific in her critique, Cynthia Weber argues that 'what makes *Fahrenheit 9/11* such an incendiary experience is that it is imbricated in every one of the themes it critiques' (2006: 116). Furthermore,

for all their disagreements, George W. Bush and Michael Moore agree on two fundamental issues. The first is that even in the increasingly morally uncertain post-9/11 era, one can hold on to a morally certain vision of America and Americans (hemispheric terms that euphemistically and some would argue imperially stand in for the citizens and state of the USA in both Bush's and Moore's constructions of some collective US subject, what I prefer to call a US 'we'). Of course, their moral visions of a US 'we' clash, but they are morally certain visions nonetheless. (2006: 113)

That liberal critique here seeks to recuperate the system as a whole will be explored in greater depth in later chapters. Indeed, the taking of a critical view while arguing around to a position where the system as a whole is valorised and thereby stabilised can be taken as an illustration in miniature of the wider process charted in some of the later chapters of this book in which parallel or competing political viewpoints are reconciled, or converge, through the work of cultural production.

Unsurprisingly, Moore's film attracted a lot of critical attention, with a number of reviewers describing it as 'dividing the nation'. One response was the production of the documentary *Celsius 41.11: The Temperature at Which the Brain... Begins to Die* (2004), which aimed to refute the main lines of Moore's argument. However, scholarly comment has been largely sympathetic to the general political direction of the film, reserving criticism for Moore's manipulative rhetorical style and factual overreach (see Porton 2004; Briley 2005; Doherty 2007; Stuckey 2007). Indeed, with the benefit of hindsight the film seems prescient on a number of issues, as Robert Brent Toplin notes:

> Serious and troublesome revelations have come to public attention about the absence of weapons of mass destruction in Iraq, the Bush Administration's incorrect association of Saddam Hussein with the events of 9/11 [...], excesses of the Patriot Act, suffering by Iraqi civilians and American troops in the war zone, problems associated with a back-door draft through service in the National Guard, and many other subjects raised in the film. (2005: 9)

Further, images of US soldiers putting hoods on POWs while referring to them as 'Ali Baba' and using sexual innuendo clearly prefigure the prisoner abuse scandal at Abu Ghraib, with Moore commenting that 'immoral behaviour breeds immoral behaviour'. Here the film gestures towards the way in which the complex ethical issues related to torture would emerge as a central preoccupation of post-9/11 cinema (see chapter seven).

When the certainty of the account of events offered in *DC 9/11: Time of Crisis* is placed alongside Moore's demand that viewers challenge everything that they have seen and heard about 9/11, we have a useful index of the deeply unstable political and cultural climate surrounding the events of 9/11 in 2004. That both ways of approaching the event are in effect mainstreamed is significant. *Fahrenheit 9/11* is indicative of how critique moved from the margins (a handful of zero-budget documentaries, a single Hollywood film, and so on) to a central position in the highest-grossing documentary in history.

On 27 November 2002 the National Commission on Terrorist Attacks upon the United States (or 9/11 Commission) was formed and given the task of examining how and why the 9/11 terrorist attacks had taken place and what might be done to prevent further attacks. In July 2004, after months of hearings conducted without support from the White House, *The 9/11 Commission Report* was published. The report identified what it called 'failures of imagination, policy, capabilities, and management' (Kean and Hamilton 2004: 339), particularly in relation to the responses of, and communication between, the FBI and CIA. However, the report was widely felt to be too little too late, especially for the way in which it offered too orderly an explanation of the motivations of al-Qaida (without examining how the organisation was funded via Pakistan and Saudi Arabia), too neat a description of the unfolding of the attacks on 9/11 and the government response and a general reticence in identifying any significant shortcomings or culpability related to those in positions of responsibility in the period leading up to the attacks. The report claimed that 'that September day, we came together as a nation. The test before us is to sustain that unity of purpose and meet the challenges confronting us now' (2004: xvi). Against the backdrop of the kind of deeply divided public opinion expressed in the films described in this chapter, the Commission's consensus-seeking report was felt by many to be inadequate, leading to a search for alternative explanations.

This frustration manifested in an increasing visibility of conspiracy theories that offered alternate views of 9/11. Peter Knight argues that the US is a nation where conspiracy thinking runs deep (widespread paranoia regarding British subterfuge and dissembling during the American Revolution is an early example) and that this has given rise to a 'conspiracy culture' that has shifted and modulated over time. Knight observes that in the immediate aftermath of 9/11, a number of conspiracy theories appeared, especially in Europe and the Middle East (2008: 167–8). However, it was not until 2003 that these were identified as a distinct phenomenon in the US, surfacing in radio broadcasts, on websites and as books (see Hufschmid 2002; Jones 2002; Marrs 2003; Fetzer 2007; Griffin 2008). Those who endorsed the conspiracy theories, including a number of celebrities such as Charlie Sheen, David Lynch and Rosie O'Donnell – in combination with a loose coalition of 9/11 sceptics – were given the label the '9/11 Truth Movement', and this 'movement' formed part of the wider anti-war and anti-Bush protests gathering momentum in 2003–04 (see Pollard 2011: 21–2). Central to this movement was the production of a number of independent documentary films made by enthusiastic amateurs and/or groups that were produced and released on the web or via commercial and non-commercial distribution channels. Titles included *9/11: In Plane Site* (2004), *Painful Deceptions* (2005), *Zeitgeist* (2006) and *The Elephant in the Room* (2008), but the best known and most widely viewed of this group is *Loose Change*.[20]

This film was made by Dylan Avery in his home in Oneonta in the Catskill Mountains, about four hours' drive north of New York. According to Avery, the film began as a script for a fictional thriller, but as he researched the story he felt he had unearthed a real conspiracy, and along with his friend (and ex-soldier) Korey Rowe he further developed the film, first as a 30-minute documentary released in early 2005, and then as a 60-minute version released in September 2005 (known as *Loose Change – Original Web Release*). A number of further versions followed, including *Loose Change – Final Cut* (2007, 128 min.) and *Loose Change 9/11 – An American Coup* (2009, 99 min.). Initially distributed for free using Google Video (where it was viewed over seven million times), the film has subsequently appeared on YouTube, as well as having a DVD release (with an encouragement to freely duplicate and disseminate copies). Distributed thus, it is estimated that the film has been viewed over seventy million times (Avery claims over a hundred million), a figure that justifies the assertion made in an August 2006 *Vanity Fair* article that *Loose Change* 'just might be the first Internet blockbuster'. Although the film attracted significant press coverage worldwide, most journalists dismissed it as unethical, politically reactionary and/or deluded. However, the impact of the film was considered significant enough to merit a rebuttal by the US government, which published an online article debunking *Loose Change* in 2009. This and other web-based challenges to the conspiracy theories notwithstanding, according to one estimate one-third of the US population (and over half of those under the age of thirty) believed that the official version of 9/11 was some kind of cover up, and it is this deeply held suspicion that explains the phenomenal success of *Loose Change* and other 9/11 conspiracy films (see Olmsted 2009: 1).

So what is the conspiracy that *Loose Change* purports to reveal? The numerous versions of the film, and the filmmakers' reluctance to pull together the different pieces of the puzzle into a coherent whole, ensure that this is not an easy question to answer. Across its numerous versions the film makes many claims that run counter to official accounts, the most dramatic of which is that because jet fuel burns at a temperature lower than the melting point of steel, the impact of the planes (and resulting fires) could not have destroyed the World Trade Center. It follows, then, that the Twin Towers collapsed as a result of a controlled demolition. In a similar vein, it is claimed that the lack of CCTV records showing the plane strike on the Pentagon, combined with an amount of debris incommensurate with a plane crash, is evidence that the damage was caused by a cruise missile or military drone strike. It is also claimed that United 93 did not crash in Pennsylvania and that the phone calls made from that plane were faked. The government is also accused of failing to heed warnings that the attacks were imminent and, in order to create confusion, of conducting military exercises on 9/11 involving the interception of hijacked civilian planes. Other 'loose ends' that the film draws attention to include the shipping of debris overseas before it could be examined forensically, the transfer of money to hijacker Mohammed Atta via the Pakistani secret service (ISI) (and with CIA knowledge), that a number of the 9/11 hijackers are alive and well and that the flying skills of the hijackers were not good enough to have controlled the planes as they did.

A number of explanations of these reconfigured facts are then offered, including that the attacks were a 'false flag' operation by the Bush administration and/or oil corporations, who, as Peter Knight notes, 'had much to gain from the subsequent invasions of Afghanistan and Iraq, and were looking for – perhaps even willing to engineer – a modern-day Pearl Harbor in order to gain support for their pre-existing war plans' (2008: 170). Another possible motive offered is that the attacks allowed an elaborate insurance scam to take place (it is claimed the Twin Towers were packed with asbestos that would have cost $1 billion to remove) and/or that the attacks concealed an elaborate heist of gold and/or state secrets held in vaults in the World Trade Center or buildings nearby.[21] A special issue of the journal *Popular Mechanics* scrutinised a number of the seeming disparities described in the film and found them to be explicable without recourse to any of the wider conspiracy theories; the findings of the journal were published on the web and as a book (Editors 2005). It is the intention here not to engage with specific claims but rather to demonstrate how critical writing on conspiracy theory might help us to understand the phenomenon of 9/11 conspiracy culture.

Writing in the early to mid-1960s, and contributing to a series of wider reflections on the breakdown of post-war consensus in the US, Richard Hofstadter coined the term 'paranoid style': a 'style of mind' prone to 'heated exaggeration, suspiciousness, and conspiratorial fantasy' (2008: 3). He wrote that for the conspiracy theorist,

> the enemy is clearly delineated: he is a perfect model of malice, a kind of amoral superman … Unlike the rest of us, the enemy is not caught in the toils of the vast mechanism of history, himself a victim of his past, his desires, his limitations. He wills, indeed he manufactures, the mechanism of history, or tries to deflect the normal course of history in an evil way. He makes crises, starts runs on banks, causes depressions, manufactures disasters, and then enjoys and profits from the misery he has produced. (2008: 32)

Hofstadter attributed the rise of a paranoid style to a certain kind of political demonology (a fear of the political class and ruling elite) and argued that those who are drawn to conspiracy thinking are usually located on the political margins. In Avery and Rowe's film the US government is described in exactly these terms, and the filmmakers' social and geographical location would fit Hofstadter's profile, with their investment in conspiracism (as a form of delusion) possibly stemming from their marginalisation; it is telling that in Nina Davenport's documentary, *Parallel Lines*, conversations with a range of disenfranchised people show them to be heavily invested in conspiracy theories related to 9/11. Timothy Melley, writing in the late 1990s, extends and refines Hofstadter's argument with his idea of 'agency panic'. For him, in the post-war period 'control has been transferred from human agents to larger agencies, institutions, or corporate structures'; this has resulted in 'intense anxiety about an apparent loss of autonomy or self-control – the conviction that one's actions are being controlled by someone else, that one has been "constructed" by powerful external agents' (2000: 5, 12). This anxiety manifests in contradictory ways:

> 'paranoid' interpretations … stem from a desire to think sociologically about agency while simultaneously retaining a concept of individual action that is at odds with sociological work. They sometimes amount, then, not only to a self-defensive posture in the face of external controls, but to a fraught and paradoxical defense of liberal individualism itself. (2000: 23)

The paradoxical desire to acknowledge the death of subjectivity *and* launch a rear-guard action to save said subjectivity fits closely with much of the discourse around 9/11 and conspiracy culture, as well as *Loose Change*, which replaces the complex factors leading into and through 9/11 with a closed, comprehensible world. Avery and Rowe claim that a powerful structural conspiracy has hoodwinked the entire world and yet conclude by demanding that viewers follow their (liberal individualist) lead and act to unveil this conspiracy and bring those responsible to justice.

One sequence in the film relates to the claim that the towers were destroyed by a controlled demolition and can be used to indicate how the conventions of film form and a certain kind of paranoid reasoning are brought together in ways that segue with Hofstadter's and Melley's claims. Here, the film deploys a range of techniques commonly associated with documentary filmmaking: montage sequences of news footage, talking heads, rostrum shots of documents and, in the 2009 version, short stylised animations, which are blended together in a loose, associative editing style. A great deal of material from the initial live broadcasts of the attacks (in which news readers and commentators speculate on what has happened) is brought together in these sequences and treated as reasoned judgement, rather than often poorly thought-through first impressions. The film notes that no other similar building in history has collapsed as a result of fire, a scientist testifies to the presence of thermite (which accelerates and intensifies an explosion), and an official report about the collapse by NIST (National Institute of Standards and Technology) is said to have ignored these difficult facts. Here the film follows conventions that Richard Barkun observes are central to conspiracist literature, namely, the mimicry of 'the apparatus of source citation and evidence presentation found in conventional scholarship' (2003: 7). The viewer's attention is drawn to telling details of evidence such as the puffs of smoke that precede the collapse of the towers, which it is claimed are the result of controlled explosions. Although it is presumed that such details speak for themselves, the 'evidence' is usually augmented with arrows indicating where to look or a voice-over directing interpretation. This 'reasoning by anomaly', as Prince calls it (2009: 161), is a technique common to all 9/11 conspiracy films, and allows suspicion of the official version to germinate and grow. If one small detail can be presented as evidence, the film argues, then this can then be scaled up, pointing to a wider conspiracy. The film is also cut to a fast tempo, making it difficult to order facts, challenge them and spot logical inconsistencies (many of which appear readily on a second viewing). As such, the 'evidence' is adjoined to misdirection in the cultivation of the film's claims of a conspiracy.[22]

Writing before 9/11, Knight had observed that 'a quasi-paranoid hermeneutic of suspicion is now taken for granted by many Americans, including the scholarly community' (2000: 10) and that this postmodern paranoid style is expressed in

> an eclectic and often contradictory manner, as part entertainment, part speculation, and part accusation [...] Whatever else it might have become, conspiracy theory is an integral part of the infotainment culture at the turn of the millennium, hovering somewhere between committed belief and the culture of consumption. (2000: 44, 45)

For Knight, 'conspiracy theories are now less a sign of mental delusion than an ironic stance towards knowledge and the possibility of truth' (2000: 2) and this ironic stance is almost a form of half-belief in which 'consumers of conspiracy don't really believe what they buy, but neither do they really disbelieve it either. Often people believe rumors with a provisional commitment, believing them *as if* they were true' (2000: 48). The way *Loose Change*'s soundtrack combines two modes of rhetorical address is indicative here. The film's voice-over (Dylan Avery in earlier versions, television actor Daniel Sunjata in the 2009 version) consists of a mild, almost monotone, voice that marshals the film's evidence in such a way as to encourage the viewer to answer in the affirmative a number of rhetorical questions. Is the official account inadequate? Should we be suspicious? Is there a conspiracy here? This sensible-sounding reasoning is adjoined to a more distanced, even ironic, tone, indicated by the use of a rock- and hip-hop-inflected soundtrack that keys the film to a subcultural terrain associated with rebelliousness and marginal groups (albeit a terrain that is now thoroughly co-opted). This blend seems to ask that viewers believe earnestly in what is being said while at the same time finding the experience hip, and thereby ironic.

At one level, then, *Loose Change* is risible – significant mainly for its symptomatic nature, pointing to political marginalisation, agency panic, understandable scepticism and no small amount of narcissistic posturing. But it may be worth entertaining a less dismissive interpretation. Writing in the mid-1990s, as part of a wider engagement with postmodernism and globalisation, Fredric Jameson argued that 'conspiracy theory (and its garish narrative manifestations) must be seen as a degraded attempt … to think the impossible totality of the contemporary world system' (quoted in Wegner 2009: 172). In this argument, the paranoiac's search for meaning, what Jameson calls 'a poor person's cognitive mapping', may well lay the groundwork for cognitive mapping proper, with a properly dialectical and materialist sense of history emerging as a result. Although Knight is sceptical of this possibility in his 2000 work, in a journal article written in 2008, he notes how online resources such as *The Complete 911 Timeline* (sic) are indicative of a conspiracy theorising that embraces complexity and may offer insight into structural historical process.[23] *Loose Change* does not obviously display such potential, but in the piecing together of a series of companies, people and interactions that are at best nepotistic and self-serving and at worst conspiratorial, the film is informed by a desire to map and note connections. The film's position in this networked culture requires it to be willing to make amendments and changes as each version is produced, with, for example, *Loose Change: Final Cut* containing no mention of the use of cruise missiles, no close analysis of the World Trade Center being demolished using controlled explosions, and no questioning of the crash wreckage at the Pentagon. This last instalment is also wary of stating what the overarching, if any, conspiracy might be. *Loose Change 9/11 – An American Coup*, the 2009 version, begins with a long preamble seeking historical precedent, including the Reichstag fires, secrecy around the Manhattan project, JFK's assassination, the Gulf of Tonkin incident and the My Lai massacre. These events are not explicitly linked together but are instead used to gesture to a certain way of thinking about history, which in finding precedent presumes a predicative power to understand contemporary events. The list of precursor events gestures towards a relatively sophisticated view of the past, which acknowledges that the state has been capable of illegal and secret actions, a view articulated (without the dressing of conspiracy thinking) in the history films described in chapter nine. Thus, the multiple versions of *Loose Change* speak to an awareness of the shifting purchase on the popular imagination of those conspiracy theories that might be said to retain some coherent and plausible relationship with the (visual) evidence, and in the main the film avoids the more outlandish conspiracies posited to explain the attacks.

Knight argues that conspiracy thinking reached its peak around the fifth anniversary of the attacks, noting that 'as with the belated flowering of Kennedy assassination conspiracy theories in the late 1960s, the troubling reality of contemporary events provokes the need to posit retrospectively a primal scene of conspiracy as a symbolically necessary origin for present woes' (2008: 181). As such, 9/11 conspiracy theories retrospectively *explain* what happened on 9/11 during a period of uncertainty five years afterwards. According to a May 2006 Zogby poll, 42 per cent of Americans claimed to believe that the US government and the 9/11 Commission 'concealed or refused to investigate critical evidence that contradicts their official explanation of the September 11th attacks' and that 'there has been a cover-up' (see Sales 2006). Similarly,

> A 2006 Scripps Howard poll found that 36 percent of Americans believed the government had orchestrated the attacks, 16 percent said the World Trade Center had actually been destroyed by hidden bombs, and 12 percent said the Pentagon had not been hit by an airplane but by a missile. (Pollard 2011: 21–2)

A majority of Americans between the ages of 18 and 29 believe these theories (see Olmsted 2009: 1). These statistics indicate how conspiracy culture has become mainstreamed. In a way not seen in the 1990s – when conspiracy theory seemed reducible to a pithy quote on an expensive T-shirt – the political earnestness of contemporary conspiracy culture appears to fit Jameson's hunch that there may be something positive in the desire to question and challenge and be suspicious (hence Knight's about-face). I do not suggest that *Loose Change* is an example of conspiracy thinking *with possibility*, but I do feel that at the saner end of the spectrum a certain politically engaged, angry desire for truthfulness has been politically significant.[24] Or, as Melley puts it, conspiracy theory provides 'important representations of

Fig. 7: 'Ask questions, demand answers': *Loose Change: An American Coup* (2009)

global capitalist networks' and 'instead of being merely a comforting form of misrepresentation, conspiracy theory is a reductive (or "degraded"), but still useful, form of political representation' (2000: 9).[25]

A film that can be profitably read into this cultural context is *Syriana* (2005), a complex, multi-stranded espionage thriller. Like *Fahrenheit 9/11*, *Syriana* is an avowedly left-liberal and political film, which grossed almost $95 million worldwide, the strong box office an indicator of the appetite for political fare in the multiplex mid-decade. The film was co-produced by Participant Productions (now known as Participant Media), a production company set up in early 2004 by Jeff Skoll, a former president of eBay, with the avowedly philanthropic aim to 'entertain audiences first, then to invite them to participate in making a difference'; a sister company – TakePart. com – allows viewers to discuss issues raised in their documentary and feature films (Participant also helped to fund *Standard Operating Procedure*, (2008) discussed in chapter seven). As with the grassroots documentary films described in chapter one, here we see a further indication of how some level of independence from the mainstream licenses stronger political statements. As the film's production context indicates, *Syriana* was intended to engage its audience and draw out reflections on the wider geopolitical landscape pertaining to oil, the Middle East and, inevitably, 9/11. Here I wish to examine a number of aspects of the film that illustrate its politics, linking to other examples of post-9/11 cinema.

As already noted, a number of responses to 9/11 pointed to the way the event made visible a series of connections linking US action (past and present) to the wider world, and this might be considered the primary aim of the film's multi-stranded narrative, which offers a complex view of the alliances, deals, betrayals and interconnections between the CIA, Middle Eastern powerbrokers, energy analysts, oil industry moguls, high-powered lawyers and Pakistani migrant workers in the Persian Gulf. Four core plotlines run in parallel. First, corporate lawyer Bennett Holiday (Jeffrey Wright) is tasked with scrutinising the merger of two US oil companies, Connex and Killeen. Connex has been refused drilling rights in Syriana, a fictional Gulf state, but by purchasing Killeen will gain access to drilling rights in Kazakhstan. Holiday discovers that Killeen bribed Kazakh officials to secure these rights and arranges for a representative from his law firm and another from Killeen to be scapegoated in order to ensure the illusion of due diligence and allow the merger to proceed. Second, Syrianian Prince Nasir (Alexander Siddig), who is about to inherit the throne, is keen to reform the country by lessening US influence and adopting progressive social and political reforms. Nasir employs US energy analyst Bryan Woodman (Matt Damon) to help him achieve this goal. However, US pressure leads the Emir to choose a different son to take charge, and Nasir plots a coup but is killed by the CIA. Third, CIA agent Robert Barnes (George Clooney) is tasked with arranging the assassination of Nasir but is thwarted (and tortured) by previously friendly Iranian agent Mussawi (Mark Strong), who is now sided with Nasir. Barnes's allegiances shift and he travels to Syriana to warn Nasir of the plot against him but is killed in a US drone strike. Fourth, a young Pakistani immigrant called Wasim (Mazhar Munir) loses his job when Connex loses its contract, and in desperation joins a madrasah, where he becomes radicalised. The film ends with Wasim conducting a suicide attack on a Connex-Killeen tanker.[26]

A number of critical terms have been used to describe the plot's complexity, including 'mosaic film' (Pisters 2011: 175), 'polyphonic film' (Bruns 2008: 189) and a shift from Hollywood's preferred 'single-hero pattern' to 'the multi-protagonist format' (Azcona 2010: 5). Whatever label is selected, it is clear that through this commitment to complexity *Syriana* seeks to show how politics, economics and military power work in a symbiotic way. The representation of corporate structure, via the Holiday character, is quite clearly driven by dismay at the Enron and Worldcom corruption scandals and the role of Dick Cheney in Halliburton (a large corporation that received billions of dollars' worth of government contracts for nation-building in Iraq), as well as pointing to the recession of 2009 (see Mayer 2004). As one of the characters states: 'Corruption is our protection; corruption keeps us safe and warm […] Corruption is why we win.' This corporate sharp practice meshes with the condoned illegal CIA operation that seeks to support an unelected ruler in order to maintain a foreign country in ways sympathetic to US national self-interest. As such, each element of the film lends further complexity to the picture portrayed in order to indicate how corruption and criminality – driven by the desire to secure power – are systemic. As Knight notes, although we may be sensible to disbelieve conspiracy theories in the main,

> given all that we have learned about the less than democratic operation of government in the United States, it is a not unreasonable working hypothesis that there exists a clandestine or tacit collusion of vested interests that verges on a conspiracy. (2000: 31)

Reviewing the film, Ryan Gilbey observed that 'handheld camera, erratic editing and occasional loss of focus conspire to create the illusion of documentary' (2006). But this seems reductive; this is not simply a question of what Roland Barthes labelled 'reality effects' (1986), but more a coherent political aesthetic, containing a number of fully realised technical motifs that interact with the complex narrative design. Each of the film's locations – Kazakhstan, Geneva, Tehran, Beirut and Washington – is shown through a series of floating handheld shots with very little by way of intertitles to indicate geographical specificity or temporal shifts. As such, cinematography and editing serve to demonstrate the fluid, interconnected relations between contemporary geopolitical spaces. This way of showing spatial complexity combines with the use of occasional high-angle/extreme long shots that establish these distinct but connected locations in ways that emphasise context and a lack of individual agency. María del Mar Azcona notes that this combination of complex plot and politicised, coherently repeated technical motifs requires the viewer to

> acknowledge the complexity of forces that shape our world and the moral ambiguity of our response to them. The resulting sense of disorientation is particularly unnerving since this confusion, carefully knitted as it is with the film's relentless suspense, shatters any hopes for the feasibility of meaningful individual action and highlights the precariousness and futility of human agency in the midst of multiple and unpredictable forces. (2010: 133)

For Azcona, the film's ending (Bryan with his family; Bennett with his father) 'is not a triumph of family values over the network logic but the only alternative left for damaged and powerless subjects' (2010: 135). Here we see something like the structural view of things articulated by *Loose Change*, and perhaps also *Fahrenheit 9/11*, but without the possibility of the individual intervening and even prevailing.

Fig. 8: Subjects in context: *Syriana* (2005)

Temenuga Trifonova argues that where 1970s conspiracy thrillers such as *The Parallax View* (1974), *Three Days of the Condor* (1975) and *All the President's Men* (1976) 'presuppose a secret conspiratorial power endowed with agency', in post-9/11 conspiracy films such as *Syriana* 'the conspiracy is no longer a secret power, but part of the very structure of contemporary global relations' (2012: 122). One criticism of this way of describing the abuse of power is that those wielding power are no longer held responsible. However, although in *Syriana* the full consequences of each individual's actions may never be fully known to them, certain powerbrokers – namely politicians and corporate leaders, and an acquiescent middle management – are shown to be in a position to understand and therefore be held accountable for the consequences of their actions. In contrast to the 1970s conspiracy films, as well as *Loose Change* and even *Fahrenheit 9/11*, *Syriana* does not presume a cabal of sinister conspirators in high office but rather represents the system working with its own inevitable force and logic. As such, the film does not maintain that small-scale intervention – such as voting Bush out of office – will be corrective. On the contrary, it suggests that wholesale progressive social change of the type envisaged by the new (and by the end of the film, dead) sheik is the type of change that is really needed. Writing in 2003, Douglas Kellner called for more films in the mould of *Syriana* that displayed a 'dialectical and contextualising optic' that might offer audiences not just a clear sense of the problem but also potential solutions (2003: 44). Arguably, films such as *The Interpreter* (2005), *The Constant Gardener* (2005), *Michael Clayton* (2007), *Traitor* (2008) and *Fair Game* (2010) sought to provide such a view, with Mark Cousins observing that the immediate post-9/11 tendency towards escapism has given way to a 'new engagement with reality' (2006). Alongside the more outlandish conspiracy films such as *Loose Change*, this cycle of complex political conspiracy films pursued the notion that 'everything is connected', implying that historical realities can be mapped out and untruths and abuses of power challenged. Set against this cycle of films that seek to show complex global power relations and express the difficulty of individual human agency, the films described in the next chapter are governed by the contrasting desire to maintain a parochial relationship with the events of 9/11.

The Return to Ground Zero

In his account of post-9/11 literature, Richard Gray criticises many 9/11 novels for their insular focus and the way in which they reduce 'a turning point in national and international history to little more than a stage in a sentimental education' (2009: 134). Against this, Gray celebrates, and calls for more, 'immigrant fictions', typified by Joseph O'Neill's *Netherland* (2008), that explore difference and hybrid identity within US society. Responding to Gray's work, Michael Rothberg argues that in addition to Gray's model of literary multiculturalism, there is a need for novels in the mould of Mohsin Hamid's *The Reluctant Fundamentalist* (2007) that attempt a

> complementary centrifugal mapping that charts the outward movement of American power. The most difficult thing for citizens of the US empire to grasp is not the internal difference of their motley multiculture, but the prosthetic reach of that empire into other worlds. (2009: 153)

While *25th Hour* (and the documentaries described in chapter one) and *Fahrenheit 9/11* might be considered part of Gray's celebrated 'immigrant fiction', *Syriana* seeks to chart Rothberg's 'outward movement of American power'. However, these inclusive and searching approaches to 9/11, indicative of resistance, uncertainty and a liberal counter-reaction that gathered momentum mid-decade, sit alongside cultural production that maintained the unity discourse by pulling away from an inclusive, historicised and global sense of things and insisted instead that 9/11 be shown only via the claustrophobic and terrifying experience of those who had direct experience of the attacks. This act of conservative reassurance is visible at work in two feature films, *United 93* and *World Trade Center*.

United 93 was released in April 2006 and depicts the hijacking of United Airlines Flight 93, one of the four planes taken on 9/11. As the terrorists prepare to fly the plane into a target (possibly the White House or Capitol Building), the passengers use their mobile phones to talk to family and friends and in doing so hear about the attacks on the World Trade Center and the Pentagon. Forewarned, they attempt to overpower the terrorists and take control of the plane. As the struggle intensifies, the plane crashes in Pennsylvania. The film was preceded by a public relations campaign that pledged a donation of ten per cent of the first weekend's box-office receipts to the Flight 93 National Memorial Fund and the inclusion in press notes of the obituaries of the passengers who had died. These moves were relatively successful in heading off the inevitable accusations that the film was returning to the events too soon and seeking to commercially exploit death and suffering.

By the time of the film's release, the events on board Flight 93 had become central to the nationalist response to 9/11. Susan Faludi points to ways in which stories of Flight 93 invariably foreground the physical size, sporting background and rugged character types of predominantly male passengers, at the expense of women (2007: 56–7). The passengers' actions were also subject to specific constructions of national identity, with a *Newsweek* article celebrating the men of Flight 93 as a 'group of citizen soldiers who rose up, like their forefathers, to defy tyranny. And when they came storming down the aisle, it wasn't Americans who were afraid. It was the terrorists' (quoted in Faludi 2007: 59). In a speech at the Pennsylvania crash site on 11 September 2002, Tom Ridge, the inaugural US Secretary of Homeland Security, repeated the phrase 'citizen soldiers', thereby 'putting the patriotic rhetoric of World War II in service of the "war on terror"' (Jaafar 2006: 80). The words 'Let's roll', which were attributed to passenger Todd Beamer and widely understood to have been shouted as the passengers confronted the terrorists, quickly became shorthand for those advocating a belligerent response, and were even trademarked by Beamer's widow, Lisa, who subsequently licensed them to Wal-Mart and the Florida State University football team, among others (see Winter 2006: 15). Positioned in culture thus, the events on board Flight 93 ran with the grain of the nationalist sense of 9/11 and formed the basis for a number of patriotic television films, including *Let's Roll: The Story of Flight 93* (2002), *Last Hour of Flight 11* (2004), *Flight 93: The Flight That Fought Back* (2005) and *Flight 93* (2006). Set against these

Fig. 9:
'Let's roll':
United 93 (2006)

more clearly ideologically aligned versions, *United 93* is relatively considered and pared down. But that is not to say that it escapes the preferred reading of Flight 93 completely.

The film undertakes a complex interweaving of narrative strands show-ing the hijackers boarding the plane, the events in the plane, and reactions to the hijackings at the Boston and New York Air Traffic Control Centers, the national Air Traffic Control System Command Center in Herndon, Virginia, and the office of NORAD's Northeast Air Defense Sector in Rome, New York. Robert Burgoyne notes that 'the technique of parallel editing here renders in a detailed way activities in six different locations, each of which is distinctively colored and clearly defined' (2010: 156). Although the con-struction of the narrative is complex, this complexity does not address the wider context: the nature and locales of the film's different points of action are circumscribed. Unlike *Syriana*, which is characterised by a formally similar narrative complexity, the film is closed off from the wider event and its consequences.

United 93's director, British filmmaker Paul Greengrass, has emulated a *vérité* style of filmmaking. This aesthetic makes the film readily readable as authentic given the widespread assumption that news events, especially those depicting violence, do not permit camera crews to maintain steady framing and careful composition. As a result, the film looks more like a documen-tary than a fictional feature film. While this technique is often described as displaying realism or verisimilitude, it is, in fact, equally congruent with the intensified continuity techniques associated with big-budget, commer-cial action films. Burgoyne notes, for instance, that 'as the film progresses, the camerawork becomes increasingly jagged, with the speed and inten-sity of movement, the fragmentary split-second images, and the whip pans of the camera creating a tachycardic rhythm that pummels the audience' (2010: 155). This editing technique, combined with our knowledge of what is going to happen, amplifies a bodily sensation of tension, terror and fear. In contrast to *Syriana*, with its stylistic attempts to place specific events in context, *United 93* provides what one reviewer calls a 'sense of claustrophobic doom' that does not bring wider understanding to the events; *vérité* is placed here in the service of pure affect rather than a desire for deeper understanding (see Jaafar 2006: 81). Stephen Prince notes that

> scenes in the control centers and on the airplane were shot using multiple cameras, with staggered start and reload times. This permitted Greengrass to obtain takes of up to one hour and offered the performers the extraordinary advantage of performing in real time for extended intervals. (2009: 108)

This extended coverage enabled the actors to improvise freely, enabling the construction of a contingent and believable range of responses to the attacks. Shooting in this way also allowed improvisation around the known facts, thereby elaborating or 'filling out' the details of what might have happened on board the flight, and rather than being edited out these are included for their 'reality effect'. In this way the film's production strategy and performance style allow for pauses, stuttering and incoherence, thereby giving events an authentic feel; this contingency is subsumed, however, by the linear blow-by-blow account that makes the (contested) events that take place on the plane concrete and certain. A number of further elements sustain the film's powerful 'reality effect'. For example, the cast includes a number of air-traffic control officials who were at work on 9/11, most notably Ben Sliney, then the US Federal Aviation Authority's (FAA) national operations manager, and Major James Fox at NORAD, both of whom play themselves. This information was made public before the film so that viewers would be on the lookout for these 'real' people who had experienced events first hand. Similarly, pre-publicity drew attention to the care taken to consult with and gain the consent of victim's families. This approach – a coherent and worked-through aesthetic that brings immediacy and drama to political events – is consonant with Greengrass's previous work, including *The Murder of Steven Lawrence* (1999) and *Bloody Sunday* (2001). But whereas these earlier films depict versions of events that have been suppressed, and are shown in order to counter preconceptions, in *United 93* this aesthetic reiterates the dominant version. The consequence is that many viewers and reviewers are likely to be convinced of the film's authenticity, with the result that *United 93* gains a privileged position in relation to claims about the meaning of 9/11.

Parallel Lines

Yet under the surface of this powerful aesthetic, a number of ideologically significant operations already noted in relation to the wider discourse can be clearly identified. For example, a key tension in the film and its relation to the wider discourse is its depiction of the response of the authorities. Here the film navigates the positions (and ideological skews) articulated in *DC 9/11: Time of Crisis* (the authorities acted with propriety and calm) and *Fahrenheit 9/11* (the authorities were bewildered and incompetent). A number of commentators have read *United 93* as gesturing towards the latter in its recognition of some of the findings of the *9/11 Commission Report*, which criticised the response of the FAA in particular. Prince notes that

> in contrast to Hollywood's action thrillers, which tend to show the nation's security forces responding to terrorism efficiently and effectively, *United 93* shows the confusion, paralysis, and incomprehension that gripped the air control and defense systems. (2009: 109)

But any potential anxiety is mitigated by the fact that federal bureaucracies are shown peopled by ordinary people who do their best in difficult circumstances. Ultimately, the film shows key managerial figures in the FAA behaving heroically at a time of great stress and uncertainty. Marc Redfield notes in relation to the performance of Sliney, for example, that 'the camera returns again and again to his urbane, middle-aged face as he struggles bravely and competently, though of course ineffectively, with the unfolding crisis' (2009: 40). J. Hoberman, in his review of the film, claims it offers a vision of the 'collectivisation of heroism' (2006: 22): a 'we're all in it together' response that disallows the valid and necessary suspicion and criticism of those in positions of power, regardless of their personal endeavour and self-sacrifice. The depiction of this quiet heroism is reserved only for some. For example, there is no evidence that, as the film shows, a German passenger panicked and attempted to warn the hijackers of what the other passengers

Fig. 10: The heroic calm of FAA National Operations Manager Ben Sliney: *United 93*

intended to do. A German businessman, Christian Adam, was on board United Airlines 93, but, as Thomas Reigler notes, 'it was the actor assigned his part who suggested his supposedly defeatist attitude [which] reinforced stereotypes about European willingness to compromise in the face of suicide terrorism' (2011: 158).

As noted, Faludi describes how most accounts of Flight 93 prioritise the role of the men on board. It seems just as plausible that the flight crew, who were primarily women, would have been in a better position to coordinate any action, something *United 93* does at least gesture towards. But this aside, the film largely conforms to and reinforces a belligerent response to 9/11. The film's use of the Lord's Prayer as the passengers steel themselves to tackle the terrorists gives it a religious anchor, and an early cut of the film reportedly ended with the words, 'America's war on terror had begun' (see Jaafar 2006: 80).[27] Although the film is understated in the way it shows the decisive 'Let's roll' moment – even implying that it might be a prosaic reference to the use of a hostess trolley as a battering ram – the film still culminates in the successful fight back, with the passengers breaking in to the cockpit and seemingly killing the hijackers. This is a significant piece of improvisation, given that the transcript of conversations taking place in the cockpit during the final thirty minutes of the flight suggested that the passengers did not get inside (see Prince 2009: 113). The film reaches an emotional climax as it shows the phone calls made from the plane to family and friends, mainly involving declarations of love (though the Beamer family are shown calmly discussing what might be done). Here the film develops a narrative trope found in a large number of contemporary Hollywood films (including many described in this book), whereby a traumatic event galvanises and crystallises feelings and emotions that without the state of emergency would remain qualified and conditional. Crucially, the feelings and emotions found of value in such a moment of crisis are traditional, conservative and, seemingly, universal, thereby underwriting specific nationalist and political discourses with the deep structures of common sense and shared human feeling. For all its seemingly liberal credentials, then, this is a narrative of collective endeavour, family values, Christian faith, justified aggression and overcoming. This reaffirms the mood in the days immediately after 9/11 that was so easily co-opted and cultivated into belligerent support of the war in Iraq.

The theatrical run of *United 93* ended in July 2006, with *World Trade Center* released just four weeks later. The film is based on the story of John McLoughlin (Nicolas Cage) and Will Jimeno (Michael Peña), Port Authority police officers who volunteered to help with the evacuation of the World Trade Center and who became buried when the South Tower collapsed. Publicity photos for the film showed McLoughlin on set with director Oliver Stone and Cage, and both McLoughlin and Jimeno worked as consultants to ensure accuracy, as well as appearing in the film's epilogue attending a memorial service. Careful hiring of extras and bit-part players ensured the participation of more than fifty of McLoughlin's and Jimeno's colleagues and co-workers (see Riegler 2011: 158). As with *United 93*, this respectful consultation and inclusion of those directly involved served to indicate the filmmakers' commitment to remaining faithful to the survivors' stories, thereby legitimating the production and heading off potential criticism.[28]

Geoff King and Mike Chopra-Gant both describe how within hours of the attacks continuity editing techniques associated with fictional film and television were used by the news channels to bring together the myriad fragments of film and photography to create a coherent cause-and-effect description of the event (see King 2005: 54–5; Chopra-Gant 2008: 89–91). This orderly presentation was then echoed and consolidated in high-profile 9/11 documentaries such as *9/11* and *In Memoriam* (see King 2005: 51–2). These documentaries impose order, edit out dissenting views and seek a redemptive through-line. Of course, as we have seen, elements of many films – Nina Davenport's decision not to film the World Trade Center site in *Parallel Lines*, the use of a desolate and empty Ground Zero as backdrop to existential soul-searching in *25th Hour*, the forensic re-examination of news footage in *Loose Change* – sought to subject 9/11 to critical scrutiny. But rather than acknowledge these more qualified views, *World Trade Center* returns to the period immediately after the attacks, when the dominant response was one of bewilderment and confusion. A character viewing an image of the Twin Towers cloaked in smoke on a television screen states: 'It's as though God put up a screen of smoke to prevent us from seeing something we are not yet ready to see.' This indicates the film's re-distancing of 9/11, separating the event from the critical discourses that had adhered to it. Karen Randall notes that 'the spectacle of the twin towers collapse is already understood to be imprinted on the audience's memory' (2010: 146), indicating that a certain understanding of the event determined in the hours immediately following the attack remained available even some five years later. *World Trade Center* seeks to return its audience to this already ideologically-framed version of the event. *United 93* works in the same way, with the events mainly depicted via television, and with only one shot of the Twin Towers (after the plane strikes but before their collapse) seen in the far distance through the binoculars of an air-traffic controller. The two films appear to be simply retelling what happened and nothing more, and yet they disinter the initial response. Robert Burgoyne notes that 'an unstated consensus seems to be emerging that 9/11 should be considered a hallowed event, that "graven images" should not be made of it' (2010: 149). This prohibition on the direct representation of 9/11 places the conspiracy filmmakers who insisted that images of 9/11 must be revisited and questioned in the role of iconoclasts and privileges those filmmakers who kept the event at a distance, thereby maintaining its integrity.

World Trade Center begins with McLoughlin waking up at 3.29am, leaving his sleeping family, and travelling into New York to begin his shift. Burgoyne compares the opening sequence to the city symphony films of Dziga Vertov and Walter Ruttman, and comments that 'like Vertov and Ruttman, Oliver Stone draws a familiar portrait of the city, picturing it as a place that is both prosaic and beautiful – the epitome of a particular historical moment' (2010: 161). This celebration of New York, casting its high-rise buildings in the light of a rising sun on a beautiful clear day, is similar to the opening sequence of *In Memoriam*. New York is presented as a shining beacon, and McLoughlin as a cipher for US rectitude and family values. Against this backdrop, the attacks are shown as a catastrophic upheaval of the everyday lives of hard-working, ordinary people, the cityscape and, by extension, the fabric of the nation. McLoughlin's stoic resolve in the face of this upheaval reinforces the sense of 9/11 as a schism, an event that comes literally out of the blue, alongside the privileged response that 9/11 must be met with hard work and dutiful conformity. McLoughlin rallies his men and seeks to help those evacuating the World Trade Center but becomes trapped underground, along with Jimeno, as the towers collapse. His ordinary heroism becomes overlaid with pain, suffering and self-sacrifice.

The film cuts between the men trapped underground and their wives watching the events on television, oscillating between an intense reconstruction of stark unknowing terror and a *repetition* of the experience of watching the events unfold on news networks (an experience which, as already noted, was subject to considerable editorial control). Even here, above ground, point of view remains limited, bound to the helpless suffering of the men's wives. The gender dynamics on display support Faludi's critique that terrified women are central to understanding the response to 9/11, with male weakness in the moment of the attacks quickly translated into a familiar idiom of female helplessness and male bravery (2007: 128). Jimeno's wife, Allison (Maggie Gyllenhaal) is pregnant, intensifying the pathos of the situation (a trope also found in *Last Hour of Flight 11*). The poignancy of Allison's potential loss and her fecundity can be read as reinforcing the sense that gender is being reconstructed in conventional ways, and as a means of putting in place a certain national identity.

The conservative version of events is structured further through allusion to Christianity. Jimeno has a vision of Jesus, and in McLoughlin's recollections of everyday situations with his wife she appears as 'a latter-day domestic non-Virgin Mary, who calls her husband back from death' (Redfield 2009: 39). As Dave Karnes (Michael Shannon), a former US Marine who will locate the men thereby allowing their rescue, contemplates whether to travel to the site of 9/11, he sits in a church under a large crucifix and reads the first page of Revelation. A coda to the film notes that after finding and rescuing the two men, Karnes re-enlisted in the military and served two tours of duty in Iraq. Karnes's story gives the film a providential and redemptive direction (as well as keying the film into the wider rescue narrative identified by Faludi (2007: 216)). The contrast between the infernal, fiery dark pit in which the men are trapped and the brilliant white light of rescue might also be read in terms of religious discourse, with the film ending as McLoughlin emerges into the light 'with a powerful sense of renewal and reunion' (Burgoyne 2010: 163). This sense of renewal extends to the film's closing scenes, in which the men attend a gathering of Port Authority police officers and their families. Marc Redfield goes as far as to suggest that the shots that rise out of the rubble of Ground Zero to a satellite orbiting the Earth constitute an omniscient, God's-eye perspective and that from this 'we cut to representative images of a global village, united by technology and sorrow: all over the world different peoples are hearing of 9/11' (2009: 38). Here 9/11 is treated as a universal catastrophe, akin to a natural disaster and the film claims universality for the conservative Christian (though multicultural) worldview depicted. Unlike *United 93*, which presents two religious groups in conflict with one another, *World Trade Center* does not give any screen time to the terrorists or their creed or cause. This constrained view of 9/11 – the conservative depiction of hard-working federal employees and their suffering wives, the foregrounding of Christian faith and its rewards and consolations, the men's survival and devotion to their families, and the straight line leading from 9/11 to war in Iraq – makes *World Trade Center* fully complicit with right-wing responses to 9/11.

For the majority of *World Trade Center*'s 130-minute running time the viewer is witness to the bodily suffering the men endure as they are slowly crushed to death and threatened by fire. The film's tagline reads simply,

'A true story of courage and survival'. This focus on bodily suffering and survival undertakes something of an elision of the fact that very few intact bodies or survivors were ever recovered from Ground Zero. Mikita Brottman describes how early news coverage showing images of people jumping from the towers and falling through space was quickly pulled by news editors (2004: 176). The *New York Times* reporter Dexter Filkins describes how when he visited Ground Zero he saw pieces of intestine standing out starkly against the rubble and that he overheard rescue workers state that they were finding a lot of spinal cords (2008: 44–7). Yet, in the days following the attacks, Susan Sontag could find published only one explicit photograph: a severed hand in the rubble at Ground Zero which appeared on 12 September in the New York tabloid *The Daily News* (2003: 61). This constraint also applied to the first wave of documentary films, with the executive producer of *9/11*, for example, explaining at the press screening that the sounds of bodies hitting the ground that had been recorded by camera microphones were edited out on the grounds that 'to have that incredible crush of sound every twenty or thirty seconds would have been very tough for the audience' (quoted in Craps 2007: 199–200). As Prince notes, 'the carnage on the streets below the towers, with hundreds of burst and shattered bodies strewn about the pavement, has never been written about or substantively photographed' (2012: 502).[29] This propriety extends to *World Trade Center*, which sequesters the bodily horror of the event behind a decorous surface of heroic self-sacrifice, suffering and survival. The film seems to promise to show what has been hidden from view but in effect tells a story of survival and bodily intactness rather than disintegration. The failure to represent or note McLoughlin's and Jimeno's long-term disabilities, which have required them to retire from the police force, is telling.

Marita Sturken argues that re-enactments of traumatic historical events must be judged according to whether or not they 'involve an erasure and smoothing over of difficult material or alternatively, a constant rescripting that, like memory, enables an active engagement with the past' (1997: 43). Neither *United 93* nor *World Trade Center* enables such an engagement. Five years after the attack the interpretation of the event offered up by these films repeats the initial patriotic reactions and relegates any call for historical contextualisation. For Faludi, the films are indicative of a mass cultural response dominated by 'slavishly literal reenactments of the physical attack [...] or unrepresentative tales of triumphal rescue at Ground Zero [that were only able to] replicate not delve' (2007: 2, 3). Burgoyne notes that the simplified view of 9/11 offered by the two films ensures that nowhere are the compound contexts, the traumatic cultural and social effects, the devastating losses, or the profound alterations of national life that characterize 9/11 registered; instead, linear narrative patterning and classical limitations of character, place and time impose a rigorous and singular structure. (2010: 149)[30]

Yet, five years after 9/11, these films, perhaps inevitably, bear the burden of representation. B. Ruby Rich asks, 'is it possible to return the imagination, even in a movie theatre, to a time before the US government destroyed world sympathy with its invasions of Afghanistan and Iraq, before one disaster became many disasters?' (2006: 18). The answer may well be no, it is not fully possible. A number of critics have suggested too that *United 93* and *World Trade Center* display an ambiguity and relative perspective. Nick James points out that *United 93* shows a 'mirroring between the behaviour of the terrorists and the passengers' (2006: 3) and Hoberman argues that Greengrass's film 'promotes official incompetence over conspiracy, eschews nationalist appeal, and shows the hijackers – as well as the passengers – addressing their God' (2006: 22). Burgoyne notes that the films are 'simultaneously disruptive and conservative' and that a 'sense of adrenalized stasis dominates … a mood compounded by their focus on the profound disconnection, claustrophobia, and sense of helplessness suffered by the characters' (2010: 148, 150). Jeffrey Melnick observes that, 'with its tense insistence on the power of these two fathers, [*World Trade Center*] barely hides its central anxiety – the one shared by so many 9/11 films – that the father has been rendered powerless by the attacks, or, worse yet, is revealed to have been powerless all along' (2009: 128). The strain of reproducing the dominant discourse manifests here in a range of subtexts and contradictions that also appear in an even more marked way in the cycle of end-of-the-world films explored in the next chapter. However, although the films bear marks of the strain of upholding a straightforward, nationalist view of 9/11, they uphold the view nonetheless.

Some forms of cultural production did try to extend the more questioning and critical attitude. For example, the book *102 Minutes: The Untold Story of the Fight to Survive Inside the Twin Towers* (Dwyer and Flynn 2005) pieces together numerous stories and vignettes of those caught up in the day's events. These are prosaic rather than heroic – 'how, for instance, to open a jammed door, or navigate a flaming hallway, or climb dozens of flights of stairs' (2005: xxi) – and the dominant tone is antiheroic, detailing confusion, chaos and the grim work of survival. The book does record redemptive moments, what the authors call 'acts of grace at a brutal hour' (ibid.), including the rescue story recounted in *World Trade Center* (2005: 259–61), but this is balanced with some less acceptable revelations – for instance, that not all the people who leapt from the upper floors of the towers did so of their own volition, some being pushed by those desperate to escape the noxious smoke; that firefighters were looting from shops during the rescue; and that a 'sclerotic emergency response culture' marred by poor communications, inter-agency rivalry and failure to make changes after the 1993 World Trade Center bombing exacerbated the loss of life (2005: xxiii). *102 Minutes* seeks to adhere to the facts and hold different viewpoints related to the terrorist attacks in tension; in contrast, *United 93* and *World Trade Center* prefer instead to iron out contradiction and present a clear, heroic and redemptive view of 9/11.

The End of the World

Describing 9/11 fiction, Kristiaan Versluys claims that 'on the whole, the narratives shy away from the brute facts, the stark "donnee" of thousands of lives lost. As an event, 9/11 is limned as a silhouette, expressible only through allegory and indirection' (2009: 14). As we have seen, however, this argument about the post-9/11 novel is not true of post-9/11 cinema, in which the attacks are directly depicted in a number of (albeit guarded) ways. Yet, like the post-9/11 novel, and as *Man on Fire* and *Syriana* suggest, some films may be read as indirect representations of, or informed by, 9/11 that extend the ways in which those attacks and their aftermath might be described and, most importantly, understood. It is in these mainstream Hollywood feature films, once removed from events, that the work of bringing together seemingly conflicting political positions in order to broker hegemony can be seen. Indeed, this work – replete with ambiguity and contradiction, but undertaken nonetheless – is a central concern of the remainder of this book. While analysis following distinct parallel lines continues, with certain films depicting torture, and Iraq War films and history films maintaining a counter-hegemonic position and resisting recuperation, these are examined alongside mainstream feature films such as *In the Valley of Elah* (2007), *Incredibly Loud and Extremely Close* (2011) and *Zero Dark Thirty* (2012) that undertake the work of seeking hegemonic reconciliation between politically irreconcilable positions.

Ideological criticism regards representation as a veiling of another reality; for example, the image of the firefighter or policeman and his ascension, a trope observable in a number of films analysed here, is a figure grounded in religious narrative and folklore that allows 9/11 to be phrased in a redemptive way. As such, ideological criticism is already considering representation to be functioning allegorically. One of the earliest ways in which 9/11 was allegorised was in the designation of the World Trade Center site as 'Ground Zero', a term first used on the evening of 11 September by CBS News reporter Jim Axelrod and, a little later the same day, by NBC News reporter Rehema Ellis, who said: 'We're now just a block away from the World Trade Center and the closer we get to Ground Zero the harder it is to breathe and to see.' In the film *The Guys* (2002), discussed in the next chapter, a character describes Ground Zero as 'reminiscent of a nuclear winter'; and as we shall see, the *mise-en-scène* and cinematography of much post-9/11 cinema has an apocalyptic look. The term originates in a military context, where 'Ground Zero' is used to refer to the epicentre of the detonation of a nuclear weapon, and entered popular usage in journalistic descriptions of the atomic bombs dropped on Hiroshima and Nagasaki at the end of World War II. Here, in short measure, we can see the ideological service to which allegory can be put, in this case amplifying the size and scale of the attacks (9/11 is equivalent to Hiroshima), as well as the potency of the threat (Iraqi WMD could lead to a nuclear strike on a US city); in both cases, the allegorical dimension may license an aggressive and expansive foreign policy. As John Dower notes, after 9/11

> Ground Zero became code for America as victim of evil forces – alien peoples and cultures who, 'unlike ourselves,' did not recognise the sanctity of human life and had no compunctions about killing innocent men, women and children. [...] To an extent almost impossible to exaggerate, 'Ground Zero 2001' became a wall that simultaneously took its name from the past and blocked out all sightlines of from what and where that name came. (2010: 161)

While Dower's point is that the use of the term is intended to evacuate history – the Year Zero effect – this preferred reading of the allegorical figure did not go unchallenged. In *Parallel Lines*, documentary filmmaker Nina Davenport travels to Los Alamos, the site of nuclear testing during World War II, as a way of drawing attention to the ways in which the use of the term 'Ground Zero' belied a number of contradictory realities, not least straightforwardly jingoistic accounts of World War II (see Dower 2010: 151–61). As Philip E. Wegner notes,

Allegories enable complex or abstract historical processes to take on a concrete form. Indeed, allegories often offer figurations of these historical movements before the emergence of a more proper conceptual or theoretical language. Allegorical representations also have the capacity to condense different historical levels and conflicts into a single figure, enabling a kind of relational thinking that is not as readily available to other forms of expression. (2009: 7)

As Wegner notes, the allegorical figure is dialectical: speaking of an event through recourse to another event, seeking simplicity but often, unwittingly, revealing layers of further significance. In this chapter I wish to consider one particular allegorical response, namely the indirect address of 9/11 through films that depict the end of the world.[31] An apocalyptic sensibility can be traced back to the initial response to the attacks themselves, when the description of the event as a national catastrophe was a central feature of news coverage. Following this, in the immediate aftermath, as well as making the term 'Ground Zero' central, the mass media reported on a series of anthrax attacks and published a number of speculative accounts suggesting that terrorists planned to use smallpox and ricin to poison water supplies, shoot down civilian planes with surface-to-air missiles and explode 'dirty' bombs in crowded city centres. The discursive amplification of the terrorist threat – which conjured any number of apocalyptic scenarios – served a crisis mentality underpinning a culture of fear.

A sceptic might point to the fact that US popular culture is, and has long been, replete with apocalyptic scenarios, and it is true that a distinct cycle of films depicting the end of the world originated in the late 1990s (as well as at numerous other points in Hollywood's history). However, I wish to argue that the diverse cycle of films appearing from the mid-2000s, including *War of the Worlds* (2005), *I Am Legend* (2007), *The Mist* (2007), *Cloverfield* (2008), *The Happening* (2008) and *The Road* (2009), all contain references that key their respective apocalypses into the experience of 9/11. In *The Road*, for example, documentary film footage of clouds of dust from 9/11 was composited into the background of one scene, with the film's director, John Hillcoat, stating:

We deliberately used America's real apocalyptic zones. We went to New Orleans to shoot our interior shots in a ruined shopping mall in post-Katrina New Orleans. We used the strip mines in western Pennsylvania [...] these places were not hard to find. There's a fair amount of devastation already in the American landscape. (Quoted in Chiarella 2009)

Here we see a literal coming together of the real and the figural in a way that corroborates the view that many of these films solicit a response that relates what is onscreen to 9/11. This raises the questions: How do the end-of-the-world films relate to this discourse and the wider culture of fear? Do they perpetuate or challenge a patriotic nationalism? And how might reading them as allegories of 9/11 help us understand the wider popular cultural response to 9/11 mid-decade?

Released in June 2005, *War of the Worlds* is an adaptation of the H. G. Wells novel and tells the story of a devastating alien invasion of Earth. With an estimated budget of $132 million, the film grossed $591 million worldwide, making it one of the most commercially successful films discussed in this book. J. Hoberman argues that *War of the Worlds* alongside two other films by director Steven Spielberg – *The Terminal* (2004) and *Munich* (2005) – constitutes a long-form engagement with 9/11, a 'trilogy of terror' that is laced with preoccupations related to the terrorist attacks and their aftermath (2006: 20). Upon the film's release numerous reviewers corroborated Hoberman's view that the film sought to activate memories of 9/11 (see Atkinson 2005). The film's opening sequences are set in New Jersey, separated from Manhattan by the George Washington Bridge crossing the Hudson. In a widely carried promotional interview for the film Spielberg stated that the images of people fleeing across the bridge on 9/11 were a 'searing image that I haven't been able to get out of my head', and this choice of location both activates a memory of 9/11 *and* maintains some respectful distance between those events and the alien attack. The depiction of the attacks includes clouds of grey dust and clothing falling to the ground, explicitly calling on memories of the media coverage of 9/11, especially those of the people falling from the World Trade Center and crowds fleeing as the Twin Towers collapsed. Unable to understand what is happening, Ray Ferrier's (Tom Cruise) daughter, Rachel (Dakota Fanning), asks her father 'is it the terrorists?' The allusions continue: missing person posters can be seen in numerous scenes, and, as Kirsten Moana Thompson observes, 'people ask each other, "Did you lose anyone?"' (2007: 147), a common turn of phrase after 9/11. Later in the film, a woman on a loudspeaker proclaims to a crowd waiting to board a ferry that no more donations of blood are needed, echoing accounts that healthcare professionals at Ground Zero had to turn away willing donors. A number of reviewers considered this way of recalling 9/11 to be in poor taste, indeed 'pornographic', suggesting that the images were challenging and unsettling (see Kellner 2010: 131). However, closer examination suggests something more familiar from earlier chapters at work.

The depiction of bodies turned to dust is perhaps the most resonant of the references to 9/11, and here the *mise-en-scène* is directly modelled on documentary footage of the terrorist attacks. Indeed, correspondences between Etienne Suaret's *WTC – The First 24 Hours* and *War of the Worlds* are too many to be coincidental. Following 9/11, the dust produced by the collapse of the World Trade Center became a public health issue that was handled with wariness by the mass media. Reporters wrote about the dangers of poor air quality in lower Manhattan, especially as experienced by rescue and salvage workers, but rarely commented on the fact that many of those killed in the World Trade Center had simply disintegrated with the building, their bodies becoming part of the dust cloud that enveloped lower Manhattan. Although evidenced by the numerous missing person posters and funeral services conducted with empty coffins, this difficult fact was rarely addressed directly.

Against this caesura, Spielberg makes explicit the connection between the grey dust and destroyed bodies, and places this at the heart of a family melodrama in which a father must decide how to explain what has happened to his children. Returning home after witnessing the initial attacks, in which many people have been killed, Ferrier's children see their father covered in dust and want to know what it is. Ferrier refuses to explain and retreats into the bathroom, where he frantically tries to clean himself. Ray's inability to

Fig. 11: Bodies turned to dust: *War of the Worlds* (2005)

wash off the dust or explain what has happened to his children presents 9/11 as something that cannot be washed away, expressed in language or moved beyond: the experience remains raw and terrifying. Like the focus on serious physical injury and the ability to endure pain depicted in *World Trade Center*, this returning of the corporeal to dust works to renew the signifier 9/11, and to reactivate memory of the initial traumatic impact of the attacks. As such, a key element – dust/bodies – is used to sustain a high pitch of anxiety and terror many years after the initial frightened reaction to the attacks has ebbed away. This aspect of the film can be read in relation to the continued centrality of a culture of fear in mid-decade politicking. For example, a key voting constituency that helped re-elect George W. Bush in 2004 was the so-called 'security moms', whose vote went to the candidate most committed to protecting the nation's children from terrorism. Peter Stearnes observes that

> after 9/11, sales of home protection devices went up massively [...] The reaction was understandable, given the level of anxiety, and it allowed people to 'do something'; it also reflected the high degree of personalisation in the reactions to the attack, as Americans somehow merged terrorism with other concerns. (2006: 215)

Here, fear generated by the terrorist attacks was used to reinforce the dominant ideological response. This meshing of fear and everyday life helps explain the tone and tenor of the films discussed in this chapter, which imagine ordinary, mundane scenarios torn apart by terrifying, all-powerful forces (with the dust/body trope a distillation of this logic). It was unlikely that Americans living away from the major cities were ever in any real danger, and yet, the fear was widespread. Unlike the British and Spanish responses to the terrorist attacks on London and Madrid, which stressed the continuation of everyday life and actively resisted the calls for a military response, the fearful reaction of Americans is said by Stearnes to be the equivalent of a 'panic attack', which precipitated a 'fear-induced excess of belligerence' (2006: 218). As we shall see, the film's narrative corrals this powerful combination of anxiety and inarticulacy and turns it in a conservative direction.

But it is the nature of allegory to be imprecise. As such, while many readings of the film focused on the aforementioned correspondences with the experience of 9/11, including the resonance of dust/bodies, other interpretations traced a different allegorical trajectory, this time related to the war in

Iraq (see Newman 2005: 83; Vest 2006: 69). Lester D. Friedman argues that *War of the Worlds*

> provides dramatic examples of what it must have been like for Iraqi civilians during the American invasion/liberation of their country. The 'shock and awe' created by the aliens in *War of the Worlds* resembles the panic generated by the American military more than it does the devastating, but as yet singular, attack on the World Trade Center. (2006: 159)

Similarly, David Holloway notes that the film undertakes 'a displacement that turned American audiences into victims of their "own" sublime battery of hi-tech weapons of mass destruction' (2008: 95). This reading is also marshalled by the filmmakers themselves, with Spielberg stating that he wished to make an actively anti-neoconservative film (Anon. 2006) and screenwriter David Koepp saying, 'I view [the film] as an anti-war film, especially an anti-Iraq War film' (quoted in Abramowitz 2005). In light of this, it is no coincidence that Ferrier's son, Robbie (Justin Chatwin), is writing a paper on the brutal, and ultimately unsuccessful, French occupation of Algeria.[32]

Undeniably, the film can be plausibly read in this way. However, my argument is that the film returns to the traumatic shock caused by the experience of 9/11 *and* imbricates this with the vicarious experience of the Iraq War as victim. Taken together, the sense of the US as a victim of terrorism on 9/11 combines with the placing of the nation into the role of victim of the 'war on terror', thereby serving to distract from the fact that the US is perpetrator in the latter. *War of the Worlds* compounds this sense of victimisation through the use of other generic images of atrocity: dead bodies shown floating in a river recall news photographs of the genocide in Rwanda; a line of dialogue – 'When they flash that thing, everything lights up like Hiroshima' – compares the alien weapons to nuclear bombs. These references call on the experience of genocide and nuclear war to amplify senses of victimhood. Critique, then, in the form of an allegory of the invasion of Iraq is made subordinate to this vicarious victimisation. As these elements of the film come together, the politically positioned and distinct responses to 9/11 – what this book has called parallel lines – converge, drawn together into a single post-9/11 trope that although replete with contradiction serves to bring critical responses to 9/11 under the command of hegemonic discourse.

Further elements confirm that this synthesis is central to the film's overall direction. As already noted, in much post-9/11 cinema, including many of the films described in this book, the depiction of relations between parent and child often work allegorically.[33] Holloway describes how strained relations between parents and children stand in for a wider anxiety regarding the state/citizen, with the former failing to protect the latter on 9/11 (2008: 110). Arguably, the mainstream media deals with this anxiety by reinforcing a conservative discourse, most obviously by placing Bush (and a number of people in positions of authority) in the reassuring role of father/protector (see Faludi 2007: 147–8). Aligned with this, the need to protect children also licenses revenge films such as *Man on Fire* (see chapter two). But even in these formulations, a negative dialectic remains. As Holloway notes, the allegory speaks to a bald fact: the state had, indeed, failed to protect its citizens, leaving many Americans with the difficult task of having to explain 9/11 to their children (see Holloway 2008: 110). This anxiety is central to the post-9/11 disaster film cycle, including *War of the Worlds*.

As noted, Ferrier is the film's main focaliser, a blue-collar worker, skilled crane operator and union man who is separated from his wife and is shown to be emotionally immature. Ferrier has a troubled relationship with his (near estranged) children, who are visiting him for the weekend when the aliens attack. The casting of Dakota Fanning as his daughter reiterates the dynamics already described in relation to *Man on Fire*: Fanning's porcelain complexion, blue-veined skin and plucky gregarious attitude signals a morally and aesthetically pure whiteness that stands as a symbol of an imperilled USA. At first, Ferrier (in denial himself) attempts to protect his children from what has happened, refusing to explain what the dust that covers him signifies. Ferrier then resolves to flee the city and return the children to their mother's house in Boston, a journey narrative observable in a number of post-9/11 post-apocalyptic films, including *I Am Legend*, *Children of Men* (2006) and *28 Weeks Later* (2007) (see Aston 2008). As the family travel north by car they are caught in chaotic scenes as they try to cross the Hudson. Here the exodus from New York turns to anarchy, with people fighting each other in desperation. Ferrier's car is stolen by the mob, and his children see him reduced to helplessness. After accusing his father of cowardice, Ferrier's son leaves to join the forces fighting against the aliens. By the mid-point of the film, the vulnerability of Ferrier is raw and clearly taps a cultural anxiety not fully alleviated by media images of strong fathers and patrician leaders.

Now alone, Ferrier and Rachel are offered refuge by a stranger, Harlan Ogilvy (Tim Robbins), who threatens Rachel in a number of ways, including talking blackly about the future (Ferrier does not want his daughter to

Fig. 12: Parental anxiety and the 'father-protector': *War of the Worlds* **(2005)**

hear that there is no hope), telling of his plan to fight the aliens (which will imperil them all) and viewing Rachel with a predatory gaze (leading some critics to suggest he is a paedophile) (see Faludi 2007: 10; Holloway 2008: 92–6). In response, Ferrier blindfolds his daughter and kills Ogilvy, stating: 'I can't let my daughter die because of you.' For most of this sequence we adopt Ferrier's point of view (seeing Ogilvy, the aliens and his daughter through his eyes), but when the murder takes place (offscreen), the point of view shifts to Rachel as she attempts to block out the sound of the killing. The sequence – a fraught scenario set out in a complex point-of-view system – is extremely dark for a mainstream blockbuster, and the moral quandary is a challenging one (*Munich* takes its central character into similar territory). However, *War of the Worlds* backs away from creating what might be called ethical deadlock – a situation with no clear way out – preferring instead to legitimate Ferrier's actions by depicting Ogilvy's character in the most negative terms. Ultimately, the killing is justified and the scene rehearses what Richard Slotkin terms 'regeneration through violence' (2000: 5), thereby aligning *War of the Worlds* with a strong father/revenger discourse.

In contrast, Cormac McCarthy's post-apocalyptic novel *The Road* (2006, released as a film three years later) takes the same figure/allegory of a father and child attempting to survive and provides an even bleaker view, showing 'the young child's awful vulnerability to the predations of the post-apocalypse (extreme cold, starvation, illness, rape, slavery, cannibalism) and the likely death of the father who protects him' (Holloway 2008: 110). The novel and film also contain a dramatic scenario equivalent to the one faced by Ferrier, but instead of a regeneration through violence the son persuades his father that the threatening stranger should not be killed, thereby seeking an ethical course of action that resists the clear-cut through-line offered in *War of the Worlds*. Similarly, an equivalent scenario in *Right at Your Door* (2006) shows a struggling writer working from home, whose wife is caught in a chemical/biological terrorist attack as she travels to work. Following instructions from the authorities the writer seals himself and, unknowingly, a Mexican handyman working for a neighbour in his house. The wife survives the attack and manages to return home, and in the fraught scenes that follow, with the wife demanding entry, the husband reasons to her that because she is probably contaminated he must refuse her entry in order to protect the life of the stranger. Here the ethical stakes are finely poised, with no (morally) clear course of action available to any of the characters. This spare, difficult pitting of one person against another, and an insistence that every course of action will result in harm, stands in sharp contrast to *War of the Worlds*, and prefigures the kind of scenario that gives shape to the torture films discussed in chapter seven.

The film's conclusion ties these different elements together. As noted, at the film's start Ferrier is depicted as dysfunctional, with his family disintegrating as a consequence of his failure to adopt a suitably patriarchal blend of action, authority and maturity. Sheldon Hall notes that many of Spielberg's films 'revolve around incomplete, dysfunctional or disintegrating families and around weak, absent, abusive or irresponsible fathers or father figures' (quoted in Williams and Hammond 2006: 167). However, where Spielberg's earlier films, including *Duel* (1971), *Jaws* (1975) and *Close Encounters of the Third Kind* (1977), remain relatively qualified in their redemption of the patriarchal status of their central characters, *War of the Worlds* is more affirmative. Through the violent defence of his daughter, Ferrier begins the process of reclaiming his position as head of the family. As the alien threat succumbs to the common cold virus, the film ends with Ferrier delivering his daughter to his mother, safe in a Boston brownstone, and discovering that his son has also reached safety. James Aston offers a persuasive reading that, as well as consolidating an overarching patriarchal logic, this fantasy of repatriation also taps into 'media attention given to New Yorkers and the need of being with or finding loved ones in the aftermath of 9/11' (2008). In combination, then, these facets of the film – the recall of 9/11 as traumatic shock, the placing of the protagonist in the role of victim and the activation of the father/protector role – indicates that although elements of *War of the Worlds* may seem left-liberal in inclination, the wider operations of the film provide order and coherence, and a clear way through the action for the viewer that aligns them with the conservative discourse.

The way in which *War of the Worlds* shows the re-establishment of patriarchal authority and closes with a redemptive image of the reunited family, combined with the placing of Americans in the role of victims of atrocity, shadows the elements of the film that might be read in relation to critique. The malleability of an allegorical rendering of 9/11 permits the convergence of left-liberal and right-wing positions, producing a synthesis that – while seemingly incompatible if expressed as clear political statements – is reconciled allegorically. *War of the Worlds*, then, is a useful indicator of the way in which left-liberal responses are held alongside right-wing constructions in the mainstream feature film, and this, in turn, is indicative of the operation of hegemony in relation to 9/11 more generally. A critical perspective will, if it defers too much to the dominant ideological frame – in this case a sense of vicarious victimisation and remasculinisation – lose its critical purchase.

Adapted by director Frank Darabont from a Stephen King novella first published in 1980, the apocalyptic horror film *The Mist* (2007) occupies much the same territory as *War of the Worlds*. However, the film's relatively low-budget ($18 million), semi-independent production set-up (financed by Dimension Films and shot and edited by the production crew from the television series *The Shield* (2002–08)) and willingness to venture into territory unexplored by the wider cycle helps to set in relief the operations of more mainstream fare.

The film is set in the small town of Bridgton, Maine. With its white picket fences and neatly tended gardens, Bridgton has a 1950s feel that recalls the opening sequences of David Lynch's *Blue Velvet* (1986). As with that film, outward appearance belies dark undercurrents and conflicts. The night after a violent thunderstorm, David Drayton (Thomas Jane), a graphic artist, and his eight-year-old son, Billy (Nathan Gamble), drive into town. While they are at the local supermarket a mist descends that sets the scene for a claustrophobic narrative in which the supermarket is besieged by an array of supernatural creatures. The mist can be read allegorically in relation to the dust cloud seen on 9/11. Characters in the film describe it variously as a pollution cloud caused by a chemical explosion, a harbinger of the apocalypse and death itself. It is eventually revealed, in contrast to the dust in *War of the Worlds*, that the mist is the result of a military experiment gone wrong. As the characters desperately try to survive, their struggle can be read as an allegory of the political tensions and divisions in US society during the mid-2000s.

The End of the World

This can be clearly seen in the film's depiction of religion. Deadly flying insects manage to break the windows of the supermarket, but Mrs Carmody (Marcia Gay Harden), a fanatically religious local woman, appears to be saved because she prays as the attack takes place. Carmody claims that the creatures are God's way of punishing a fallen mankind, while also vehemently denouncing stem cell research, abortion and sexual immorality. Her survival seems to legitimate her views, and she gains the confidence of other survivors, who together call for a human sacrifice by way of expiation. The group capture and stab a soldier before throwing him outside, where he is killed by a praying-mantis-like creature. With Carmody now calling for a child sacrifice, Ollie Weaks (Toby Jones), the mild-mannered, effeminate assistant manager of the supermarket, shoots her dead. The depiction of this strongly religious response – one character states, 'If you scare people bad enough they'll turn to whoever offers a solution' – models the wider culture of fear but also suggests that this way of reacting to crisis is hysterical and unfounded. Indeed, by the film's logic, it merits violent suppression.

However, *The Mist*'s anti-religious stance is exceptional, especially when read against the wider cultural/religious response to 9/11, which, as already noted, was underpinned by a Christian value system. Bush called for a crusade against the evildoers responsible and, in what Stuart Croft calls the 'crisis narrative' constructed after 9/11, religious rhetoric gave shape to the understanding of the 'war on terror' as a battle against a rising, all-encompassing evil (2006: 27–33). Although criticism of this rhetoric led to statements that Islam was to be considered a peaceful co-religion with Christianity, with only Islamic fundamentalism a force of evil, the sense of Christian religious purpose and providential meaning continued to adhere to policy statements and to circulate in the wider culture. Indeed, between 18 September and 15 December 2001, one million Americans signed up to

Fig. 13: The violent suppression of Christian fundamentalism: *The Mist* (2007)

a National Prayer programme, with Bush addressing the National Prayer Breakfast in February 2002, stating: 'Many, including me, have been on bended knee. The prayers of this nation are a part of the good that has come from the evil of September the 11th, more good than we could ever have predicted' (quoted in Croft 2006: 91).

With less prominence in the media, Christian fundamentalists such as Jerry Falwell and Pat Robertson 'interpreted the events of 9/11 precisely as the just desserts of "sinful" American hedonism and materialism' (King 2005: 49). Peter Stearnes argues that this response can be traced back to an American tradition stemming from the experience of European Christian sects exiled to North America in the seventeenth and eighteenth centuries, who longed for God's apocalyptic judgement of a sinful mankind so that the fallen might be punished and the chosen saved (see 2006: 64–72). According to this interpretation, precisely the one pilloried in *The Mist*, 9/11 was a God-given punishment, 'a cleansing destruction of centres of government and urban decadence' (King 2005: 49). This apocalyptic sensibility can be seen in the sixteen bestselling *Left Behind* novels released from 1995 by Christian evangelists Tim La Haye and Jerry B. Jenkins. The books, which, according to Jonathan Vincent, saw a sixty per cent increase in sales following 9/11, have also been turned into films (*Left Behind* (2000), *Left Behind II: Tribulation Force* (2002) and *Left Behind: World at War* (2005)), as well as inspiring other films such as *2012: Doomsday* (2008) (2010: 45). Certainly, the initial code-name for the 'war on terror' – 'Operation Infinite Justice' – would not be out of place in this kind of religio-fiction.

Like the conspiracy films described in chapter three (with which they share some territory, especially the belief that the federal government is evil, or at least deeply untrustworthy), these novels and films, and the wider sensibility of religious hysteria, have been widely dismissed as marginal and without merit. However, although often given short shrift, an apocalyptic sensibility seems to be habitual and ingrained in US popular culture. Ian McEwan observes that this belief in end-time biblical prophecy, or 'premillennial dispensationalism', 'extends from marginal, ill-educated, economically deprived groups, to college-educated people in the millions, through to governing elites, to the very summits of power' (2008).[34] Kevin Rozario notes that 'according to a Time/CNN poll conducted in 2002, a quarter of all Americans believed the events of 9/11 were predicted in the Bible. The same survey found that 59 percent of Americans expected the world to end as prophesied in the Book of Revelation' (2007: 185). This sensibility can be traced into post-9/11 film plots. For example, In *I Am Legend*, scientist

Robert Neville (Will Smith) searches for a cure for a disease that has turned the world's population into flesh-eating zombies/vampires. Crucially, the disease is the result of a mutation of a genetically engineered variant of the measles virus, which it was hoped would cure cancer. The film's sombre mood and persistent sense of loss, as well as scenes of panic in New York, arguably activate a connection to 9/11. The final scenes of the film have Neville finding a cure in part through scientific enquiry but only because he has tempered his scientific zeal with a commitment to an unquestioning religious or spiritual belief (as marked by the arrival of a devout Latin American woman who has travelled to New York following a sign from God, and the film's butterfly motif, which suggests some kind of divine intervention). Neville martyrs himself in defence of the vaccine and his surrogate nuclear family, who as a result of his actions escape to a religious community in Vermont. The ending of the film asserts a need to annihilate difference (the zombies figured as threat) driven by a powerful, religiously inflected self-belief. Similarly, *The Reaping* (2007), *Knowing* (2009), *The Book of Eli* (2010) and *Legion* (2010) all have apocalyptic religious narratives in which fundamentalist Christian religious views are shown to have foundation (belief in the supernatural and in God is encouraged) and positive purpose (the apocalypse provides grounds for the betterment of humankind). As seen in an earlier chapter, in *World Trade Center*, Dave Karnes, the former US Marine who helps to rescue the two police officers trapped in the collapsed Twin Towers, decides to join the search party while sitting in church under a large crucifix reading the first page of Revelation. Although in *War of the Worlds* any sense of a religious dimension remains dilute (Morgan Freeman's voice-over notwithstanding), it remains the case that the near-end times provide the catalyst for the shouldering of patriarchal responsibility.

As already noted, *The Mist* engages head on with 'end times' theology in its plot, actively refuting it – indeed, through the killing of Carmody, suggesting that the religious viewpoint would be better eradicated. There is no brokering of compromise here, no consensus-seeking gathering of the different parts into an uneasy whole. This is in line with the film's uncompromising narrative structure in general. For instance, it becomes apparent that rather than some form of divine retribution, the lethal mist – and the terrifying creatures contained therein – is the consequence of experiments by a military-industrial complex seeking to harness supernatural energies to form weapons, a conceit that can be read in relation to Chalmers Johnson's concept of 'blowback', namely, that clandestine actions of the CIA and the military eventually have consequences in the form of unanticipated and unpredictable events.

The Mist also contains the central father/child dynamic as found in *War of the Worlds*. However, the father is relatively passive and while trying to escape finds that he and his son are about to succumb to the monsters in the mist. Rather than submit to this fate, he uses a pistol to kill his son and the others escaping with him, before (now without bullets) awaiting his fate. At that point the fog clears and the military arrive. Where a more conventional film might show the townsfolk banding together in the face of the threat, *The Mist* shows people to be divided, with tensions playing out in relation to geographical, racial, class, religious and gender difference. In this sense the supermarket (which Aviva Briefel and Sam J. Miller claim is a symbol of consumer society (2011: 8)) might be read as an attempt to map the fraught and irreconcilable forces shaping US popular and political culture after 9/11: an allegory of the difficulty of brokering and maintaining consent for any of the forms of nationalism on offer. The film rejects outright, through the treatment of the issue of religion, the strident, patriotic nationalism of the neoconservatives. In addition, the military are shown to be the source of the problem and are ineffectual in dealing with the situation. Nor does the film seek a 'conscience liberalism' position, in which some kind of concession to right-wing positions might permit the brokering of consensus, but rather allegorises the divisive cultural politics as they play out in the post-9/11 culture of fear, before following this through to the bleak apocalyptic ending, in which the townsfolk, through their failure to cooperate, produce the conditions of their own downfall. This pessimistic rendering of political realities can also be seen in other horror films, including *Dawn of the Dead* (2004), *Land of the Dead* (2005) and the television film *Homecoming* (2005), forming a cycle that recalls the apocalyptic scenarios identified by Robin Wood in a strand of 1970s horror film that he argued had progressive potential. For Wood, in films such as *Night of the Living Dead* (1968),

> the apocalypse, even when presented in metaphysical terms (the end of the world), is generally reinterpretable in social/political ones (the end of the highly specific world of patriarchal capitalism) ... and this is progressive in so far as their negativity is not recuperable into the dominant ideology, but constitutes, on the contrary, the recognition of that ideology's disintegration and its untenability, as all it has repressed explodes and blows it apart. (1986: 191–2)

In general, this kind of explosive, radical political energy remained marginal in post-9/11 cinema, being found only in semi-independent horror films like

The End of the World

The Mist, with the centre-ground ceded to films such as *War of the Worlds*, in which the recognition of demonstrable political differences was accommodated in the allegorical figure of the nuclear family in peril.

The September 11 Syndrome

In this chapter, I examine another discourse that gave shape to post-9/11 cinema, namely, the treatment of 9/11 as an event experienced as a psychological trauma. Reflecting on television news coverage in the immediate aftermath of the attacks, Pat Aufderheide observed that alongside the jingoistic rallying cries to war ran a 'therapeutic patriotism', with news networks assuming 'a therapeutic role as grief counsellor … nurturing insecure viewers who had been stripped of their adult self-assurance by the shock of the attacks' and providing 'emotional reassurance' (2001). This therapeutic patriotism gave shape to news coverage of the cycles of funerals, eulogies for the dead and ritualised mourning practices surrounding the burial of those killed on 9/11, invariably with a focus on the recovery (or the struggle to recover) of survivors and family and friends (see Kitch 2003). In Karen M. Seeley's account of the work of mental health professionals in New York following 9/11, she notes that

> based on a rapid assessment of mental health needs conducted by Columbia University's School of Public Health, the New York State Office of Mental Health warned that residents of New York City and its environs would suffer an epidemic of psychiatric problems, including depression, anxiety, substance abuse, and, especially, PTSD. (2008: 147–8)

Tom Pollard calls on a number of studies to indicate how post-traumatic stress disorder (PTSD) – a severe condition first diagnosed in the 1980s that may develop after a person has experienced (directly or indirectly) a traumatic event, and which results in symptoms that include flashbacks and high levels of debilitating anxiety – was the primary problem reported. According to Pollard,

> 7.5 percent of New Yorkers and 20 percent of those who were near the World Trade Center when the attacks occurred suffered from PTSD [and] in the weeks and months following September 11 a signifi-cant number of children and adults exposed to media coverage of the attacks developed full-fledged cases of PTSD (over 5 percent). In addi-tion, an astonishing percentage of children (18.7 percent) and adults (10.7 percent) developed some symptoms of PTSD but did not develop full-blown cases. (2011: 7)

In response, through schemes such as the Project Liberty programme, the federal government made available $155 million for mental health support, with up to 1.5 million New York state residents seeking treatment (see Seeley 2008: 165).[35] The fact that a mental health problem was often an important precursor to a successful compensation claim further consolidated the high incidence of this way of responding to the attacks. As these accounts of the wider response show, 9/11 was 'effectively medicalized' (Seeley 2008: 4), with Seeley describing how 'one therapist maintained that, instead of encourag-ing people to rationally analyse the events of 9/11, the government [through the distribution of leaflets by FEMA, NIMH and other federal organisa-tions and through the wider public health response] consistently advised them to pay attention to their feelings' (2008: 157). Frustrated by this use of the therapy paradigm, Susan Sontag warned that 'the politics of a democ-racy – which entails disagreement, and which promotes candour – has been replaced by psychotherapy' (2001).

Psychologised thus, 9/11 is made available to the redemptive moves of a therapeutic patriotism. Susan Faludi argues that the political campaign ad 'Ashley's Story', in which a female who has been traumatised by 9/11 is 'cured' on receiving a heartfelt embrace from George W. Bush, is an example of the preferred right-wing response (see 2007: 147–8). Here, the wounded, traumatised (usually female) subject has little agency and retreats from the public sphere to await the state's paternal/therapeutic cure. What is more, the traumatic experience of 9/11 acts as a catalyst that precipitates a strong, action-driven response: in this discourse, those wounded by the attack are made safe in the family home while father/protectors make the US safe.

Between $14 million and $17 million was spent to screen the ad more than 30,000 times in the final week of Bush's successful re-election campaign (see Faludi 2007: 163).

At the same time, this neoconservative response – in which being traumatised by 9/11 is bracketed as a gendered reaction in need of strong male guidance and leadership – works in parallel with a more liberal, less obviously gendered, version that extends the wounded state to all. Harriet B. Braiker's self-help book *The September 11 Syndrome: Anxious Days and Sleepless Nights* (2002) is indicative. Braiker writes that

> following the events of September 11, and continuing to this day, an intense sense of vulnerability and loss of control has taken hold. These troubling feelings may linger beneath the surface producing heightened anxiety at any time, stimulated by replaying news footage of the September 11 attacks or by current news events from the war on terrorism. These jolts cause the embers to reignite into a flame of heightened anxiety and from there into more serious feelings of stress, depression, anxiety and loss – the September 11 syndrome. (2002: 5)

Braiker's self-help approach deals with these difficult emotions and feelings via Cognitive Behavioural Therapy (CBT): a 'worry-timer' to restrict time spent worrying, an elastic band to twang when feeling anxious, choosing to not watch the news or read a newspaper, and so on. The latter suggestion, to turn away from media coverage of 9/11, to effectively avoid thinking about the event, to retreat into the realm of the personal and the domestic, signals clearly the political stakes. This chapter argues that a cycle of post-9/11 films, including *The Guys* (2003) and *Extremely Loud and Incredibly Close*, places the experience of 9/11 in this liberal therapeutic framework and that this serves to sequester the experience of 9/11 squarely in the realm of the personal and in doing so turn away from more expansive senses of the event that had become central to critical views of the attacks. Spanning nearly a decade, this cycle signals the longevity of this way of framing the experience of the terrorist attacks and is especially important in indicating the continued centrality of therapeutic nationalism to the brokering of consensus in relation to 9/11 and its aftermath.

In Anne Nelson's stage play *The Guys*, a fire captain and ex-soldier asks a female journalist to help him prepare eulogies for eight of his men who were killed on 9/11. Opening less than twelve weeks after the attacks, the play was first staged at the Flea Theatre in Tribeca, New York, very close to the ruins of the World Trade Center, with Sigourney Weaver and Bill Murray in the central roles. The play was a success and transferred to Los Angeles in July 2002 and to the Edinburgh Festival in the same year. A modestly budgeted film version, starring Sigourney Weaver and Anthony LaPaglia, premiered at the Toronto film festival in September 2002, followed by a limited release in the US in April 2003.

As a stage play written within days of the attacks, *The Guys* is readable as part of the very first wave of responses to 9/11 described in chapter one, and also an addition to the variety of voices, many based in New York, who resisted the call to arms. In interview, Nelson has described the play as a self-conscious attempt to produce a counter-hegemonic response to 9/11, stating:

> In the weeks after September 11, I felt as though New York's grief was being appropriated for all kinds of other political and commercial inter-ests. I thought that if I wrote this small play, it would be claiming a little patch of ground for the way I and the people around me were actually experiencing the event. (Quoted in Finn 2006)

In some respects the film version embodies a left-liberal sensibility. Joan (Weaver) is a cultured, middle-aged photojournalist who has reported on 'dirty wars' in Latin America. Perhaps her background is here intended to point to clandestine US involvement in that region in much the same way Ken Loach intended with his contribution to *11'09"01 September 11*, which describes the CIA-supported coup that brought Augusto Pinochet to power in Chile on 11 September 1973. However, the loose, associative way this fact sits within the narrative of *The Guys* suggests that it functions more as a mark of a certain middle-class, left-liberal cosmopolitanism than as a political comment. Joan reflects on the vernacular used by New Yorkers in the days following 9/11. She notes how people ask, 'Are you okay? Are your family okay? Are your people okay? Are your acquaintances okay?', the careful and varied choice of words negotiating racial, national and eth-nic difference, and implicitly pointing to the city's diversity and complexity. In a coffee shop, Joan's server tells her that he has lost two people and says 'God Bless America', leading Joan to ruminate on how difficult it is to use the term 'God Bless!' in New York because of the multiplicity of religions at large. Reinforcing this, cutaways show grief-stricken multi-ethnic New Yorkers going about their daily lives. By these means the film seeks to show how loss affects a widely varied New York community and not only the res-cue services that were given privileged status in much mass media coverage.

Considered thus, it might be argued that in its humanism and commitment to community the film stands apart from the mainstream media response and offers potential for left-liberal critique. However, to the extent that it also offers an early working through of the PTSD/therapy paradigm, it may be regarded as forming part of the outpouring of therapeutic patriotism.

First and foremost, for all its evocation of a multi-ethnic, polyvocal New York, the film focuses primarily on the experience of white Anglo-American Nick (LaPaglia), a war veteran and fire captain. The film's opening scene, seemingly from a surveillance camera, shows a lone firefighter standing outside a fire station at 08.39am on the morning of 11 September; pieces of paper fill the air and a fire engine leaves amidst a cloud of smoke and debris. Later, we learn that these images are haunting Nick (who was not on duty on 9/11) as disruptive flashbacks. He sees his men begin the journey that will lead to their deaths, but their bodies have not been recovered and he doesn't even know which of the Twin Towers they attended. In the stage play these and further images of the terrorist attacks were projected behind the actors, functioning, like the intrusive flashbacks Nick suffers, as a constant reminder of the way in which the trauma of 9/11 infiltrated and disrupted the everyday lives of those who experienced it.

The film then shows how Joan's therapeutic support allows Nick to come to terms with these images (and the trauma they connote), indicating how the wider discourse around the firefighters' heroism and their heroic victimisation dovetails with a narrative of recuperation and redemption. The specific plot moves are as follows: the primary problem faced by Nick is how to write eulogies for his men. Joan encourages him to search for the telling detail or anecdote that might unlock something of each man's character. They discuss writing the eulogy for Bill Doherty, an Irish churchgoer, whom Nick describes as ordinary and unremarkable. Joan teases out the fact that Bill was also a mentor to the younger firefighters, that he had a fascination with the history of New York and that he was the self-appointed fire station food critic. This process is repeated with each of the men, with the eulogies emphasising the quiet, modest surface appearance of each man and their characterful and colourful inner lives. This is then extended to the city as a whole, with Joan observing, 'I knew then that whenever I saw a person on the street I only saw their public shadow'. While their dialogue contains some critical comment on the ways in which firefighters were cast as heroes, it also affirms the men as extraordinarily strong and good-natured.

Here the film aligns with the 1,910 300-word obituaries published in the *New York Times* in the weeks following 9/11 under the heading 'Among the

Missing' and later 'Portraits of Grief'. These vignettes – which represent a therapeutic response in microcosm – were widely celebrated as embodying

> the utopian moment of solidarity right after the attacks, when the unity of the population, transcending usual dividers of gender, race, and class, was also concretized in candlelight vigils, small-scale classical concerts, and the more mournful than defiant flying of the American flag. (Versluys 2009: 9)

However, as Nancy Miller, in an extended analysis of the portraits, observes, the telling anecdotes that allowed the lives to be condensed and celebrated were assembled according to a specific formula. She writes:

> If you have attended a funeral lately, or watched one on television, these anecdotes will sound familiar. Like the subject of the eulogy, the subject of the portrait always appears in a good, often humorous light – and the story told, like the desirable details the reporters typically sought for, is meant to illuminate that something 'true and essential' [and] always reveals something good, like virtue – often civic, or at least domestic, virtue. (2003: 117)

Miller's critique of the 'Portraits of Grief' may also apply to *The Guys*, with Nick and Joan's eulogies focusing on civic virtue and celebrating the values of family, community and friendship. As Richard Gray observes, 'through talking about the dead and making them come alive again in memory and eulogy, the two characters achieve a kind of catharsis' (2011: 153). Miller argues that the consequence of subjecting all deaths to this positive form is that 'they are crafted to serve as the microcosm of family life, of community values, of a valiant and, though wounded, above all, happy America' (2003: 122). On a wider scale, this process aims for catharsis by sidestepping any political or historical framework in which to place 9/11 and the focusing on the spirit of individuals who make up the nation. While the efficacy of therapy for those suffering mental health problems and the important palliative role of funerals and eulogies are undeniable, it is significant and consequential that these personal responses become a cultural trope (financially underwritten by the state, amplified in the mass media and rehearsed again and again in the cinema). At the film's close, Joan describes the attacks in reverse, undertaking a fantasy that what has happened can be undone. This is edited with footage of actual funeral services, and the combination

Fig. 14: therapeutic nationalism: *The Guys* (2002)

of words and image sets a redemptive tone; the final scene has Nick addressing a large remembrance service, overcoming his fear of public speaking and celebrating the lives of his men. Grief and anger are recognised but are pressed to the service of therapeutic nationalism seeking closure and redemption. Gray notes that the film ends with advice to avoid thinking about 9/11, recalling Braiker's advice to avoid watching the news or reading a newspaper: 'Nick confides in Jean that "I lie awake at nights thinking, 'What was the reason?'" … And Jean speaks for the play when she replies simply, "No reason"' (2011: 153).

We might reasonably expect a clash between the value systems of the two protagonists: it seems unlikely that a liberal journalist and a fire chief would share the same worldview. Yet it turns out that their meetings are relatively conventional in tone. Gender difference does rise to the surface (Nick's inarticulacy; Joan's empathy), but this is resolved through a moment of transcendence. Nick mournfully comments on how post-9/11 nobody has fun any more, and Joan replies by describing a 'tango wedding' she attended which was carefree and full of laughter. This prompts Nick to reveal that, like his men, he too has an unexpected side: he's been taking dancing lessons for years. The scene proceeds with the two dancing, and Nick telling Joan, 'you have to let go' and 'learn to follow'. Here Joan's gender is emphasised and her power (to narrate, to articulate) de-emphasised. This keys her character into a gendered construction that stresses her role as an enabler, a healer – in her voice-over narration she expresses the 'primal' need to hug a baby in the week after 9/11. This episode is described as 'a dream intermission in the middle of all this', and we later learn that the dancing scene never happened. But its work – masculine capability providing direction to a wounded female – is done.

Writing in the *New York Times* in 2005, Stephen Farber noted that a cycle of films including *Fear X* (2003), *Winter Solstice* (2003), *Bereft* (2004), *Imaginary Heroes* (2004) and *The Upside of Anger* (2005) features protagonists who are faced with the sudden, traumatic death of a loved one. Farber argues that this cycle of films is 'suffused with a deep, enduring sense of grief' that can be read as an early attempt to address the experience of 9/11; he notes how

> healing figures in some of these new movies but it is a minor part of the story; most of the films survey characters who remain stuck in a syndrome of grief and anger that overpowers them for months or even years after the traumatic event. They convey a profound sadness that in some cases has more than subliminal connection to the post-9/11 mood in which the pictures, with their typically long lead times, took shape. (2005)

These films may well describe something of the kind of pain experienced by those grief-stricken by 9/11. However, as already noted, this raw experience, not easily reconciled or overcome, was, in cultural terms, arguably subject to a therapeutic nationalism shaped by the wider discourse and (albeit in a qualified way) by films such as *The Guys*. *Reign Over Me* (2007), directed by Mike Binder, also responsible for *The Upside of Anger*, is indicative of the two tendencies being brought together, with the raw anger of loss subjected to a therapeutic steer towards resolution. The film tells the story of Charlie (Adam Sandler), who lost his family on 9/11 and who has subsequently spiralled into a depressed existence and displays symptoms that fit with a diagnosis of PTSD. He behaves childishly, wears headphones at all times to drown out intrusive thoughts, obsessively plays a violent computer game (the 'boss' characters can be read as an allegory for the Twin Towers) and has sleep problems due to vivid nightmares. Five years on from 9/11, Charlie meets former college roommate Alan (Don Cheadle), who is suffering marital problems. As they reconnect, a therapeutic relationship allows Charlie to begin the process of recovery and Alan to mend his broken marriage. Here we see how the general melancholy registered in the cycle of films described by Farber is given structure by the therapeutic discourse, and how this structure inevitably moves towards closure, even against a background of considerable consternation and critique related to 9/11 and prevalent in the wider culture.

Extremely Loud and Incredibly Close was given a limited release on 25 December 2011, and a full theatrical release on 20 January 2012. However, the film, based on Jonathan Safran Foer's bestselling novel, has its origins mid-decade, alongside *Reign Over Me*, when the book was published and when director Stephen Daldry and producer Scott Rudin began work on the adaptation. The film tells the story of a hyper-intelligent, hyperactive and by some accounts autistic 11-year-old boy, Oskar Schell (Thomas Horn), who is seeking to find the meaning of a key (marked with the label 'Black') that belonged to his father, who died in the World Trade Center on 9/11. The film renders the symptoms of PTSD in two ways. The first is the intrusive thoughts that Oskar has resulting from hearing the desperate phone messages left by his father, Thomas (Tom Hanks), as he was stuck in the North Tower, and especially Oskar's failure to answer the sixth message, which was being recorded as the building collapsed. And the second is Oskar's fixation with the image of a man falling from the World Trade Center, an image that appears at a number of crucial points in the film's narrative, including the beginning of the film layered with images of Oskar watching his father's funeral, in a scene where Oskar downloads from the internet photographs of people falling from the Twin Towers, in a sequence on the subway where Oskar has a vision of a falling man, clearly identifiable as his father, and at the film's close.[36] Both elements have an intensely personal meaning for Oskar (he feels guilt that he didn't pick up the telephone and imagines that the falling man may be his father), but both are also central aspects of the wider cultural response to 9/11.

The phone calls made during the attacks – especially those made to family and friends from the passengers on board United 93 – functioned discursively to galvanise traditional and seemingly universal senses of family, love and community, and thus underwrite specific nationalist and political discourses with the deep structures of common sense and shared human feeling. Oskar's failure to answer his father's call has thereby (momentarily) disrupted the way in which these acts of communication helped to consolidate a redemptive account of 9/11. The figure of the falling man is more complex: footage of people falling/jumping from the Twin Towers had been shown in television news reports during the attacks, but within a few hours an editorial decision was taken not to show it. As already noted, documentaries depicting 9/11 were extremely careful in the ways they negotiated this, with *9/11*, for example, using only an abbreviated audio-only version of camera footage of bodies hitting the ground. Despite this self-censorship, the images were revisited, appearing on websites such as Ogrish.com, in Alejandro González Iñárritu's contribution to the portmanteau film *11'09"01 September 11* and in visual artist Sharon Paz's *Falling* (2002), an installation of falling figures silhouetted on the windows of the Jamaica Center in Queens, New York. These early attempts to explore the significance of the figure of the falling people were widely condemned as exploitative, and Paz's installation was withdrawn after public protests (see Swartz 2006). However, from mid-decade, following an extended article in *Esquire* which sought to identify a man featured in one of the most widely reproduced photographs, the singular image of a falling man became central to the wider responses to 9/11 (see Junod 2006). Here the general issue of people falling from the building (seeking air, falling by accident, deciding to die, being pushed by others) is replaced by a singular image of a particular individual. The central thrust of Junod's article (and the wider media response, including a documentary film called *9/11: The Falling Man* (2006)) is that this person must be identified in order to allow his family to grieve, thereby activating the therapeutic mechanisms called upon to alleviate wider anxieties regarding 9/11. We might relate this to an observation made by Jeffrey Melnick that mid-decade there is a wholesale shift from metaphors of rising (such as Bruce Springsteen's important post-9/11 album *The Rising* and myriad images of ascension) to those of falling (Tom Junod's article, for example, and Don DeLillo's novel *The Falling Man* (2007)) (2009: 91); this discursive shift points to a move from a jingoistic to a therapeutic nationalism, with *Extremely Loud and Incredibly Close*, as book and then film, a measure of the increasing centrality of the latter.

Oskar's quest to track down everyone in New York with the surname Black, thereby finding the owner of the key, brings him into contact with a diverse range of people: a black woman who is grief-stricken and estranged from her husband, an evangelical Christian who states that if he finds the owner of the key it will be a miracle, an OCD Asian woman, a drag queen, and so on. Oskar tells his mother: 'So many of them had lost somebody or something.' Kristiaan Versluys offers a positive reading of these encounters, describing how Oskar's expedition aggregates a range of different cultural and ethnic experiences, which 'produces epic momentum and psychic uplift [and points to a] rich and complicated collective destiny' (2009: 115). Taken together, Oskar's journey and encounters provide, for Versluys, 'a counterbalance to personal devastation' (ibid,.). But read in relation to the wider discourse of therapeutic nationalism, this aggregation, or archive, of suffering places the whole city (and by inference the whole country) in a parlous psychological state. As Holloway notes in relation to Foer's novel,

> The New Yorkers Oskar encountered were invariably as damaged, scarred, unstable or fixated as he … each of them gripped, like Oskar, by private tragedy so all-consuming that they became private universes in which their victims endured blighted and asocial lives. (2008: 116)

Described thus, Oskar's visits (and one might argue the experience of 9/11 in general) point to suffering as a central facet of contemporary experience (the traumatised state of the 'Blacks' is not just a consequence of 9/11). Here, the film has correspondences with *25th Hour* and *Parallel Lines*, shedding light on inequality, economic difficulty, and so on. However, in contrast to these films, *Extremely Loud and Incredibly Close* seeks some redemptive note to tie this collective grief to the possibility of uplift and therapeutic overcoming resulting from the successful completion of Oskar's quest.

While Oskar searches for the owner of the key as a means for coming to terms with his father's death, a secondary narrative strand shows him establishing a relationship with his paternal grandfather. Oskar's grandfather (Max von Sydow) accompanies him on his quest, and together they listen to the answering machine messages left by Oskar's father, including the one Oskar ignored. A key aspect of Oskar's grandfather's mental state is that he experienced first-hand the Allied bombing of Dresden in World War II, during which his parents were killed, along with over 20,000 people. His experience was so devastating that Oskar's grandfather chose to never speak again, resulting in the failure of his marriage, estrangement from his son and grandson and a near feral existence on the margins of family life. Where, as noted earlier, *War of the Worlds* calls on the experience of Iraq, the genocide in Rwanda and the bombing of Hiroshima, this conflation of the Dresden bombing and 9/11 has the effect of both amplifying the significance of 9/11 (as with Ground Zero, Pearl Harbor, etc.) and reducing history to a level playing field of traumatised victims. While the grandfather's psychological derangement appears, at first glance, to indicate that this kind of trauma cannot be overcome, as the film's narrative proceeds, 9/11 is folded into this wider trauma; and as the 9/11 syndrome is alleviated so too is his traumatic experience of World War II. As Oskar's grandfather's aids Oskar's recovery (accompanying him in the quest for the owner of the missing key) his own traumatic experience undergoes rehabilitation. As a result he is able to return to the family fold, thereby healing the film's multiple historical ruptures.[37]

The search for the key culminates in a similarly resolute way: we learn that the key, found by Oskar in a vase, belongs to the father of a 'Mr Black' and that it was acquired by Oskar's father accidentally when he bought the vase at an estate sale. Oskar's search eventually allows him to identify William Black (Jeffrey Wright) as the owner, and the key allows Black to access a letter his father wrote to him just before his death which will allow him to resolve issues of his own. Oskar confesses to Black about the answering machine message and receives a form of absolution.

With the film's preoccupation with fathers and sons comes a marginalisation of the experience of Oskar's mother and grandmother. In the novel Oskar's mother (Sandra Bullock) has a boyfriend who makes Oskar feel resentful; however, it has been reported that a scene from the film where Oskar's mother meets a man (James Gandolfini) at a grief counselling session was cut due to negative test audience reactions (see Appelo 2012). The film is also clearer than the novel in the way it signals that Oskar's mother knows about his quest and arranges for people to meet him, thereby ensuring that she cannot be accused of placing her son in danger. These changes from novel to film have the effect of depicting Oskar's mother in a less complex way: she remains loyal to her dead husband and her mothering is at all times strong and capable despite her great suffering: the messy reality acknowledged in the novel is thus simplified into a schematic gendering.

In the penultimate scene of the film Oskar compiles a scrapbook recounting his journey and creates a final page in such a way as to allow him to have the falling man move upwards, or return, to safety: a redemptive image that echoes earlier instances of apotheosis already described in other post-9/11 films. Having found some comfort in his travails, the final scene has Oskar discovering a note left by his father on a swing in Central Park that he has

Fig. 15: The falling man as motif: *Extremely Loud and Incredibly Close* (2011)

previously been too frightened to play on (throughout his life his father had devised puzzles that required him to confront his autism). The note quietly reminds Oskar that the authority and comfort of his father will remain in memory, and thus reassured he overcomes his fear and rides the swing, a freeze frame catching this positive image of transcendence and offering it as a salve to the traumatic images of the falling man interspersed throughout the film. As such, the film takes two tropes by which the experience of 9/11 was mediated – the highly symbolic figures of the telephone calls and the falling man – and brings them into the service of a story of grief, anger and an existential search for meaning. Oskar's quest reveals itself to be a therapeutic journey that enables him to alleviate the symptoms of PTSD caused by the death of his father on 9/11 and thereby subject the wider event to the logic of therapeutic nationalism.

There may be significant costs to the reliance on therapeutic nationalism in coming to terms with 9/11. Didier Fassin and Richard Rechtman argue that, as a cultural phenomenon, focus on the traumatised individual tends to offer an ahistorical and apolitical reading of any event that 'obliterates experience' and 'operates as a screen between the event and its context' (2009: 281). Karen M. Seeley argues that the medicalisation of 9/11 and the emphasis on the psychological harm done by the attacks promoted 'clinical solutions to an act of international political violence' (2008: 4) and conferred a status of victimised innocence on the sufferer: this becomes central to the commemoration of 9/11, in which 'victims of the attack were considered heroes who had made sacrifices for their country' (2008: 155). This broader criticism

Fig. 16: Fathers and sons and overcoming: *Extremely Loud and Incredibly Close* **(2011)**

of therapy culture is certainly applicable to films such as *The Guys, Reign Over Me* and *Extremely Loud and Incredibly Close*. The logic condenses in a dramatic scene in the latter where, frustrated with Oskar's persistent questioning, his mother shouts, 'Not everything makes sense! I don't know why a man flew a plane into a building!' The line of dialogue works to sum all the films described in this chapter: 9/11 cannot be explained; it can only be carried as a burden of pain and worked through via therapeutic frameworks. And this way of bracketing 9/11 extends to other films already discussed in this book: in the revenge film *Man on Fire* a traumatised special forces assassin, John Creasy, finds redemption (and therapeutic closure) through the sacrifice of his life for a child in his care; in *World Trade Center* a paramedic troubled by alcoholism finds redemption in his heroic actions helping the trapped policemen. We will have cause to return to this theme in chapter eight in discussion of how PTSD is also a central feature of films depicting the Iraq War.

That said, a number of films discussed in previous chapters engage the therapeutic discourse as a key structuring element but resist easy solutions.[38] *Parallel Lines* is couched in therapeutic terms: Davenport cannot face returning to her home in New York and is haunted by what the view of the Manhattan skyline from her apartment will look like. However, her journey engages difficult questions and pulls into play a number of wider political, social and historical discourses to give structure to her personal struggle and make her return a positive experience. *25th Hour* activates a therapeutic mode, but the journey to well-being is shown to require atonement for past sins. In *Margaret* (2011), another film set in post-9/11 New York and described by Ben Kenisberg as 'a definitive post-9/11 film' (2011), a young woman experiences a traumatic and life-changing event for which she is partially responsible. The film follows her struggle to reconcile the different views and responses of family (her mother counsels an ethically unclear approach), victims (who resolutely refuse to behave like victims) and peers. The film links this personal quandary with explicit references to 9/11 made through high-school debating groups and numerous shots of planes leaving vapour trails high above the Manhattan skyline. Though the final scenes do offer a moment of resolution (as mother and daughter set aside their differences), the film celebrates resilience as opposed to victimhood and upholds a dialectical sense of the difficulty of coming to terms with traumatic experience. Roger Luckhurst claims that after the 7/7 bombings in London clinicians shifted to a resilience-based approach, which rather than imposing a framework related to PTSD instead responded to the attitude of the victims, many of whom did not present PTSD-related symptoms (2008: 210). *Margaret* is a film that might be said to explore how individuals and communities who experience traumatic events should be permitted to respond to their experience in ways other than a predetermined 'post-traumatic afterwardsness' (see Luckhurst 2008: 211–12). Cynthia Weber claims that

> September 11 is a liminal moment in US history, not so much as a trauma that requires a national therapeutic response but rather as a 'confrontation' or an 'encounter' with questions that haunt the US relationship both between self and other and with(in) the self. (2005: 2)

The complex view offered by films such as *Margaret* indicates that the encounter/confrontation valued by Weber was being explored in US popular culture. And as we shall see in the next chapter, there is also evidence of its further staging in a cycle of post-9/11 'torture' films.

Torture

At a press conference held six days after 9/11, Vice President Dick Cheney stated:

> We'll have to work sort of the dark side, if you will. We've got to spend time in the shadows in the intelligence world. A lot of what needs to be done here will have to be done quietly, without any discussion, using sources and methods that are available to our intelligence agencies … it's going to be vital for us to use any means at our disposal basically, to achieve our objectives. (Quoted in Froomkin 2005)

The 'dark side' refers to the clandestine operations that might be required to confront and combat terrorist organisations such as al-Qaida. Although the US military and intelligence agencies had considerable experience and protocols for such work, the administration believed that it was necessary to challenge the constraints placed on imprisonment and torture by the constitution, the Geneva Conventions and legal and historical precedent. Philippe Sands describes how lawyers at the Justice Department were drafted into service to provide a context in which illegal imprisonment without due process and the use of 'enhanced tactics' during interrogations could be permitted and condoned (2008: 154). The interpretation of law produced by this 'torture team' as Sands called it – the Haynes Memo – was signed by Donald Rumsfeld on 2 December 2001, providing what Stephen Prince terms a 'legal shield' for the use of torture against suspected terrorists (2009: 176).

Securing consent for this policy took place across a broad cultural terrain, from statements by key politicians to the television series *24* (2001–10), which frequently presented its central protagonist, Jack Bauer (Kiefer Sutherland), with a stark dilemma:

> a resistant suspect can either be accorded due process – allowing a terrorist plot to proceed – or be tortured in pursuit of a lead. Bauer invariably chooses coercion. With unnerving efficiency, suspects are beaten, suffocated, electrocuted, drugged, assaulted with knives, or more exotically abused; almost without fail, these suspects divulge critical secrets. (Mayer 2007)

24's producer Joel Sarnow has openly stated that the series was designed to be 'patriotic' and to corroborate the policy initiatives of the president and his team (see Mayer 2007), leading Prince to note that 'killing for the state, and for the greater good, is *24*'s gold standard of moral behaviour' (2012: 247). Investigating the use of torture post-9/11, Sands even unearthed evidence that the scenarios depicted in *24* directly influenced interrogators in Iraq, who modelled their practices on scenes from the series (see 2008: 88–9). Bauer often faced a 'ticking bomb scenario' in which torture was shown to be the only way of soliciting information in a time-critical situation in order to save the lives of a great many innocent civilians. John Ip notes that this time-critical framing appeared in various official government documents and statements that assert the legality of torture and was designed to overcome the absolutist nature of its legal prohibition (2009: 43). The same rationale can be found in a range of feature films in a number of different genres, including the revenge film *Man on Fire*, discussed in chapter two. In that film, ex-CIA agent John Creasy achieves his goals by torturing those who have knowledge of where an abducted child, formerly under his protection, is being kept prisoner. Similarly, in *Five Fingers* (2006) the protagonists conducting torture (in this case, the cutting off of fingers) appear to be Islamic terrorists but are later shown to be CIA agents whose work reveals and prevents a terror plot. In *Unthinkable* (2010) a terrorist has planted nuclear bombs in three (or possibly four) US cities. Only when interrogators are shown to be willing to kill the terrorist's wife and torture his children is the threat allayed. The message in these films seems clear: torture is necessary and it works.

However, this stance came under considerable pressure mid-decade. In *Against All Enemies* (2004), the administration's former anti-terrorism chief,

Torture

Richard A. Clarke, argued that the response to 9/11 had been muddled and ineffective, with George W. Bush and key policymakers distracted from targeting al-Qaida by an obsession with Iraq. Topping the *New York Times* bestseller list for eleven weeks, Clarke's book indexed growing dissatisfaction with and distrust of the government. Another key figure drawing attention to uncomfortable facts was journalist Seymour Hersh, who between 2002 and 2004 published 26 stories in the *New Yorker* describing, amongst other things, the intelligence failures leading up to 9/11, the lack of post-war planning in Afghanistan and Iraq, the reliance on dubious intelligence related to Iraqi WMD and the widespread use of illegal rendition flights whereby terrorist suspects were flown to countries in which due process was not followed and torture was permitted (see Hersh 2004b). Hersh revealed that according to an internal military report, guards at Abu Ghraib military prison in Iraq had committed numerous instances of 'sadistic, blatant, and wanton criminal abuses' and that army regulations and the Geneva Conventions had been routinely violated. The abuse included

> breaking chemical lights and pouring the phosphoric liquid on detainees; pouring cold water on naked detainees; beating detainees with a broom handle and a chair; threatening male detainees with rape [...]; sodomizing a detainee with a chemical light and perhaps a broom stick, and using military working dogs to frighten and intimidate detainees with threats of attack, and in one instance actually biting a detainee. (Hersh 2004a)

On 28 April 2004, CBS's *60 Minutes* covered the story and illustrated the abuse with a number of sensational photographs taken by prison guards, resulting in large-scale media coverage. A PBS documentary, *The Torture Question* (2005), also raised awareness of the issue. In the wake of the Abu Ghraib scandal, a less uncritical view of 9/11 and the 'war on terror' became more widespread, with a shift from endorsement of Bush's 'legal shield' and tacit consent for torture to acknowledgement of, and willingness to tackle, the shifting and morally compromised realities of the 'war on terror'. As Holloway notes, torture became 'a revealing and representative discourse of the times', standing in for widespread scepticism towards the official response to 9/11 (2008: 53).

Indeed, most observers agree that by 2004 popular support for the government's foreign policy commitments in Afghanistan and Iraq had ebbed, with a critical view of the neoconservative presidency and the wider terrain of the 'war on terror' gaining considerable traction (see Holloway 2008: 91; Kellner 2010: 1). Holloway argues that 'by the fifth anniversary of 9/11, American artists and audiences seem to have agreed that the major taboos that structured immediate responses to the attacks had now been lifted' (2008: 91). As a result, much of the critique levelled by the documentaries and feature films described in previous chapters, including *25th Hour*, *Parallel Lines*, *Fahrenheit 9/11* and *Syriana*, was retrospectively acknowledged as valid. This chapter focuses on a group of films that were made against this background, films which feature scenes of torture that implicitly (in the 'torture porn' cycle) and explicitly (in *Rendition* (2007) and *Standard Operating Procedure* (2008)) reference events at Abu Ghraib.

A number of commentators have noted how a post-9/11 cycle of horror films emerged from this ambivalent, conflicting reality (see Briefel and Miller 2011; Wetmore 2012). Films such as *Saw* (2004) and *Hostel* (2005) contain scenes of prolonged, graphically portrayed, torture and were given the label 'torture porn' by film critic David Edelstein. Edelstein's review of the films claimed that they showed how 'fear supplants empathy and makes us all potential torturers [and that post-9/11] we've engaged in a national debate about the morality of torture, fuelled by horrifying pictures of manifestly decent men and women … enacting brutal scenarios of domination at Abu Ghraib' (2006). How, then, do these two films relate to the post-Abu Ghraib context?

A number of plot elements in *Hostel* can be read as uneasy recognitions of rendition and torture. In a dramatic central sequence a US tourist wakes up in a torture chamber, wearing a hood like those worn by the prisoners in the Abu Ghraib photographs, and asks his captor, 'Who are you? Where the fuck am I? What is this shit?' He gets little by way of explanation and is tortured to death. Here the viewer is offered the point of view of someone 'extraordinarily rendered', with no sense of what is about to happen to them or why. In another scene a character is beheaded and a photograph of his head is sent by mobile phone, recalling gruesome jihadi films of kidnapping and beheading. In colour, tone and lighting, *Hostel*'s *mise-en-scène* is also broadly similar to the photographs of torture chambers at Abu Ghraib. These elements have led Brigid Cherry to claim that the film's 'shock and gore' is symptomatic of the war on terror's 'shock and awe' (2009: 58) and underpin readings of the film as a progressive critique of the dangers of unbridled US power (see Hollyfield 2009).

However, other elements point to a more conservative logic at play. Arguably, by putting Americans on the receiving end of torture, the film once again places the US in the position of victim. Those responsible for running the torture chamber in *Hostel* are marked by their otherness: Eastern Europeans, women and homosexuals conspire to terrorise American men. One character says that 'nowadays everyone wants to kill Americans' and states that the torturers are willing to pay extra to kill a US citizen, thereby indicating that, although a number of nationalities are subjected to torture, Americans are the most endangered. As Kim Newman notes, 'in a world where foreigners worry about winding up at the mercy of Americans, *Hostel* is about Americans being terrified of the rest of the planet' (2006: 30). In concert with its depiction of otherness, the film's ending has the main protagonist escape and then torture and kill his captors, activating the logic of the revenge film. If 1970s horror films like *The Last House on the Left* (1972) and *The Hills Have Eyes* (1977) have their protagonists wreaking revenge only to show that they have become monsters themselves, *Hostel* offers no such reading. The logic here is, as Newman points out, that 'torture is an atrocity when perpetrated on Americans but is justified when used by Americans against those responsible for starting the conflict' (2006: 31). In this view, *Hostel* encourages Americans to be fearful of difference, to draw in their horizons in order to keep themselves out of harm's way and to relish the performance of retributive (and in the film's terms self-defensive) violence. For all its activation of, and immersion of the viewer in, places that recall extraordinary rendition and torture, the film ultimately provides an extension of the logic of *24* that torture is a necessary evil when conduced for the sake of self-preservation and justice.

Douglas Kellner claims that the *Saw* franchise displays a similar logic to *Hostel*, a 'brutal Darwinian vision [of] kill or be killed' (2010: 7), noting that *Saw IV* (2007)

> reveals a backstory that indicates [that the film's central protagonist] Jigsaw became crazed when his pregnant wife was accosted by a junkie in a violent encounter and lost their child. Thereafter, Jigsaw turned his energies as engineer and builder to construct elaborate torture mechanisms and tests to punish 'Evil' of various sorts, just as the Bush-Cheney administration was constructing apparatuses of torture in Afghanistan, Iraq and Guantanamo, and other sites throughout the world to punish its alleged enemies and 'evil doers'. (Ibid.)

Here Kellner reads *Saw*, the first film in the series, privileged with narrative information taken from *Saw IV*, a later instalment, as a moralising revenge film (see also Sharrett 2009). However, closer examination suggests that this is overly simplistic. *Saw* suggests that the victims of Jigsaw's (Tobin Bell) games are chosen as a result of their lack of moral rectitude; their failure to live good lives has drawn them into their current predicament. The hinterland here seems to be that of a corrupt society forced to face its sins. There is a correspondence here to *25th Hour*'s depiction of a personal reckoning modelling a wider cultural/national reckoning. As such, *Saw* might be read allegorically as signifying, again, Johnson's concept of 'blowback' – namely, events in the past (in Johnson's case, terror precipitated abroad by agencies; in the film's logic, the past misdeeds of Jigsaw's victims) eventually have unpredictable, and often bloody, consequences.

The original pitch for the film showed a man in a cell with a 'reverse bear trap' fitted to his skull and with a clock ticking; to release himself from the trap, and armed only with a knife, the man was required to retrieve the key from the stomach of an unconscious man sharing his cell.[39] *Saw* is basically a reiteration and amplification of this initial dramatic scenario, with two imprisoned men informed that their families will be killed and they too will die if one does not kill the other. This central scenario – two protagonists in a fraught situation in which they attempt to achieve different goals (with their lives at stake) – can be traced to the time-critical ordeals confronted by Jack Bauer in *24* but with a crucial difference: there is no obvious way out in narrative terms. In *Saw* each protagonist is aware that pursuing their goal will result in pain, injury and death to someone else, and the film shows that the protagonists prefer inaction and self-mutilation to the harming of a stranger/other. Hence, in its dramatic scenario, the film indexes an equivocal post-9/11 reality. Whereas in *24* this scenario is shown to be fraught – Jack Bauer is often in the throes of an existential crisis – it is also always clearly scripted to contain a preferred course of action: torture is a last resort, but it is necessary in order to find information that will save countless innocent people. By contrast, *Saw*'s tagline – 'How much blood would you shed to stay alive?' – points to how conflict takes place within a series of bounded choices, none of which offers an easy ethical or moral course of action; as such, the film functions as allegory for a complex view of the 'war on terror' that emerged in the aftermath of Abu Ghraib. That a dark underworld (akin to the torture chambers at Abu Ghraib) is shown beneath and within the safe suburban lives of the film's central characters conveys how the two distinct realities of the US homeland and the 'war on terror' are thoroughly interdependent.

Released in 2007, *Rendition* sought to draw public attention to rendition flights and the clandestine outsourcing of torture. The film is based on the true story of Syrian-born Canadian engineer Maher Arar, who was placed on a rendition flight to Syria, where he was imprisoned for one year and subjected to torture before being released without charge. Directed by South African Gavin Hood, the film was part-funded by Participant Productions, which was also involved in the production of *Syriana*. By 2007 rendition flights had become a regular occurrence. Between 2001 and 2007 the CIA and allied intelligence agencies detained over 3,000 individuals worldwide and transported them to 'black sites' in countries where torture was permitted; the number of 'erroneous renditions', such as that experienced by Arar, has not been recorded but is likely to be high (see Rejali 2007: 504).

Responding to the news that a US citizen has been killed in the suicide bombing shown in the film's opening sequence, CIA director Corinne Whitman (Meryl Streep), whose character is a cipher for the hawkish initial responses to 9/11, authorises a rendition order with the words, 'they got one of us'. However, Whitman's standpoint is called into question through a layering in of multiple points of view, in particular that of CIA analyst Douglas Freeman (Jake Gyllenhaal). Freeman is shown in hospital after the suicide bombing with the blood of a fellow American on his clothes, in a long-held shot that allows the viewer time not just to register Freeman's anguish but also to see alongside him the injured civilians who have also been caught up in the bombing. Later, Freeman directly refuses to consider the dead CIA colleague one of 'us', stating that they were not friends and thereby refusing the allegiance expected to exist along national lines in favour of a more reciprocal relation with the other (significantly, Freeman is in a relationship with a North African woman).

Tasked with overseeing the interrogation of rendered Egyptian-American Anwar El-Ibrahimi (Omar Metwally), Freeman becomes increasingly

Fig. 17: Acknowledging the suffering of the other: *Rendition* (2007)

frustrated and cynical as he realises that the torture is not working, indeed that it is precipitating a cycle of violence that is actually counter-productive. The film's mid-point consists of a hiatus where all the characters, including Freeman, are shown in moments of introspection. In these sequences, a strong noirish contrast drops faces into half-shadow, signalling moral quandary and the high stakes in determining future courses of action within a scenario in which there are no easy choices. After a period of soul-searching, Freeman acts on his conviction that rendition and torture are unethical and at the cost of his own career arranges for the release of El-Ibrahimi.

A distinctive feature of *Rendition* is the space given to the film's other characters. Freeman's personal journey, for example, is mirrored by the experience of Isabella Fields El-Ibrahimi (Reese Witherspoon) as she struggles to discover what has happened to her husband. In ways comparable to *A Mighty Heart* (2007), Isabella is shown to be a woman capable of rational action, political lobbying, resilience and resourcefulness. In this respect, the film moves beyond the tendency observable in post-9/11 cinema to attribute agency to male protagonists only. The motives of the suicide bomber, Khalid El-Emin (Moa Khouas), are also presented in some detail (his brother died under torture and interrogation by the secret police), and in telling his story, and showing him victim to both social deprivation and manipulation by a clandestine fundamentalist group, the film figures terror in relatively human (and knowable) terms. The film also humanises the head of the secret police, Abasi Fawal (Yigal Naor), who is shown conducting his brutal work while also wrestling with mundane family problems, in particular his daughter's refusal to agree to an arranged marriage. Through its cosmopolitan approach to point of view the film extends screen time to an American other (Anwar is an Egyptian citizen with a green card) and to a Third World other, in this case, a suicide bomber politicised by the brutal treatment of his brother at the hands of the secret police.[40]

In cross-cutting between Cape Town, Chicago and Washington, DC, as well as North Africa, *Rendition* also attempts an ambitious mapping of geopolitical space via international air travel, rendition flights, long-distance telephone calls and intertitles that place the viewer in discrete (but connected) national contexts. A steely-grey Washington, DC, appears to stand in stark contrast to a sun-burnished North Africa, marking a clear divide between the west and the Arab world; but the film then undermines this neat separation as the brutal work of waterboarding and electrocution is shown to have consequences far beyond the North African prison in which it takes place. On a number of occasions the conventional markers that might be expected to denote a transition from one time frame or geographical location to another are not deployed, producing moments of disorientation as characters appear to have slipped from one realm to another. The effect of this (and the film's elliptical narrative structure) is to collapse the safe distance between 'us' and 'them', between the US and the wider world: here the film shares some formal characteristics with *Syriana*, whose tagline, 'Everything is connected', might also serve to sum up the organising principle in play in *Rendition*.

It seems at first that the film's multiple perspectives and locations are ordered according to the conventional rules of continuity (with characters inhabiting different locations at the same time). However, a pivotal sequence at the film's close has Abasi (in search of his daughter Fatima (Zineb Oukach), who has run away from home with terrorist El-Emin) climbing the stairs to El-Emin's apartment. At the same time, seemingly, Fatima descends the stairs. The viewer expects the two characters to meet, but when this does not happen it becomes apparent that they are ascending and descending the stairs at two different moments in time. What has thus far been presented as two parallel narrative strands is revealed instead to be a contemporary action intercut with an event from the past. With this information, the viewer is able to work out that the bombing that opens the film is, in fact, the work of El-Emin and that Fatima has been killed in the same explosion. The film's structure here points to the way in which actions will have (often unforeseen) consequences, with Abasi's role as torturer of El-Emin's brother resulting eventually in the death of his daughter. Not only this, but Abasi's attempt to trace Fatima has in fact been futile, since he is not preventing terrorism (in a ticking-bomb scenario) as the narrative has momentarily led us to believe, but is actually only dealing with its aftermath. The implications for Abasi's character are clear enough, but perhaps this play with narrative structure can be read more ambitiously. For much of the film the viewer is made to feel that they are immersed in the kind of dramatically charged and time-critical situation that typifies television shows like *24*. As already noted, these situations tend to show that it is necessary to be violent towards one person (usually a terrorist) in order to ensure the safety of innumerable others; torture is shown to be necessary, to work and to be in the interest of the greater good. The narrative twist in *Rendition* actively challenges this logic, with the events under investigation being shown to have already happened, and with the act of attempting to prevent them using violent means furthering the likelihood that they will be repeated. As such, *Rendition*'s complex structure contrasts markedly with the caesura that the events of

9/11 are usually deemed to represent, suggesting instead a continuity of violence, with both sides locked into an escalating struggle.

The multiple perspectives and complex non-linear narrative can be contrasted with the closed, claustrophobic construction of *World Trade Center* with its hemmed-in point of view (victim, victim's family, rescuer) and clear narrative resolution (rescue, survival, resolve to wage war). As such, *Rendition* can be seen as a response to Susan Sontag's (2003) request that Manichean constructions of 'us' and 'them', and the bracketing off of 9/11 from history, should be resisted and that this act of resistance must address issues of cosmopolitanism (and the interconnected world) and the vulnerability of those in positions of (economic, social, physical) disadvantage (see also Brassett 2010). Similarly, Judith Butler counsels that it is necessary to 'emerge from the narrative perspective of US unilateralism and, as it were, its defensive structures, to consider the ways in which our lives are profoundly implicated in the lives of others' (2004: 7–8). And, reflecting on the different ways in which the commemorated dead of 9/11 and the uncounted dead of the wars in Afghanistan, Iraq and elsewhere are valued, she asks: when is life grievable? (Butler 2009). Butler's question points to the ways in which value is placed on life differentially across social and geographical territories, something to which *Rendition* also seeks to draw attention. Although earlier films had been inflected with the desire to make this inclusive ethical gesture – the acknowledgement of culpability and otherness in *25th Hour*, the dynamic multicultural and multivocal depiction of New York in *Seven Days in September* – *Rendition* addresses the issue as a central element of its story and via its innovative narrative structure, making it an important post-9/11 film. Describing the post-9/11 novel, Versluys observes that there is a move from books that shift away 'from the perpetrator-victim dichotomy, which the trauma paradigm implies, to a triangulating discourse in which the confrontation with the Other is the central concern' (2009: 183). *Rendition* allows us to make a similar observation in relation to post-9/11 cinema in the latter part of the decade.

A note of caution must be sounded, however. Although there is no suggestion in the film that the CIA will self-correct – Freeman has very little agency and must disobey orders, losing his job as a result – the ending shows El-Ibrahimi being freed. Freeman contacts the media, implying that the story will surface and policy will be changed (in reality, Maher Arar was not released because of a conscience-stricken CIA operative and nor was his story widely reported in the press). In this redemptive gesture *Rendition* shares much with a film like *All the President's Men*, which suggests that the press is a key check on the excesses of a malign imperial presidency. Indeed, *All the President's Men* provides a touchstone for a wider hopefulness that the system contains the mechanisms to allow it to self-correct. *The Green Zone* (2010), which is scathing in its depiction of the Iraq War and the issue of WMD, makes a similar move, with Chief Warrant Officer Roy Miller (Matt Damon) turning whistle-blower and leaking a report to a journalist to salvage credibility for the system. By contrast, the pessimistic resolutions of *Syriana*, *The Quiet American* and *The Constant Gardener* show individuals accepting that they have very little agency and retreating from any attempt to change things for the better. This desire for a way out sits with the maintenance of the status quo and is consonant with the fact that the public debate about the legal, ethical and practical matter of torture did not become subject to the exacting ethical rigour demanded by Sontag and Butler. While *Rendition* went some way to depicting the issues in their complexity, the subject of torture arguably remained open to recuperation and revision on behalf of the conservative ideological discourse.

As already noted, Abu Ghraib became a focal point for protest against the use of torture. Organisations such as the Center for Constitutional Rights, the American Civil Liberties Union and the International Justice Network and left-liberal websites such as the *Huffington Post*, *Salon* and *The Nation* combined with the *New York Times* and the *Washington Post* to offer substantial coverage. Seymour Hersh explored how responsibility for the torture resided in the high offices of government (2004b), while Jane Mayer's investigative journalism (2008) and Philippe Sands's legal expose (2008) traced the complex web of political and legal rulings that allowed a torture regime to originate at Guantánamo and spread to Iraq, Afghanistan and 'black sites' in North Africa and the Middle East.

In addition, a number of political documentaries sought visual means to convey the large amounts of data, leaked documents and complex legal backstory circulating around the torture debate. *Taxi to the Dark Side* (2007) tells the story of Dilawar, an innocent Afghani taxi driver who was tortured to death at Bagram prison in Iraq in 2002. The film pieces together the testimonies of military police, military interrogators and the journalists who uncovered the story in 2003 (when, as Julia Lesage reports, the *New York Times* 'sat on the story for a month and then buried it on page A14, running it on March 4, 2003 under the headline, "US Military Investigating Death of Afghan in Custody"' (2009)). The film shows how, over the course of five days, Dilawar was suspended in a stress position and his legs repeatedly beaten, leading the coroner to rule that Dilawar's legs had been 'pulpified' and would have needed amputation had he survived (ibid.). In its sustained presentation of legal documents and handbooks and the revelation of the consequences of Dilawar's death for his family, this film challenges the view that Guantánamo, Bagram and Abu Ghraib were simply necessary evils where well-trained interrogators practised 'torture-lite' or, to use Rush Limbaugh's formulation, that the interrogation techniques amounted to little more than fraternity-type hazing rituals.

Standard Operating Procedure, directed by Errol Morris and released in 2008, can be seen as a further contribution to consciousness-raising around the events at Abu Ghraib.[41] The film might be understood primarily as a kind of ideology critique: it seeks, using the conventional techniques of documentary as well as a number of innovative practices pioneered by Morris, to bring together four audiovisual components – still photographs, interview testimony, re-enactments of events recounted by the interviewees and an orchestral score by Danny Elfman – to get beyond the version of Abu Ghraib established in relation to the infamous photographs.

In contrast to Hersh's claim in the *New Yorker* that 'the photographs tell it all', Morris believes that the photographs misled people into thinking that the military personnel in the images were to blame for the torture. *Standard Operating Procedure* can be seen as an extended attempt to move through the photographs to the complexities of the event from which they originate (see Hersh 2004a). For Morris, the meaning of the photographs is not self-evident – they, in his words, 'reveal and conceal' (from DVD commentary) and it is necessary to subject them to forensic scrutiny in order to illuminate the complex reality they elide. Indeed, an organising principle of the film is that the photographs must be *both* placed back into a complex context (to reground their meaning in relation to the event they depict) *and* subjected to an iconoclasm that submits everything about them to suspicion. As Thomas Austin notes, Morris sought to make 'visible some of that invisible whole – context, setting, background' (2011: 347).

The main method by which the film goes about this is the juxtaposition of the photographs with testimony and re-enactments. However, the mode of presentation of the photographs is also an important facet of the film's aesthetic. They are displayed in a variety of ways, often with a white framing border, sometimes as singular items, sometimes in groups; at times they move across the screen in arrays, which gather chronologically or in terms of a specific location. Often they are held up to the viewer for as long as ten seconds, allowing considerable time for contemplation. On occasion they are shown under the steady gaze of one of the prison guards. This formal attempt to unsettle preconceived senses of the photographs is extended through the inclusion of photographs not shown in the media and the re-presentation of well-known photographs with any cropped-out elements recovered. Released from their media context thus, the images slew off pre-held assumptions and connotations and their meanings are reconfigured. This can be seen in the sequences that show Military Intelligence Specialist Roman Krol peering into the camera lens to analyse a picture showing him and several other soldiers throwing water and Nerf balls at detainees. As Benson-Allot notes,

> Krol's scrutinizing gaze highlights the role of the apparatus in the interview and reminds the viewer that his interview is both an image and an engagement with images. Krol bridges the roles of viewer and subject during his photographic analysis, thereby reminding the viewer that he and Morris's interviewees possess a similarly imperfect interpretive relationship to the Abu Ghraib photos. (2009: 41)

With their meaning already destabilised through the form of their presentation, the photographs are subject to a forensic parsing by Special Agent Brent Pack, a military investigator. During the court martials of the Abu Ghraib prison guards, Pack was tasked with extracting the metadata from the 12,000 digital photographs in order to place them on a timeline. Benson-Allott notes that Pack was asked to decide

> whether a given interaction constituted a violation of military protocol or 'standard operating procedure.' Pack's job authorized him to plumb only digital – not human or historical – depths; he could look inside a photo for its metadata but could not read anything into the faces of its subjects or infer causal relationships. (2009: 42)

Briefed thus, Pack judged that by far the majority of photographs depicted standard operating procedure rather than criminal acts, thereby making one of the film's strongest points: what we see is routine. In *Torture Team* Philippe Sands offers a detailed description of the interrogation of Detainee 063 at Guantánamo Bay in 2002, an account that is similar in many respects to the photographs of prisoner abuse at Abu Ghraib (2008: 5–15). Sands' description confirms Morris's point that the photographs generally depict what is actually permissible (and indeed, encouraged). By demonstrating that the guards improvised within a bounded set of legally specified

Fig. 18: Parsing
the photographs
of prisoner abuse:
*Standard Operating
Procedure* (2008)

behaviours, embellishing but generally not transgressing what was deemed permissible, the film serves to refute the 'bad apple' claim that a few untypical individuals of bad character had invented a dark fantasy inflected with the mores of hard-core pornography and sadomasochistic sex and that this bore no relation to wider practices.

But *Standard Operating Procedure* also signals to the viewer that Pack's belief that he is being objective should by met with scepticism. Pack professes to adhere only to the facts, but he regularly judges the guards' expression and notes, judgementally, that they seemed to be enjoying what they are doing. The film also uses computer-generated imagery (CGI) to illustrate the process of parsing the photographs, which appear to at first to conform to neat timelines and an orderly narrative of cause and effect but then dissolve 'into streams of binary code that finally render their contents invisible' (Benson-Allott 2009: 42). So, in the film's presentation of, and sceptical distancing from, Pack's investigation, we have an oscillation between the pinning down of meaning and the constant and recursive questioning of it.

The photographs are also brought into a complex relationship with other elements of the documentary. The most dramatic of these is the human face in close-up. Linda Williams notes that 'all of Morris's films concern judicial processes. If they are not about actual trials, they are about the process of bearing witness to disputed facts' (2010: 34). Central to this courtroom metaphor, as Williams observes, is a desire to enter into the record what lawyers call 'demeanor evidence', the effect of a witness's or defendant's appearance under this close scrutiny (2010: 37). But the metaphor of a witness standing trial is not completely apt. As Lesage points out, by the time the prison guards appear in Morris's film they have had

> their memories, rhetoric, and public personae filtered through their prepared and delivered testimony at over a dozen military tribunals and at their own or others' courts martial, as well as numerous media appearances and news interviews. We might also add that they have learned to inhabit the version of events the US public prefers. In the process,

they probably developed a version of events that they came to believe and prefer. (2009)

Faced with this, Morris searches for techniques that can capture demeanour evidence yet also point to the ways in which the interviewees are often caught up in elaborate constructions of self. To this end, Morris used a specific apparatus called the Interrotron, which, via an adapted two-way teleprompter, allows him to appear on a screen in front of the interviewee's field of vision. The interviewee looks directly at Morris and the camera as he asks questions and records the interviewee's response. The effect is a mediated but direct and intimate interview process that creates apparent direct eye contact between interviewee and viewer of the documentary. Williams notes, 'as viewers we see the interviewees' eye movements and facial gestures as they encounter, or resist encountering, Morris's own face and eyes in the lens that films them' (2010: 36). As such Morris

repeatedly explores his human subjects' self-presentation, and how they 'narrate themselves' even via self-deceptions; but these performances of self are not simply collected and relayed, they are arranged for viewers to assess and evaluate, with some shown to be more plausible than others. (Austin 2011: 345)

Analysis of two witness testimonies will serve to indicate how this apparatus operates. The first is from Lyndie England, a diminutive female prison guard seen holding a prone Iraqi prisoner on a leash in one of the most widely circulated photographs. Williams notes that

the microphysiognomy of England's face as revealed in the Interrotron does not dramatically catch her lying, nor does it catch an admission of guilt. But her very difficulty phrasing the description of what she saw – 'unusual ... weird ... wrong' – combined with her initial avoidance and then final acceptance of eye contact when she admits that it was 'OK,' illustrates the mind-set that made it possible for such acts of abuse to be understood as 'standard operating procedure.' (2010: 40)

For Williams, the complex series of looks requires England to be considered neither villain nor misunderstood victim, but instead displays how she, at one and the same time, excuses herself by claiming that 'the example' of abuse was already set and indicates with her face that she feels culpable for

Fig. 19:
'Demeanour
evidence':
*Standard
Operating
Procedure*
(2008)

not resisting the example set. As such the image is one of 'an ethical being wrestling with her acquiescence to an unethical situation' (2010: 40).

The second testimony is that of Sabrina Harman, the prison guard who appeared next to the corpse of Manadel al-Jamadi, smiling and giving a thumbs-up. As she appears in *Standard Operating Procedure* Harman is articulate, unapologetic and open. She is also able to submit further evidence: her letters to her wife in which she states she is shocked about what is happening at the prison and claims that she is seeking to behave ethically by documenting events. The layering of Harman's plausible testimony with the bleak and seemingly irredeemable photograph in which she appears leads Benson-Allott to note that

> Both photograph and film hold some truth – al-Jamadi really did die, and Harman really did pose with his body – but neither can show why the photograph was taken, what Harman was 'really' thinking, or who killed al-Jamadi. Furthermore, the images' juxtaposition reminds the viewer that both are staged for the camera, and by offering these two contrasting moments of direct eye contact together, Morris seems to reconsider his own ability to master the history of Abu Ghraib. For if Morris is indeed suggesting that Harman possesses no better understanding of the woman in the photo than any other viewer, then he is also acknowledging the limits of his documentary. (2009: 41)

In both England's and Harman's cases, then, *Standard Operating Procedure* ensures that 'the familiarity of the images is both invoked and repudiated' (Austin 2011: 345). We are asked to reimagine the scenarios depicted in the photographs as complex and multi-fold, often veiling even darker realities.

While the different perspectives build to create a complex picture, *Standard Operating Procedure* does not include the views of any of the prisoners at Abu Ghraib. As Austin notes, although the film 'manifests outrage and concern at the plight of the prisoners, it reproduces and repeats their de-individuation into nameless, voiceless objects' (2011: 351). By way of contrast, the HBO documentary *Ghosts of Abu Ghraib* (2007) is more expansive, including interviews with prison guards, military intelligence personnel, legal figures and scholars. The film also features interviews with former Iraqi prisoners who – appearing anonymously – testify to their experiences of torture. One of the prisoners states:

> The most painful thing for the inmates there were the cries of the people being tortured. One day they brought sheets to cover the cells in order for no one to see anything. They began torturing one of them, and we could hear what was happening. We listened as his soul cracked. The sound of his voice really twisted our minds and made our hearts stop. We later learned that this man was Manadel al-Jamadi.

The third structural component of *Standard Operating Procedure* – after the forensic treatment of the photographs and the nuanced handling of the interviewees – is the use of re-enactment. This aspect of the film has been subject to criticism for its 'over-aestheticised' style. However, Morris has responded by stating that the re-enactments were designed not to look like the rest of the material in the film, noting that they are not asking an audience to suspend their disbelief 'in an artificial world that has been created expressly for their entertainment; they are asking the opposite … to study the relationship of an artificial world to the real world' (2008). Formally speaking, this principle is consonant with the wider operation of the film. The re-enactments relate only obliquely, one might say dialectically, with the acts depicted in the photographs. They do not show the events depicted in the well-known media images, instead layering in telling details that extend the visual sense of the prison and the events therein. Benson-Allott, for example, notes how the film details the dust motes that 'circulate around Gilligan's sensory-deprivation hood' and 'lingers on the golden skin of a man's back as MPs pull him from an isolation cell on a leash' (2009: 43). In another scene the dogs used to threaten the prisoners are reduced to slavering jaws shot in slow-motion. These details destabilise the known images and the rehearsed testimonies, hovering somewhere 'between display and concealment' (Austin 2011: 348).

Standard Operating Procedure might be accused of relativism – destabilising meaning around the event to allow multiple interpretations and thereby dulling the imperative nature of the images: the way they express that the abuse is ethically wrong and should be subject to punishment. But this is

**Fig. 20:
Re-enactment
as juxtaposition:
*Standard
Operating
Procedure* (2008)**

precisely what enables the film to depict realities as slipping, folding one into the other, like the torture chamber of *Saw* situated beneath a comfortable suburbia. This can be seen most clearly in the way the film handles the depiction of the interrogators who subject Manadel al-Jamadi to the beatings that lead to his death. These interrogators appear in the film almost as ghosts, and Lesage notes that

> both interrogators and their prisoners were officially ghosts ... the interrogators often made themselves known by only a first name, clearly fabricated, and did not log in their prisoners. As one of their spectral detainees, Manadel al-Jamadi was thus not officially there. (2009)

The overall effect is that the film tries to make the secret and clandestine visible, while acknowledging the intentionally shadowy operating procedures explicitly sought by policymakers, and evidenced by the Rumsfeld quotation at the beginning of this chapter. As Thomas Austin notes,

> to this end, photographs are sometimes used in the film to undercut or challenge statements made in interview, while at other moments interview testimony clarifies or complicates what the still images appear to show. In other words, there is no consistent epistemological hierarchy governing the two sets of sources. (2011: 347–8)

As a result of this indeterminacy something of *Taxi to the Dark Side*'s emphatic, fact-based political commentary is lost. Yet something is also gained: there are no easy answers to be found in the prison, in the photographs, in the words of those accused of the crime. As Benson-Allott puts it, the relationship of the Abu Ghraib photographs to history 'is still tenuous and representational' and understanding them requires movement into the data and the documents, the legal rulings and the responses to and causes of

9/11 (2009: 44). Ultimately, this is a dialectical juxtaposition, not a postmodern intertextual gesture.

In his book *The Lucifer Effect*, Philip Zimbardo, an expert witness on behalf of one of the officers court-martialled for their behaviour at Abu Ghraib, traces how systems can produce unethical behaviour and how the scapegoating of low- and mid-level soldiers at Abu Ghraib has distracted from an analysis of how the military command and policymakers created a situation in which abuse was encouraged and permitted (see 2007: 324–80). Following Zimbardo, the film demands that accountability be extended beyond the vilified MPs to the operation of Abu Ghraib as a military/penal institution and to the larger context shaped by the ambitions, policies and practices of US foreign policy under Bush. Seen in this wider context, *Standard Operating Procedure* suggests that, as Austin puts it, 'the "bad apples" were the fruit of a poisoned tree' (2011: 348). There are correspondences here with the way 9/11 pointed to unethical behaviour in the middle realms of US society – financiers, lawyers, and so on – with the principle of complicity collapsing the overly neat differentiation of the innocent and the guilty (see Sands 2008: 30). Films such as *25th Hour*, *Syriana* and *Rendition* seek to scrutinise societal structure and the relationship between this structure and those with power; although it does not pursue such a tactic itself, *Standard Operating Procedure* points to the necessity of this type of cultural production.

With the exception of *Hostel*, the films described in this chapter form a cycle of forceful, politicised and aesthetically adventurous attempts to critique the worst excesses of the torture policies (and their wider ramifications) and to encourage a critical view of the 'war on terror'.[42] David Simpson writes that, following the fallout from the Abu Ghraib scandal, 'the neat distinctions between them and us, between civility and barbarism [could not] be mouthed as confidently as they once were' (2006: 110), and that

> the photographs do not show that we are all monsters, nor do they confirm that the tortures can be blamed on a few morally delinquent soldiers; they open a disturbingly ambiguous territory inbetween, where the question remains a question not yet resolved and not easy to resolve. (2006: 117)

The cycle of torture films described here, appearing through the latter part of the decade, explores this ambiguous territory. They may be open to criticism on some points – for example, the drift of the *Saw* series away from the difficult ethical scenario that was its point of origin, the liberal redemptive implication that the press will save the day in *Rendition* and the neglect of the victim's perspective in *Standard Operating Procedure* – but like the films described in chapter one this cycle acknowledges and explores a range of challenging realities in a manner that is almost without precedent in the US cinema.

There is a temptation here to pursue a teleological line of argument: that this cycle of films marks a trend in popular culture that – ten years after 9/11 – indicates that the US is now more willing and capable than ever before of questioning the 'relationship both between self *and* other and with(in) the self' (Weber 2005: 2). Douglas Kellner, for example, claims that a progressive and liberal vision of US national identity had, by the late 2000s, come to dominate, and that in this new cultural climate the success of *Slumdog Millionaire* (2008), an account of life in the slums of Mumbai, India, at the 2009 Academy Awards 'constitutes a rejection of the narrow nationalism and chauvinism of the Bush-Cheney years [and marks] a yearning for diversity, complexity, critical vision, and sympathy for the marginalized and oppressed' (2010: 12). As we have seen in this chapter, there are some grounds for this claim. Indeed, it might feasibly be argued that a dynamic and critical popular culture provided a context for the Supreme Court to rule that the Haynes Memo (condoning the use of torture) had no legal standing, which in turn led to Barack Obama rescinding all legal cover for interrogation techniques deemed torture in a memo dated 22 January 2009 (see Sands 2008: 293). Although Guantánamo Bay remains open at the time of writing (described as 'a legal black hole' by Sands (2008: 22)), the films discussed in this chapter, alongside important works of investigative journalism and myriad online repositories of leaked documents, successfully challenged the use of torture and cultivated a critical sensibility that has required policy-makers to move cautiously.[43]

The Iraq War

On 14 September 2001, US congressmen and senators voted almost unanimously to grant George W. Bush the power to wage war in response to the 9/11 attacks, with the invasion of Afghanistan quickly following. The subsequent extension of the 'war on terror' to Iraq in 2003 was preceded by a public relations campaign that claimed Saddam Hussein's regime was a threat to US security (through its development of chemical and nuclear weapons, as well as its relationship with al-Qaida). Arguably, the cycle of patriotic war films, including *We Were Soldiers*, *Behind Enemy Lines* and *Black Hawk Down*, which were produced before 9/11 but fast-tracked into cinemas in the weeks and months following the attacks, consolidated the prevailing jingoistic mood (see the introduction). At the same time, a number of high-profile post-9/11 films, including *9/11*, *United 93* and *World Trade Center*, linked Ground Zero to the battlefields of Afghanistan and Iraq in ways that could be taken to imply that the waging of war was a natural, inevitable extension of the national will. Nonetheless, even in the immediate aftermath of the attacks, the diverse, often anti-war, views of those New Yorkers shown in the documentary film *Seven Days in September* indicated that the move to war was a contentious issue from day one. In the present chapter, a cycle of post-9/11 war films is examined as they relate to a decade of both continuous war and continuous anti-war protest.

By 2003 the 'shock and awe' invasions and military campaigns in Afghanistan and Iraq had slid into ill-prepared nation-building, much of it contracted to private companies – including Halliburton, which received single-source contracts to the value of $19.3 billion in their military support role and whose name became synonymous with accusations that the war was a self-interested exercise in capitalist expansionism (see Stiglitz and Bilmes 2008: 15). After an initial period of accommodation, the presence of US forces began to be regarded as an occupation and was fiercely contested, with insurgents using improvised explosive devices (IEDs) to harry and frustrate US troops. A protracted guerrilla war led to the US military operating in heavily fortified military bases and with increasingly indiscriminate tactics. For example, the 'reduction' of the city of Fallujah included the levelling by artillery and aerial bombardment of all possible enemy strongholds and the house-to-house clearance of all resistance, resulting in a large number of Iraqi civilian deaths. Atrocities conducted by US troops in Haditha, Hamdaniya and Mahmoudiya, including the rape and murder of civilians, as well as other violations of the Geneva Conventions were reported in the media. Against this backdrop news of the widespread abuse of inmates in military prisons at Abu Ghraib and elsewhere intensified criticism of the war: indeed, the popular cultural response to the news of torture cannot be easily separated from the reactions to the war more generally (see Greenberg and Dratel 2005: xiii–xxxi). The *New York Times*'s retraction of its coverage of the build-up to the war in Iraq in May 2004 is indicative of how, from mid-decade, a critical view had gained traction. By 2008, Joseph E. Stiglitz and Linda Bilmes estimate, the cost of the war in Iraq was close to $3 trillion, with ever-diminishing public support (see 2008: 3–32).

A cycle of documentaries (appearing from 2004) and feature films (from 2007) marks this shift from jingoism to anti-war cynicism. Pat Aufderheide (2007) estimates that there have been around twenty feature documentaries showing the war in Iraq that have received limited theatrical releases.[44] These films critique the war in a number of ways. *Fahrenheit 9/11, WMD: Weapons of Mass Deception* (2004), *Iraq for Sale: The War Profiteers* (2006) and *No End in Sight* (2007), for example, take a broad historical perspective in which the Iraq War is seen as one part of a neoconservative project that seeks to secure a strategic hold over Middle Eastern oil supplies and to generate large profits for civilian contractors involved in reconstruction. These partisan and (at times) polemical films view the Iraq War as the consequence of the self-interested, semi-criminal actions of a small group of policymakers in high office. In contrast, *Occupation: Dreamland* (2005), *The War Tapes* (2006), *Ground Truth* (2006) and *Body of War* (2007) focus on the experience of US troops and draw attention to the mismatch between the pro-war discourse and the frustrating, ineffectual and often debilitating experience of the war on the ground. Most unusually, a number of films, including *Voices of Iraq* (2004), *The Blood of My Brother* (2005) and *My Country, My Country* (2006), in seeking to depict the war from an Iraqi perspective, exemplify how one of the demands that followed the Abu Ghraib torture controversy – that the US must seek a more reciprocal relation with those people in other countries upon which it is dependent – became a feature of post-9/11 cinema.[45]

Iraq in Fragments fits within this group. The film received a limited theatrical release in 2006 and won Best Director, Best Cinematography and Best Editing awards at the 2006 Sundance Film Festival, as well as being nominated for an Academy Award in 2007. The film's title refers implicitly to Iraq's formation in 1921 as a colonial amalgamation of 'fragments' of the disintegrating Ottoman Empire and to the present-day disintegration of the country as a result of the war. The title can also be read as a self-reflexive comment on the process of editing itself, whereby stories are selected and deselected and disparate images of the world are assembled into a coherent picture of a particular time and place. The film's director, James Longley, is American but studied at the All Russian Institute of Cinematography in Moscow, and also spent time working in Russia as a journalist. These experiences perhaps allow Longley to see Iraq through the lens of Marxist concepts such as class conflict and to seek cinematic form for the expression of these concepts. In the majority of documentaries that show the war in Iraq, filmmakers foreground individual experiences (of US soldiers, generals, policymakers and politicians) and describe history as a process driven by the actions of individuals as historical agents. In contrast, Longley seeks a way of extending the range of narratives in play through including multiple Iraqi perspectives and telling the stories of groups of people who are dispossessed and marginal and have little historical agency. He also searches for ways of telling these stories so that the structural elements of class, religious difference, geographical complexity and generational change are foregrounded. His distinctive approach – which I would suggest is informed by a Marxist framework – is particularly clear in the arrangement of the stories into three, strictly bracketed, thirty-minute sections. I would contend that this narrative design, which has no corollary in the wider cycle of Iraq War documentaries, offers a challenging, thought-provoking view of the war.

The first section, titled 'Mohammed of Baghdad', focuses on the story of 11-year-old auto-mechanic Mohammed Haithem, who lives in the Sheik Omar district of Baghdad, a poor working-class area. It begins with a montage sequence composed of shots of bridges across the Tigris, vignettes of city life, US troops in tanks on patrol and a surreal superimposed image of a goldfish swimming in a tank. This opening is followed by a description of Mohammed's life – his struggle at school, his relationship with his violent adoptive father – over which is layered a soundtrack composed of his thoughts, feelings and hopes for the future. Here the luminous and vivid colour palettes of digital video (and the vivid light conditions of Iraq itself) are fully explored, offering a contrast to the denotative, plain images seen on the television news and the washed out, bleach-bypass processes used in numerous Iraq War feature films. Another montage sequence – Aufderheide calls these sequences 'visual poems' (2008: 92) – captures the beauty, vitality, violence and confusion of Iraq under occupation, and makes the transition to the film's second section, titled 'Sadr's South'. This focuses on the followers of the cleric Moqtada al-Sadr, as they rally for regional elections in the Shiite South. We follow in particular 32-year-old Sheik Aws al Kafaji, who is in charge of the Sadr office in Naseriyah. The film shows political strategy meetings, religious rallies, the Mehdi Army militia enforcing the prohibition on the selling of alcohol, a violent encounter with NATO forces and an Islamic festival which features violent self-flagellation. The third section, titled 'Kurdish Spring', focuses on a family of sheep farmers in the village of Koretan in the Kurdish North of Iraq. As with the first section, there is an emphasis on the experience and thoughts of children, in particular the friendship between two boys and their fathers who live on neighbouring farms. This section also shows scenes of workers making bricks in large ovens, the observance of Islamic religious custom and enthusiastic voting in regional elections amidst clear signs of a strong Kurdish nationalism.

In his production notes, Longley (2006) describes how, at the time of filming, the Sunni Arabs in Baghdad and other areas were boycotting elections and consequently falling outside the official political process. At the same time, the Supreme Council for Islamic Revolution was lobbying for a separate Shiite state in the oil-rich south and the Kurds were pressing for independence and seeking to retain control over oil-rich Kirkuk. Observing these events, Longley noted that 'the fracture lines had been drawn that would permanently split Iraq', and so he sought out micro-narratives that would speak to these complex historical forces (each pulling in a different direction) in a suitably complex way. The film thus invites viewers to question preconceptions of the Iraq War as a singular unified event defined in relation to the US invasion and instead to hold in tension the deterioration of security in Baghdad, the strengthening of a well-organised sectarian insurgency in the South and the depiction of a region of relative peace. The documentary's structure is driven by a concept of history in which context and deeper structures of historical change are placed in a dialectical relation with day-to-day events. The selection of these events and their placement in juxtaposition with one another is not organised via a continuity system or ordered by voice-over narration. Rather, the editing system in play is closer to that of dialectical montage, that is, the theorised approach to film editing associated with early Soviet cinema – and especially the historical films of Sergei Eisenstein – that claims that it is via editing that meaning is made, especially through the 'collision' of distinct and different shots that, in the mind of the viewer, combine into explosive new concepts (see Robertson 2009: 1–13). The lack of explicit linking or explanation between the different parts of the film asks the viewer to make sense of them in relation to their own knowledge of Iraq and the Iraq War. Selmin Kara observes that this dialectical relationship is also integral to the film's sound design, noting that

> the sonic contrasts among the vernacular urban noise of Baghdad streets in the segment on the Sunnis, the overpowering sectarian sounds of the Shiites, and the suspenseful quiet of the rural Kurds up north open up a dissonant space in which each fragment of the film becomes a testimony to both the cultural, ethnic and religious disquiet of the nation and the heterogeneity of its sonic landscape. (2009: 264)

Kara concludes that 'together the fragments portray Iraq as an assemblage of discontinuous noises, sights, sounds, voices, and music, which implies that it is impossible to capture the nation (or life under occupation) in its totality' (ibid.).

The dialectical relationship between the three parts of *Iraq in Fragments* means that Longley's film contrasts sharply with the feature films (described below) that show the war in relation to the 'shock and awe' invasion stage and the ensuing military stalemate. Against this, the structure of the film asks the viewer to understand the war as a fluid, changing and complex reality within which the US invasion is formative, but not absolutely so. This is signalled through the way the dominant Western news discourse is presented in the film, where, at one point, we see Bush's acknowledgement that prisoner abuse had taken place at Abu Ghraib military prison as part of a news report playing on a television in the background in a small textile shop – and barely noticed by the workers. In *Iraq in Fragments* this pivotal news story – so central to the shaping of Western public opinion – is shown

Fig. 21:
Revealing
the lives of
others: *Iraq
in Fragments*
(2006)

... those disgraceful acts
do not reflect our character

as something blended into everyday life under occupation and, crucially, relatively unremarkable.

The dialectical design of narrative structure, editing, sound design, and so on, in *Iraq in Fragments* extends to the orchestration of point of view. Longley spent over a year with some of his subjects and more than two years in Iraq between September 2002 and April 2005, shooting over three hundred hours of film. This commitment to inhabiting the war alongside ordinary Iraqis stands in contrast to the embedded and securitised filmmaking that typifies almost all other documentary films, which tend to approach Iraq either from afar or from within the military's security cordons. Where films do seek an Iraqi perspective (as in *The Blood of My Brother* and *My Country, My Country*), the filmmaker is usually placed alongside primarily middle-class Iraqi families in relatively safe areas, and as we shall see, fiction films tend to emulate this embedded and securitised perspective.

Aufderheide claims that *Iraq in Fragments*' montage sequences 'underscore the way in which the foreigner's gaze soaks up surfaces where a resident would see only background' and signal to the viewer 'the multi-faceted, partial knowledge of the foreign observer' (2008: 91). In other parts of the film we are made aware (especially through the decision to leave considerable amounts of speech untranslated) of the difficulty (perhaps impossibility) of ever fully understanding the experience of the people we see on screen. Aufderheide concludes that the film 'says much, and gracefully, about Iraqis, but much more about what Americans do not know about them and, even more, if indirectly, about the wealth of ambiguity in cross-cultural encounter' (ibid.). While in agreement with this observation, I wish to argue that it is only part of the picture. As the above description of the film's structure indicates, the filmmaker was keen to find ways of bringing together different perspectives, and the film attempts to offer points of view different from his own (while still acknowledging that these are, to a great extent, his own constructions). Thus, the film details a number of key characters: a 13-year-old boy in the first section, a Muslim cleric in the second, and two families (focusing on two children) in the third. We might think of Longley looking as if from their perspective, acknowledging that he (and likely the viewer) is an outsider but at the same time attempting – through a strategic editing together of voice-over, dialogue, ambient sound, music and sound effects – to offer the viewer some sense of how the war is being experienced from that particular person's perspective. The film can here be placed alongside those described in the previous chapter, especially *Rendition* and *Taxi to the Dark Side*, in that it seeks a complex point-of-view system that might resist what Judith Butler calls 'the narrative perspective of US unilateralism and, as it were, its defensive structures [via description of] the ways in which our lives are profoundly implicated in the lives of others' (2004: 7–8).[46]

Longley's focus on the child's perspective invites comparison with the narrative trope – observable in a number of the films described in earlier chapters – of disrupted child/parent relations. In much post-9/11 cinema this trope is used to acknowledge anxiety, which is then conditionally disavowed through depictions of parents recovering their authority and protecting the children in their charge. Longley refuses this somewhat reductive construction. In one scene we see Mohammed watching a group of adult Iraqi males (including his violent adoptive father) discussing the whys and wherefores of the war: the men are cynical and angry; Mohammed's face is blank, his brow furrowed. Here the viewer witnesses a small child trying to understand the adult world at a time of war. To this is added a voice-over consisting of Mohammed's thoughts – a heartfelt description of his ambition to become a pilot which provides a powerful counterpoint to the difficult reality of his work as a car mechanic and the dark fatalism of the adults' conversation.

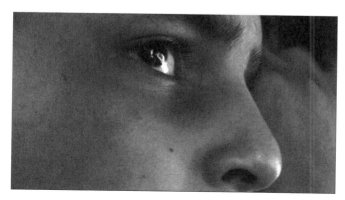

Fig. 22: An Iraqi child's perspective of war: *Iraq in Fragments* (2006)

This layered and unsentimental presentation of Mohammed's lived experience – the *mise-en-scène* of the machine-shop registering Baghdad as an urban, industrialised city with a marked class divide, the father's physique displaying injuries sustained during the Iran/Iraq War, Mohammed's diminished size bespeaking the malnutrition suffered during the UN sanctions period following the Gulf War – speaks of the ways in which structural historical factors have impacted on Mohammed's everyday life, making him who he is. The power of the scene stems from its recording and revealing of the contrast between grim, everyday reality and Mohammed's thoughts and hopes for the future and provokes the viewer's understanding that in war-torn Iraq these hopes will never be realised. Empathy and sympathy are activated (there is some ethical demand being made here that the lives of these children should be better than they are), but this response conjoins with the intellectual work demanded by the film in its entirety; these children are historical subjects and their futures will be dictated by the interplay of forces modelled by the film's dialectical structure and composition. Here the film demonstrates something of the searching quality of *Parallel Lines*, the interconnectedness and structural analysis sought by *Syriana*, and the awareness of otherness displayed in *Rendition*. This combination – a sharp riposte to the reassuring parent/child melodramas at the centre of *Man on Fire* and *War of the Worlds* – arguably makes *Iraq in Fragments* one of the most important post-9/11 films.

Following the documentary film cycle, a cycle of Iraq War feature films entered production, appearing from late 2007 and into 2008, including *GI Jesus* (2007), *The Situation* (2007), *Home of the Brave* (2007), *In the Valley of Elah* (2007), *Redacted* (2007), *Badland* (2007), *Grace Is Gone* (2008), *Conspiracy* (2008), *Stop-Loss* (2008) and *The Lucky Ones* (2008). Both *The Hurt Locker* (on wide release in the US from mid-2009) and *Green Zone* originate in this period, but the releases of both were held back after the poor box-office performance of their predecessors.[47] Most of the films are contemporaneous, that is, they are set in the period of the war immediately preceding their release, a period in which jingoistic 'mission accomplished' rhetoric confronted the reality of a strengthening insurgency and public recognition of prisoner abuse and atrocity. Douglas Kellner argues that 'the cycle testified to disillusionment with Iraq policy and helped compensate for mainstream corporate media neglect of the consequences of war' (2010: 222).

The remainder of the present chapter is devoted to a close reading of one film from this cycle, *In the Valley of Elah*, and the placing of this film and the cycle as a whole in relation to the wider US war film genre. During World

War II, the US war film functioned as propaganda, celebrating individual and group heroism, the sacrifice of individual desires to higher ideals and goals and the effectiveness of military command and technology, as well as emphasising the importance of strong leadership and celebrating war as an exciting and spectacular experience, and as a (male) rite of passage. The war film typically embodied a severely restricted point of view (usually via the experience of a small military unit or patrol) and a prejudicial construction of cultural otherness. A grim, bloody realism was also an essential element of the genre, reminding the viewer that the nation (and the ideals it embodies) was, and continues to be, built on the honourable sacrifice of young citizen soldiers. In post-war films, these propagandist elements (what Thomas Schatz calls 'Hollywood's military Ur-narrative' (2002: 75)) remained a key generic feature, with even the bloodiest war films tending to show war as a 'progressive' activity, entered into reluctantly but ultimately proving necessary and productive. The subsequent experience of losing a war in Vietnam marks films such as *The Deer Hunter* (1978) and *Apocalypse Now* (1979) which challenged and questioned many of the genre's core myths (while never escaping them completely) (see Boggs and Pollard 2007: 90–1). However, after a brief cycle of what might be considered critical (if not resolutely anti-war) films, earlier features of the genre (and the positive view of war enshrined in it) reasserted themselves. A series of revisionist war films – from the *Rambo* trilogy (1982, 1985, 1988) to *In Country* (1989) – depicted the war primarily through the experience of the ordinary combat soldier (or grunt) and alleviated the traumatic experience of the veteran through the application of discourses of therapeutic overcoming (see Sturken 1997: 85–122). Subsequently a cycle of films released in the late 1990s and early 2000s – including *Saving Private Ryan* (1998), *Pearl Harbor* (2001) and *We Were Soldiers* (2002) – presented war in ways proximate to the propagandist genre staples of the 1940s (see Westwell 2006). This reclaimed sense of war as a noble and necessary activity interlocked with forms of banal US nationalism in the period immediately following 9/11, prompting Andrew J. Bacevich to argue that in the contemporary period 'Americans have come [once again] to define the nation's strength and well-being in terms of military preparedness, military action, and the fostering of (or nostalgia for) military ideals' (2005: 2).

Significantly, though, Bacevich's claim was made before the release of the cycle of Iraq War films noted above, raising the question: do his claims still hold true? Post-Abu Ghraib, is US culture governed by what he calls the New American Militarism? While Kellner's view of the cycle – that the films are engaged in anti-war protest – would suggest that the answer is no, analysis in this chapter suggests that such unguarded optimism may be misguided. *In the Valley of Elah* contains many elements that would seem to be a very difficult fit with Bacevich's claim, especially the acknowledgement of atrocities committed by US troops and the depiction of generational angst and republican crisis. By showing these aspects of the war in Iraq the film appears to function very strongly as critique. However, the way in which the film shows that (finally) atrocity can be recuperated is, in the final instance, reconcilable with the New American Militarism, and serves as a further example – following *War of the Worlds* and *Extremely Loud and Incredibly Close* – of the way in which parallel lines converge in the service of hegemonic constructions of the war in Iraq and war in general.

In the Valley of Elah, which is based on events described by journalist Mark Boal in an article for *Playboy* (2007), focuses on the experience of Hank Deerfield (Tommy Lee Jones), a retired former military policeman and Vietnam veteran, as he investigates the disappearance of his son Mike (John Tucker), an Iraq War veteran. The film shows Hank's investigation revealing that Mike was murdered by his fellow soldiers. The scene in which Corporal Steve Penning (Wes Chatham) describes to Hank, without emotion or remorse, how he and his fellow soldiers murdered Mike and dismembered and disposed of his body shows how the war has reduced young men to sociopaths unable to feel empathy or even recognise the loss of their ethical bearings. In the same scene Hank is told that his son was a drug addict and alcoholic who took sadistic pleasure in abusing Iraqi prisoners. Here, as with *Redacted*, which is also based on real events and recounts the rape and murder of an Iraqi girl and her family, the film seeks to acknowledge the role of US troops, and the culpability of the US more generally, in war atrocity. This leads Joan Mellen to claim that the film shows how 'America's young men drilled and educated to fight America's expansionist foreign wars have been morally damaged at the same time as the national ethos' (2008: 24). Adding to this bleak view of post-Iraq realities, Deerfield's investigation takes place against a backdrop of apathy and uninterest: as Martin Barker notes, 'the film is full of people – the police, the military, men at a strip club, some café owners – who simply do not care' (2011: 29).

The details of fratricide and atrocity are revealed through the perspectives of different family members and via generational difference, especially the relation between fathers and sons (and in more dilute form, mothers and sons). The first perspective is that of a grief-stricken and guilt-ridden father. In Boal's *Playboy* article Hank is described thus: 'Staff Sergeant Lanny Davis, retired, a United States Army veteran, husband, father and proud owner of a tidy ranch home in serene St. Charles, Missouri, lives a life you could call squared away'. The film shows Hank's carefully tended garden, sharply pressed shirts and carefully organised luggage, the film's *mise-en-scène* cultivating the sense of Hank's character as 'squared away' found in Boal's prose. Tommy Lee Jones's performance also seeks to articulate this sense of a man deeply committed to a military ethos, leading Michael J. Shapiro to note that Hank's 'body and his verbally expressed allegiance to military protocols … convey the ways in which the Deerfield home is militarized' (2011: 119). Indeed, the film has identified Hank (as synonymous with a military value system) as the source of the problem: he has made his son in his own image and this sense of self has then been found to be irreconcilable with the experience of the war in Iraq. Mellen notes: 'When Mike telephoned and pleaded, "Dad, get me out of here!" Hank, a Vietnam veteran, urged him to carry on. That call, repeated several times in flashback, expresses cinematically the father's sense of his own guilt' (2008: 26). In contrast to the reassuring return of patriarchal authority found in most films that depict disturbed parent/child relations post-9/11, here the father's failure to protect his son cannot be redeemed.

Two further points of view – those of a mother in each case – give shape to the film. The first is that of Hank's wife, Joan (Susan Sarandon). Shapiro notes how the *mise-en-scène* brackets her domain (the kitchen) from the rest of the house, which is associated with Hank (2011: 119). Although, on

Fig. 23: Atrocity and post-traumatic stress disorder: *In the Valley of Elah* **(2007)**

the surface, Joan is supportive of her husband, the film hints at how she resents Hank and the military, identifying his upbringing of their sons as the cause of both their deaths. As Shapiro puts it, 'For Joan, her son's death is a result of the way her militarized household left him no option other than enlisting. As she puts it, "Living in this house, he sure never could have felt like a man if he hadn't gone"' (2011: 122). Joan's quiet grief – 'Both of my boys, Hank?' she cries at one point, 'You could have left me one' – clearly attributes blame in a way that confirms the impression conveyed through the narrative that a military ethos produces the kind of destructive violence unleashed in Iraq and felt by families of soldiers killed or physically and psychologically damaged by the war. The second point of view is that of police detective Emily Sanders (Charlize Theron), who helps Hank investigate his son's disappearance. The real-life figure on which Sanders is based is described in Boal's article as a large, bluff middle-aged man named Drew Tyner. By rewriting the character as female, the film doubles Joan's critical gaze, thereby reinforcing (from another female's/mother's perspective) a point of view external to the world of masculine militarism. The final shot of the harrowing central interrogation scene is a cutaway to Sanders's reaction to Penning's confession. She holds the gaze of the confessing soldier and then averts her eyes. Refusing to align herself fully with Hank's shocked, guilty reaction, her turning away seems to offer some kind of alternative moral/ethical position whereby Penning's sociopathy and Hank's suffering are shown to be connected. With no easy way of detaching the two realms of experience, it is necessary, the film suggests, to look elsewhere, to seek an alternative viewpoint.

Taken together, these aspects of the film (a willingness to show atrocity and to reflect on the structural elements in US society that underpin the military and that create the conditions for such atrocity) culminate in Hank's decision, in the film's final scene, to fly the US flag upside down: something that he has earlier explained to an El Salvadorian caretaker is a signal that there is an emergency. Barker observes that

> over these final scenes, a slow ballad accompanies Hank's acts. It is a woman's lament that from the moment we are born we are touched by death. The final image is of a dead body in the road, captioned with the words 'For The Children'. (2011: 31)

Thus, the film shows the republic in crisis, a theme in post-9/11 cinema observable through the documentary films described in chapter one, the conspiracy films in chapter three and the torture films in chapter seven, and which is appropriated late in the decade as a principal response to the war in Iraq.

Can it be concluded from this that *In the Valley of Elah* challenges a wider societal militarism through an unflinching depiction of atrocity and the structural rootedness of this in a certain male military mind-set? Yes, to a point. However, the focus on young soldiers so brutalised by their experience in Iraq that they have spiralled into abuse of drink and drugs to allay their traumatic experiences may also activate the therapeutic discourse at work in the films described in chapter six, and this resolute focus on the suffering of US troops (extended here to the wider family) also constitutes a turning away from the acknowledgement of the other demanded in films such as *Iraq in Fragments*.

Another look at the narrative structure of *In the Valley of Elah* opens up the potential for a more qualified reading of its description of the Iraq War. The events depicted in a fleeting image and aurally at the start of the film (where they remain opaque) are finally revealed as Hank discovers and has decoded the camera footage from his son's mobile phone. The footage shows that during a military operation a child is run over and left to die by the side of the road. This provides the point of origin for Mike's descent into despair, and subsequent desensitised, sadistic behaviour. In a world in which a child's death is barely registered, the moral bearings of young Americans in a war zone are quickly lost. Throughout the film Hank is haunted by the phone call made by his son from Iraq in which Mike pleads for help in the aftermath of the death of the Iraqi child by the roadside; the reason Hank is troubled is that he failed to offer Mike any counsel or support. Here, again, we see how an intervention (support, understanding, empathy) might have headed off Mike's subsequent breakdown and violent sadism. As Barker notes, 'Mike's agony over [the death of the child] becomes the post-facto explanation for his abusive behaviour towards prisoners' (2011: 30). Indeed, in another scene camera phone footage shows Mike playing with Iraqi children. Barker also draws attention to the fact that Boal's article considers the possibility (revealed to him by more than one source) that the real-life soldier Mike is based on was killed because he was about to report his fellow soldiers for their involvement in the rape of a young Iraqi girl (see 2011: 81–2). That this event – tackled head on in *Redacted* – does not feature in the film suggests that the filmmakers had sought to amend the nature of the atrocities committed in order to retain some audience sympathy. Similarly, Mellen reports that 'in a scene from the shooting script that did not make the final cut, Mike visits a girlfriend now in hospital, a double amputee returned from Iraq. The parts he was interested in still work, he tells her' (2008: 31). Cutting this out suggests a toning down of Mike's capacity for violence and casual misogyny to retain the possibility of redemption. Barker argues that 'this whole process of misleading and disclosing creates a space in which soldiers' cruel and inhuman treatment of Iraqis becomes *excusable*. We see their brutality simply as a mistake arising out of stress and sickness' (2011: 32). For Barker, Mike

> becomes an exemplar of ordinary soldiers, basically good men, but stressed beyond their limits by the war. Their murderous behaviour, their torturing of prisoners becomes explicable, even excusable, because they must be suffering from that syndrome known as PTSD. (2011: 82)

Here the film keys into the wider discourse: for example, follow-up stories to the iconic 'Marlboro Man' photograph – which showed a US Marine taking a cigarette break during desperate fighting in Fallujah – described how on his return home Marine Lance Corporal James Blake Miller had succumbed to PTSD. As such, an image of heroic stoicism segued into a more complex narrative of psychological injury and recovery, and as a result a questionable military operation that resulted in considerable loss of civilian life is subsumed by the wider therapeutic discourse as shaped by the media, including the cinema. Also part of this wider response, Boal's follow-up articles in *Playboy* focus on PTSD as experienced by troops who had served in Iraq. Indeed, Boal's 'The Man in the Bomb Suit' (2005) provided the basic plot of *The Hurt Locker*, the most successful, and arguably the least critical, Iraq War film.

Aligned with critics of the therapy paradigm (see Seeley 2008; Fassin and Rechtman 2009; see also chapter six), Barker argues that PTSD 'shifts uneasily between being a medical category, a legal manoeuvre and a fictional explanatory device' and that its centrality to post-9/11 culture is 'part and parcel of a depoliticising tendency, which needs people to be victims before they can be said to need help' (2011: 83, 86). Put simply, 'PTSD has come to function as a key metaphor for America inspecting itself within safe margins' (2011: 99). A key aspect of this is the way in which PTSD licenses dialogue and agreement between those with differing political points of view (Barker notes how left-liberal cartoonist Garry Trudeau and Republican John McCain both rely on the PTSD paradigm (2011: 87)), leading Barker to argue that the therapy paradigm forms a 'bridge across conservatives and liberals in America' (2011: 99). As such, PTSD as it appears as a narrative trope in the Iraq War film cycle is a key marker of one of the main themes of this book, namely the way in which a left-liberal critical perspective cedes ground to the right, thereby backing away from the radical direction critique might otherwise lead, with therapy in this case the key ground upon which the convergence of seemingly irreconcilable positions takes place.[48]

So, how might we reconcile these two claims regarding the film? Is it a forensic account of US atrocity and the dangers of a militarised domestic realm? Or does the leeway permitted by the PTSD trope constitute a turning away from, and even a redemption of, these difficult issues? Of course, in this specific case the answers to these questions are not clear-cut – the film is ambiguous and contradictory. However, things become clearer if the film is considered in the context of the cycle to which it belongs, and the relation of this cycle to the war film genre more generally. In an article for the *New York Times*, A. O. Scott (2010) tracks the widespread denial of politics in Iraq War films and argues that this is a consequence of a focus on PTSD leading the Iraq War (like Vietnam before it) to being reduced to a psychologised and thus ahistorical experience. Scott is here referring to the way in which the difficult legacies of the Vietnam War were subject during the 1980s to a widespread revisionism as part of the consolidation of the wider culture of Reaganism and the rise of the New Right. This revisionism sought to reclaim credibility for the military and rebuild national self-esteem. One of the key strands of this revisionism was a focus not on the war itself (and its political, geographical and symbolic complexity) but on the suffering of the Vietnam veteran, who, according to revisionist logic, had merely done his patriotic duty in difficult circumstances. In relation to cinema, a number of films showed Vietnam veterans overcoming their struggle with PTSD, and this process of 'healing the wounds' became the dominant metaphor for rendering the war less divisive a decade after its end (see Beattie 1998: 142). As a result of this process, Scott argues, and in continuation with many others, by the late 1980s the divisive and troubled memory of the war in Vietnam had been settled and this enabled a reclamation of foundational narratives of masculine, military, technological and political superiority, arguably ensuring the necessary preconditions for further wars in the 1990s and 2000s. Scott suggests that a similar strategy (this time working contemporaneously with the war rather than following it) is at work in relation to the Iraq War, with the resolute focus on the suffering of US troops used as a way of screening off more complex views of the war. The US is figured here as a skilful, decent, young soldier who has engaged in war in good faith and then suffered great psychological harm as a result of their experience.

At first glance, a move towards resolution of this sort is not an obvious feature of *In the Valley of Elah*. The film strikes a provisional note: the redemptive ending is deferred because the war is still being fought, and as a result of the film's drawing of attention to the structural dimension of militarism, the lines of responsibility and recuperation remain unclear. Kellner notes how in *The Hurt Locker*, *Home of the Brave*, *The Lucky Ones* and *Stop-Loss* the characters display a compulsion to return to the war. This suggests both an incompleteness and a desire for a different kind of resolution, pointing to the way the cycle acknowledges difficulty but also retains the possibility of a positive outcome (2010: 223–33). However, this critical and provisional quality notwithstanding, the wider cycle does tend to signal that a therapeutic narrative resolution may, with time, be possible: for instance, in *Grace Is Gone* a father whose wife, Grace, has been killed while serving in the military in Iraq takes his daughters on a road trip to Florida; in the final scene he visits the 'Evolving Planet' exhibit at the Enchanted Garden theme park, the *mise-en-scène* suggesting acceptance and personal growth. The redemptive trope can be seen in *Brothers*, a film about the war in Afghanistan, which ends with Captain Sam Cahill (Tobey Maguire) finding the courage to tell his wife (again named Grace) of the atrocity he has committed (the murder of a fellow soldier, a fratricide that recalls the murder of Mike in *In the Valley of Elah*). The final scene shows Grace's and Cahill's families pulling together to help heal the wounds the war has inflicted. If the films are read alongside one another, *In the Valley of Elah*'s guarded movement towards redemptive possibility segues into the more determined therapy narrative of *Grace Is Gone* and *Brothers*, thereby enfolding the figure of the returning traumatised combat veteran in discourses of healing and forgiveness.

So what is to be made of claims of an all-pervasive New American Militarism shaping US popular culture in the early twenty-first century? This chapter has demonstrated that the late 2000s witnessed the release of a cycle of films operating at the absolute limits of the war film genre. Within the set of bounded possibilities available to filmmakers working in Hollywood, and at a time when US troops were still being killed on the battlefield, a cycle of war films appeared that could be said to be largely critical of war. Filmmakers have been willing to face up to the facts that US troops have committed atrocity, that the wars have not been a success, and may even have been counter-productive, that the main beneficiaries have been large US corporations, that jingoistic constructions of national identity can be harmful, and so on. Taken together with the myriad documentaries focusing on the war, this critical coverage is almost without precedent, leading one right-wing critic to dub the cycle 'Bin Laden cinema' (Philpott 2010: 326). However, and crucially, many of the films that might be said to display this new complexity have been unpopular with audiences in the US (Barker labels the cycle 'toxic' (2011)), and the dominant trope emerging is one of the war being brought home, that is, figured as the experience of individual soldiers suffering PTSD, and made available to discourses of forgiveness and healing. This therapeutic closure – described also in chapter six – as well as the reclamation of the possibility of purposeful military action, also inflects *Zero Dark Thirty*, described in the next chapter.

History

A central thread through this book is the question of the place of 9/11 in history. Jacques Derrida observed that the term '9/11' quickly become a way of marking the attacks as a 'singular' and 'unprecedented' event, thereby signifying that the attacks somehow existed outside of, or beyond, history (see Habermas *et al.* 2003: 85–6). In the same vein, David Simpson argues that 9/11 was 'widely presented as an interruption of the deep rhythms of cultural time, a cataclysm simply erasing what was there rather than evolving from anything already in place, and threatening a yet more monstrous future' (2006: 4). The appropriation of the term 'Ground Zero' is indicative of this stripping away of history, leading John Dower to observe how its origins in World War II were replaced by connotations that placed

> America as victim of evil forces – alien peoples and cultures who, 'unlike ourselves,' did not recognise the sanctity of human life and had no compunctions about killing innocent men, women and children. [...] To an extent almost impossible to exaggerate, 'Ground Zero 2001' became a wall that simultaneously took its name from the past and blocked out all sightlines of from what and where that name came. (2010: 161)

The consequence of this turning away or repression of both history and historical complexity, especially of events in the recent past which might explain the attacks, marginalises the calling into play of historical explanations produced by historians and political scientists following 9/11, as well as evidencing a degradation of the ability of the wider culture to think historically, that is, to place contemporary events in relation to earlier events in a way that might help explain and contextualise.[49]

And yet, this is not quite the full story: in a key speech, Bush stated that 'history has called our nation into action' (quoted in Croft 2006: 126), signalling the importance of a providential, nationalist sense of history to the initial response to 9/11. The introduction to this book described how the photograph *Ground Zero Spirit* called on a nostalgic and jingoistic sense of World War II and how this provided ballast for the call to arms in Afghanistan and Iraq; as Marianna Torgovnick notes, mythologised accounts of World War II 'can make things happen' (2005: x). The height of World Trade Center One, or the 'Freedom Tower', the central building in the complex built to replace the World Trade Center, is 1,776 feet (541 metres). This height was chosen to commemorate the year in which the US declared independence from Britain, thus beginning the War of Independence. Devin Zuber notes that the building's 'cornerstone ceremony was conveniently sped up to occur on the 4th of July preceding the 2004 Republican National Convention' (2006: 291) and that the symbolic architectural gesture of the building's height was a way of garnering credibility for the ongoing 'war on terror' through symbolic association with 'the most patriotic war in American history' (2006: 271). These examples show how the banal nationalism that shaped the cultural response to 9/11 relied on a simplified view of the past that legitimised war as moral, proportionate and with historical precedent. Previous chapters have shown how, in terms of cinema, this particular dilute relation to history underpins the jingoistic sentiments of the unity and revenge films, the apocalyptic sensibility of the end-of-the-world cycle and the individualised/medicalised narratives of the therapy film. In each case, history is at once effaced (9/11 comes out of the blue; historical explanation, from the scholarly to the conspiratorial, is deemed inappropriate) and activated (traditions are reaffirmed, a positivist and partial view of the nation's history is brought to the fore, and personal and family histories are preferred over the political and geopolitical). The erasure of historical complexity and the deployment of what might be termed a historical nationalism is associated with a neoconservative response to 9/11. However, as the decade progressed, the discursive combination of dehistoricised present and mythic past became increasingly unsustainable and a more questioning and critical approach to 9/11 and its aftermath began to shape popular culture, something seen most clearly in the cycle of torture films described in chapter seven. A key element of this critical approach was a willingness to reach for a greater historicity: a view of the past that might frame 9/11 in a more complex way. This chapter argues that a cycle of history films displays this desire for a more serious engagement with past events, and focuses on the revisionist account of World War II found in *The Good German* (2006), which exemplifies the desire to seek out complex and critical counter-histories through which to reframe the experience of 9/11. This is followed by an analysis of *Zero Dark Thirty*, a film that at first glance appears to belong to this cycle of critical history films, but which activates history in a carefully calibrated way that serves to shore up the hegemonic response to 9/11.

The Good German depicts a world of political subterfuge, counter-espionage and black marketeering in occupied Berlin in the period immediately preceding the Potsdam conference of 1945. The city (and its subsequent partition) is symbolic of the complex forces at play during World War II, not least the quickly disintegrating alliance between the US and the USSR. Events in the hinterland of the narrative include the Holocaust and war crimes, the mass rape of Berlin women by Soviet soldiers and the emergence of what would become the Cold War arms race. Christine Sprengler argues that the film's opening montage sequence, composed of footage of Berlin shot by Hollywood filmmakers William Wyler and Billy Wilder, who were seconded to the US military to make propaganda films, allows a comparison to be drawn between *The Good German* and films such as *Rome Open City* (1945) and *Paisa* (1946) (2009: 165). The use of newsreel in this way seeks a neorealist affinity with actual events that 'testifies to very real destruction caused by conflict in an age where death and battles are sanitized and footage censored to accord with the Pentagon's closely regulated image of war' (2009: 167–8). Indeed, the film's setting – with US president Harry Truman's Potsdam speech talking of freedom, peace and prosperity, while the events of the narrative reveal clandestine power struggles and political assassinations – suggests that political rhetoric has long been used to surface over historical complexity. A *mise-en-scène* rich in historical detail, including, as Sprengler notes, 'the 1937 Rolls Phantom 3 owned by Field Marshall Montgomery, a 1936 Chrysler Airflow limousine driven during the Potsdam conference and countless antique props flown in from Germany including telephones, light switches, toilets, stoves and street signs', adds to the sense of authenticity (2009: 163). The depiction of Berlin in this way offers an alternative to the stock images of World War II that had given shape to post-9/11 popular culture, an alternative that points to aspects of World War II that are repressed in contemporary culture, including 'internment camps for Japanese and

Japanese-Americans; incendiary bombings of cities in Germany and Japan; the atomic bombings at Hiroshima and Nagasaki; and, operating in a different register, the vital Soviet role in defeating the Nazis' (Torgovnick 2005: 4). As a counterpoint to the post-9/11 effacement of history and the activation of a mythologised version of World War II after 9/11, *The Good German* engages historical complexity, and acknowledges the deep roots of US involvement in clandestine activities during the Cold War.

In the scenes following the opening credits US serviceman 'Tully' (Tobey Maguire, playing against the grain of his star persona) is introduced as a seemingly amiable driver to US journalist Jake Geismer (George Clooney), who has been commissioned to write an article on chief production engineer of the V-2 rocket Franz Bettmann. The film quickly reveals Tully's violent abusive relationship with German prostitute Lena Brandt (Cate Blanchett) and his unprincipled black marketeering. Later scenes show him beating a cripple and using racist invective, showing him as a sociopath with little respect for human life. While Tully strikes a casual and naïve pose in public, in private he enthuses that the war has been the best thing that ever happened to him, leading Sprengler to argue that while

> Tully's innocent act is the United States personified and envisioned through its own political rhetoric (young, enthusiastic, well-intentioned, moral, and courageous), Tully's true self is the United States as envisioned by its critics (opportunistic, corrupt, hypocritical, ignorant and ruthless). (2009: 216)

While the character of Tully lends itself to this unambiguous reading, the film as a whole reveals a greater complexity in order to show that history is not so one-dimensional.

The central thread of the narrative has Geismer searching for missing German scientist Emil Brandt (Christian Oliver). Brandt, a former SS officer, had been the secretary of Bettmann at a Nazi concentration camp. While stationed at the camp, Brant kept careful notes detailing the abuse and extermination of Jewish prisoners that implicate Bettmann in war crimes. Soviet, British and US intelligence agencies are also seeking Bettmann in order to solicit his expertise in the development of rocket technology and nuclear weapons. In return they are willing to overlook his culpability in war crimes. To protect Bettmann's reputation, Brandt must be assassinated. During his investigation Geismer meets his ex-lover, Lena Brandt (Blanchett), who is Emil's wife and a Jew. Lena gives Brandt's notes to Geismer for use in his expose. After Brandt is assassinated Geismer gives his papers to the US authorities in exchange for an exit visa that will allow Lena to leave Berlin. The notes are then destroyed in order to ensure that Bettmann can travel to the US with impunity. Geismer later learns that Lena has survived the Holocaust by doing 'what she had to' – that is, betraying the whereabouts of Jewish Germans in hiding, who were then sent to concentration camps.

As this plot summary indicates, the authorities are shown to behave, without exception, in ways that are self-interested and without recourse to moral principle or law. The successful recruitment of Nazi scientists (and war criminals) does, with time, allow the US to prevail in the Cold War, thereby ensuring post-war prosperity. As Sprengler notes, the film 'questions the extent to which domestic prosperity came to postwar America at the expense of justice' (2009: 167). There are strong parallels here between the clandestine activities of the intelligence agencies at the tail end of World War II and the actions and terror campaigns perpetrated by US intelligence agencies and surrogates of US power in the Middle East and elsewhere during the Cold War. Situated thus, characters are faced with a bounded set of choices often offering no easy course of action: Lena must betray others in order to survive, Geismer must sacrifice the truth in order to save Lena, and so on. Brandt's willingness to atone for his sins by testifying (even under threat of assassination) identifies him as the good German of the film's title – though his principled stance results only in his own death.

As he investigates, Geismer is cheated by Tully, is beaten up three times without response and repeatedly fails to grasp the full significance of the story he is investigating. It is suggested that Geismer is Jewish (he declines the offer of a ham sandwich), yet he retreats from going public with his evidence of war crimes in favour of protecting Lena, ethically compromising himself. Indeed, for a central character in a Hollywood film Geismer's almost complete lack of agency is a way of refusing an understanding of history as driven by the will/actions of determined individuals. Clooney plays a similar character in *Syriana* and *Michael Clayton*, both of which seek to reveal how structural forces will determine the actions of individuals trying to challenge the system. That Geismer is shown to be naïve and ineffectual and to lack agency stresses how historical forces are paramount and that any account of events that foregrounds the experience of the individual will inevitably be found lacking. In contrast to the famous final scene of *Casablanca* (1942), which the film recalls through strong intertextual referencing, the ending of *The Good German* has Geismer insisting that Lena leave alone (in the absence of a Victor Laszlo character, Geismer could accompany her), eschewing romance in favour of ethical judgement on what she has done. It is a bleak ending, with all characters seemingly helpless, unfulfilled and compromised in one way or another.

The Good German undertakes a wholesale revision of the dominant senses of World War II, doing so through its depiction of characters who even if seeking a moral course of action are unable to carry it through. Marianna Torgovnick argues that in the US context, any properly complex understanding of World War II has been replaced by a focus on a heroic narrative of D-Day and victory (2005: 6–8); alongside this, a simplified version of the Holocaust (constructed as a scenario of evil fascistic hatred overcome by freedom-loving liberal democracy) now forms 'a kind of citizenship for everyone after 1945' (2005: xii). For Torgovnick, as a result of this view of World War II, it has become likely and 'even logical, that we have difficulty imagining – steadily and unblinkingly – our nation in oppressive or even murderous roles' (2005: 9). It is this difficultly that *The Good German* seeks to address. It does this, first, by showing the US state undermining its own stated principles in a naked power struggle as former allies quickly become enemies, and, second, in the depiction of US characters who are shown to be evil and exploitative, and with no easy options available for those who wish to try to maintain some ethical stance in the face of this complex situation. The complex geopolitical allegiances and ethically fraught scenarios shown in *The Good German* serve to model the historical intricacies of self-interested US involvement in the Middle East (including financial and military support for a number of Middle Eastern states). Indeed, the film's revisionist view of World War II offers a model of history that helps us to understand the ways in which clandestine intervention (often once removed) shapes present and future events in complex and unpredictable ways.

While the opening sequences, and the care with which the story is meshed with actual historical events, suggest a realist aesthetic in play, the film, in fact, adopts a complex formal aesthetic through which to explore this view of history. It is careful in its recreation of the black-and-white cinematography associated with films of the period in which it is set; indeed, the filmmakers used, where possible, 'vintage' equipment (uncoated 1940s lenses, boom microphones, and so on) and filmed everything in a stripped down 1940s-style studio. Techniques such as wipe dissolves, back-projection and model work all actively recall the classical Hollywood film style, as does the acting technique and use of expository voice-over. Thomas Newman (son of famed Hollywood composer Alfred Newman) crafted a 'score reminiscent of 1940s

Fig. 24: History and
intertextuality:
The Good German (2006)

film noir that was used to punctuate dramatic moments and in a way that called attention to itself' (Sprengler 2009: 166). Little attempt is made to smooth the segue from the black-and-white film footage (actually shot on colour film and stripped of colour in post-production) into the archival material, the ensuing disjunction serving to remind the viewer that the film is a constructed object.

There is also a strong intertextual dimension to the film. As already suggested, it self-consciously recalls but ultimately refuses the propagandist inclination of *Casablanca*, instead paying homage to the cynical and pessimistic tone of *The Third Man* (1949). In contrast to, say, *United 93*, which emulates news/*vérité* camera techniques to create a powerful reality effect, *The Good German* calls attention to the process of reproducing the style associated with an earlier period of filmmaking. The objective here appears to be to encourage the viewer to think about the relations between past and present, the world on screen and the world outside the cinema, in a dialectical way. The result is complex: the past is recalled as something real, imperative, dialectical, but there is also a careful commitment to reminding the viewer that they are watching a film as construct. Sprengler concludes that

> these visually distinctive oppositions between fact and fiction, past and present serve to remind viewers of the contemporary political lens that *The Good German* offers, one adept at exposing parallels between American involvement in each of the two conflicts [World War II and Iraq]. (2009: 169)

Many reviewers found in the film's style (and its failure to deliver an unqualified nostalgic experience) grounds for criticism. Sprengler, on the other hand, suggests that it is precisely the way in which the film's visual style 'puts the viewer at arm's length' and constitutes an 'intricate play of fact and fiction and past and present' that enables it to 'facilitate political critique' (2009: 212).

The Good German is indicative of how much of the initial clarity of purpose and strong public support that the 'greatest generation' interpretation of World War II had garnered in the immediate aftermath of 11 September had dissipated by 2005. For example, one appropriation of the *Ground Zero Spirit* photograph circulating on the web shows the flag-raisers working together to put in place a McDonald's sign, complete with Arabic script. The image suggests that the military campaign in Iraq is one of economic and cultural imperialism, and one with strong historical precedent.[50] Another indication of this critical historical perspective is the centrality of the flag-raising photograph to two films directed by Clint Eastwood, *Flags of Our Fathers* (2006) and *Letters from Iwo Jima* (2006). *Flags of Our Fathers* is a conventional war film in which the ferocious fighting on Iwo Jima, the raising of the flag and the Seventh War Loan bond drive are described from a US perspective. The film establishes a critical perspective through a focus on the story of Ira Hayes, a Native American flag-raiser who we see become victim to institutional and petty racism on his return to the US. The film also shows those directing the war to be cynical, hard-nosed and unsentimental, offering some corrective to the hagiography of the 'greatest generation' view of World War II. *Letters from Iwo Jima* is based on a bestselling collection of letters written by Japanese soldiers during the fighting on Iwo Jima. The Japanese see the flag being raised in the far distance and from their perspective the event is full of portent (gesturing to a future of defeat and humiliation). Through this scene, and the resolute focus on their experience, the film points to a different cultural perspective and in doing so inevitably casts the dominant senses of the flag-raising photograph in a new light. The crucial aspect here is recognition of the other, and the attempt to figure history from an alternative point of view.

Many of the films examined in this book have brought a revisionist history to bear on 9/11. In *25th Hour*, a personal history is unearthed and reckoned with in a way that requires dramatic change; in *Parallel Lines* a road trip is punctuated with stops at places with deep historical significance in relation to the US narrative of Manifest Destiny; in the conspiracy films a paranoid history comes to the fore, with the filmmakers seeking historical precedent in 'false-flag' operations such as the Reichstag fire, the Gulf of Tonkin incident, and so on; *Syriana* searches for a suitably complex style to depict the interplay of corporate, colonial and political histories as they shape geopolitical realities and narrow future possibility. These films can be situated alongside a wider cycle of historical films that might be said to display an interest in a darker, contingent and less self-regarding version of US history, including *The Assassination of Richard Nixon* (2004), *Kingdom of Heaven* (2005) and *Good Night, and Good Luck* (2005). Westerns such as *The Assassination of Jesse James by the Coward Robert Ford* (2007), *Appaloosa* (2008) and *Meek's Cutoff* (2010), as well as the western-influenced *No Country for Old Men* (2007), can also be read as revisiting the (mythic) past in order to critique the present. Douglas Kellner considers *There Will Be Blood* (2007) to be an important post-9/11 film, writing that the depiction of oil prospecting and evangelical Christianity in the early twentieth century 'attempts to get at the roots of American's malaise and madness and shows its problems rooted in its core institutions and values, ultimately providing a critical commentary on the contemporary moment' (2010: 15–16). We might also add the counter-factual documentary *Death of a President* (2006), shown on television in 2008, which reconstructs – via talking heads, archive footage, and so on – the imagined assassination of George W. Bush in 2007. This wider cycle, to which *The Good German* belongs, is evidence of how a critical response to 9/11 sought to draw attention to the ways in which historical complexity had been sacrificed to a reductive nationalist history underpinning the 'war on terror'.[51]

In the Bourne film series – *The Bourne Identity* (2002), *The Bourne Supremacy* (2004) and *The Bourne Ultimatum* (2007) – CIA agent Jason Bourne (Matt Damon) is an amnesiac spy who fights to break free from a corrupt CIA. The films initially suggest that his past is unsullied and that he is a principled person victim to government persecution. However, as the cycle plays out, Bourne's memory returns in the form of PTSD-style flashbacks (akin to those suffered by many characters in post-9/11 cinema). These flashbacks show political assassinations undertaken by Bourne, including those of US citizens, thereby turning the trauma trope into something more difficult and complex. The final scenes of *The Bourne Ultimatum* show that he volunteered to join a programme devoted to this clandestine, illegal intelligence work, thereby pointing to culpability, the refusal of deniability and a lack of closure: historical processes, the film suggests, that still have some way to run. As Vincent M. Gaine writes, 'the franchise does not present Bourne as a passive victim in his trauma but rather as at least partially responsible for what has happened to him' (2011: 161). The trilogy's narrative arc offers a corrective to the ideological direction of the therapy film (Bourne is not cured; instead he must learn to live with a murderous past that cannot be altered) and demands a return of history that will result in a reckoning with no easy answers. As Gaine notes,

> At the end of *Supremacy* [Bourne] apologizes to Irena Neski (Oksana Akinshina) for killing her parents. His apology is futile and pathetic, and crucially so; he cannot be absolved for what he did, but he can accept shame ... and he can *live* with that shameful knowledge. Similarly, we, the Western viewing and voting public, can regard 9/11 and the war on terror as something we have nothing to do with, or we can regard ourselves as bearing some responsibility for what our leaders do, and act against them through democratic processes. (2011: 163)

Although commercial demands require that Bourne escape rather than stand trial for his crimes, moral quandary remains: might the series have been called 'The Good American'? It is significant, perhaps, that a further instalment, *The Bourne Legacy* (2012), steps back in time to replay the same scenario, this time experienced by other agents in the programme, suggesting a certain failure to find, but desire to have, closure.

In the introduction I described how in the immediate aftermath of 9/11, *The Quiet American* had its release date held back. The complex view of history offered in this film, with US-sanctioned terrorism shown as an integral part of an imperialist foreign policy, was deemed unsuited to the prevailing climate of jingoistic nationalism. Instead, dominant discourse ceded to the kind of mythologised view of World War II found in films like *Pearl Harbor*. Yet by mid-decade, following abortive wars in Afghanistan and Iraq and the scandal at Abu Ghraib prison, memories of the experience of the failed Vietnam War returned to public prominence. Aligned with anti-war activism, a number of new films were released, and older films re-purposed, to foster a critical historical consciousness. This cycle includes *The Fog of War* (2003), Errol Morris's searching interview with Robert McNamara (Secretary of Defense during the Vietnam War), the re-release of the anti-Vietnam War documentary *Hearts and Minds* (1974; 2009) and David Zeiger's *Sir! No Sir!* (2005), a history of anti-war mutinies within the military during the Vietnam era. Perhaps the most important re-release in 2005 was the documentary film *Winter Soldier*. Originally released in 1972, the film shows the 'Winter Soldier Investigation', an event staged by the Vietnam Veterans Against the War (VVAW) in which soldiers were invited to Detroit over a three-day period and asked to describe (and have recorded) the atrocities they had witnessed while on tours of duty in Vietnam. The events described included the torture and murder of enemy prisoners and the torture, rape and murder of Vietnamese civilians. The name of the hearings and the film's title refers to a soldier willing to patriotically defend their nation in the most dire and desperate of circumstances, and the phrase originates from a pamphlet written by Thomas Paine on 23 December 1776 that was designed to motivate the colonial militia in their fight against the British during the American Revolution. The soldiers who testified at the Winter Soldier Investigation and the VVAW organisers (including future presidential candidate John Kerry) believed themselves to be patriots, holding onto core principles of US national identity in the face of tyranny and corruption (with the US state now in the place of the British crown). The re-release of *Winter Soldier*, and the wider cycle of which it is part, sought to reveal how the 'war on terror' echoes and extends the experience of an earlier failed war, pointing to the way in which US foreign policy is driven by self-interest and runs counter to all stated moral principles and avowed reasons for intervention. The cycle also shows how resistance to the war requires acknowledgement of culpability in war crimes, structural critique of the state, a willingness to consider alternative viewpoints and a commitment to civil disobedience (burning of draft cards, mutinies within the military, testifying to atrocity, and so on).[52]

Set against this complex view of history, *The Path to 9/11*, a $30 million five-hour ABC television mini-series which aired on 10 and 11 September 2006, sought to provide a singular and orderly account of the history leading to the 9/11 attacks. The series shows a series of missed opportunities to tackle the terrorist threat resulting from inter-agency rivalry and a lack of political will, which it associates with the Clinton administration. The film's politics become clear in a scene where Condoleezza Rice (Penny Johnson), as a representative of the incoming Bush government, is briefed about the threat, and replies: 'We're on it.' Kellner objects to the series' clear separation of 'an incompetent Clinton administration and a resolute Bush-Cheney administration committed to fighting terrorism' (2010: 108). Indeed, the overly didactic and partisan tone of the series – set in stark relief against the more complex historical films described above – caused controversy, and as Thomas Riegler reports, 'the program became so discredited in the process that no DVD edition has yet been released' (2011: 160–1).

Against this backdrop of a cycle of films that seek historical complexity there was some cause to presume that *Zero Dark Thirty*, which recounts the hunt for, and killing of, Osama bin Laden, would retain a critical historical consciousness. Unlike *United 93* and *World Trade Center*, which revisited the attacks with some historical distance but constructed 9/11 as a hemmed-in and ahistorical experience, *Zero Dark Thirty*'s account of the CIA's decade-long hunt for Bin Laden does have significant historical scope. The film also brings together (in ways superficially comparable to *Syriana* and *Rendition*) a range of locations, including torture chambers at 'black sites' around the world, well-appointed CIA briefing rooms in Washington, DC, embattled US military bases in Afghanistan and bustling, dangerous Pakistani cities. In its ambitious timescale and global coverage the film appears to offer a definitive summation of a complex and contested history.

However, although the film is a detailed 'procedural' seemingly interested in the particularity of the CIA's post-9/11 work, a complex account of history is not forthcoming. In the opening sequence we hear audio recordings made during the 9/11 terrorist attacks, including radio chatter from first responders and a harrowing telephone call made by a woman trapped in the World Trade Center who states that she is being consumed by flames before the line goes dead. The next scene shows CIA investigators Dan (Jason Clarke) and Maya (Jessica Chastain) torturing a terrorist, seeking information about the Saudi Group and the whereabouts of Bin Laden. This transition (two years in real time; two seconds of screen time) establishes a direct connection between terrorist atrocity and an unbridled CIA response, leading Manohla Dargis to argue that the film here asserts 'a cause and effect relationship between the void of September 11 voices and the lone man strung up in a cell' (2012). In historical terms, the edit elides two years in which, as this book has clearly indicated, critique, contradiction and political struggle were predominant in the wider culture, especially with regard to the 'war on terror' and the legality of the use of torture.

In an extended analysis in the *New York Review of Books*, Steve Coll (2013) describes how the film's wider narrative suggests that torture was imperative in securing the information that led to the tracking down of Bin Laden. Coll notes that the film shows how the most important leads come from al-Qaida prisoner Ammar (Reda Kateb), who is subjected to prolonged torture (as shown in the opening sequence). Although Ammar initially resists, while he is in a physically and psychologically traumatised state he is tricked into believing he has confessed, and thereby unwittingly confirms intelligence that leads to the identification of an al-Qaida courier, known by the alias Abu Ahmed al-Kuwaiti. Using this information the CIA trace al-Kuwaiti to Abbottabad and then to Bin Laden. Some critics point to the fact that Ammar 'confesses' only when the torture stops, but Coll argues that torture, trickery and reconciliation (the interrogators are kind to Ammar) are shown to be a 'joined up' strategy, with each part ineffective without the other. Later in the film Maya gleans further leads from videotaped interrogations of a number of prisoners who bear the marks of torture. This is followed by two interviews conducted by Maya: one in which a prisoner talks, claiming that he does not wish to be tortured again (the threat of torture proving enough to elicit his cooperation); the second with Abu Faraj al-Libi, an al-Qaida operations leader, which results in no information, even under torture (the only such case in the film). Coll concludes that 'in virtually every instance in the film where Maya extracts important clues from prisoners … torture is a factor' (2013). Hence, while beatings, waterboarding, sexual humiliation and the use of stress positions are shown in some detail, the work of torture is also shown to be conducted with professionalism and intellectual purpose by highly qualified CIA operatives (we even learn that Dan holds a PhD). Although torture is unpleasant, the film says, it is necessary, it is undertaken professionally and it pays dividends.

Like the causality and historical elision stressed in the opening sequence, the depiction of torture in *Zero Dark Thirty* differs from the sadistic and counter-productive actions described in *Standard Operating Procedure*, *Taxi to the Dark Side* and *Rendition*. The film runs counter to what, by mid-decade, had become a truism: torture does not work. As the films described in chapter seven indicate, torture is largely ineffective because, as Darius Rejali observes in an exhaustive study, its use inculcates 'organizational decay [with] torturers tend[ing] to disobey orders and regulations' and 'induces false positives [while burying] interrogators in useless information' (2007: 500). Indeed, the efficacy of torture has even been denied by (then) acting CIA director Michael Morell, who wrote to agency employees following the release of *Zero Dark Thirty* to state that such an 'impression is false'.[53] Morell's views were consonant with the wider political establishment, with the

> Senate Intelligence Committee Chairman Dianne Feinstein and the two senior members of the Armed Services Committee, Democrat Carl Levin and Republican John McCain, similarly co-author[ing] a letter stating that the film would 'shape American public opinion in a disturbing and misleading manner'. (Coll 2013)

Against these (relatively conservative) markers of the received wisdom on the use of torture, *Zero Dark Thirty* arguably articulates an ideological position on torture that is consonant with that advocated by Bush and his policymakers in the immediate aftermath of 9/11. As such, the film is engaged in

Fig. 25: Embedded filmmaking: *Zero Dark Thirty* (2012)

historical revision, undoing a complex view and returning to a simplistic description of events.

The clear causal logic shaping the film's narrative structure reinforces this straightforward account of history. After 9/11, Maya is posted to the US embassy in Islamabad, Pakistan, where she begins her investigation. While at work there she learns of a terrorist attack on the Khobar Towers residential complex in Saudi Arabia. In 2004, as the investigation shifts its focus to a terrorist named Abu Ahmed, Maya travels to a 'black site' in Gdansk, Poland, and to Bagram Airbase in Afghanistan, where she oversees further interrogations. We see her watching the 2005 7/7 attacks in London being reported on the news. In 2008 back in Islamabad, Maya, and fellow CIA investigator Jessica (Jennifer Ehle), are caught up in a bomb attack at the Marriott hotel. In 2009, Jessica makes contact with a source that has infiltrated a terrorist cell in the tribal territories in Northern Pakistan. In a meeting at Camp Chapman in Afghanistan the source detonates a bomb, killing Jessica and six other CIA operatives. In response, Maya redoubles her efforts, and a covert surveillance operation in Rawalpindi and Peshawar leads her to Bin Laden's suspected hiding place in Abbottabad. As this plot summary indicates, the film's neat chapter-like structure intercuts terrorist attacks and the CIA's response (one provoking the other), showing agents (and society) under constant threat and driven by the imperatives of professional obligation, self-defence and a desire for justice. Although *Zero Dark Thirty* is superficially similar in style to *Syriana* and *Rendition* in its mapping of an array of global locations, the historically clear relation between the work of the CIA and imminent and ongoing threats (between us and them) in the film is actually in marked distinction. Unlike these films, where relations are complex, *Zero Dark Thirty* maintains the clarity of the classical narrative structure, thereby bringing a purifying coherence to the chaos and contingency of past events.

Maya is central to this resetting and re-establishing of a more orderly account of the recent past. The film shows the work of tracing Bin Laden as an almost single-handed quest and hints at some kind of providence at work; after Jessica is killed by a suicide bomber, Maya states: 'I believe I was spared so I could finish the job. I'm going to smoke everybody involved. And then I'm going to kill Bin Laden.' In a key scene, the Navy SEAL team tasked with killing Bin Laden are at first cynical about their mission but Maya's self-confidence provides a palliative for their experience of failed wars in Afghanistan and Iraq (which are otherwise completely elided). Frustrated by a risk-averse CIA and White House, Maya hectors her managers: when a CIA investigator states that he is only 60 per cent certain that the intelligence is accurate because it was obtained, in part, as a result of torture, Maya responds that she is 100 per cent certain (sardonically downgrading her estimate to 95 per cent to reassure those around her who can't handle such certainty). Through sheer force of personality, then, Maya prevails. Here the film provides a stark contrast to the ineffectual central protagonists of *Syriana* or *The Good German* and the Iraqis living in poverty in *Iraq in Fragments*. Maya's absolute focus also leaves no space to articulate the points of view of the terrorist prisoners or suspected terrorists. This reclamation of agency and extreme 'sidedness' – also in stark contrast to the ways in which a number of films in this book have sought to accommodate difference – leads Michael Atkinson to label *Zero Dark Thirty* 'the definitive 21st-century Asymmetrical War Film' (2013) and Peter Maas to suggest that it is an example of 'embedded filmmaking' (2012).

Realised by another actor (say, Tom Cruise), the kind of unwavering self-belief displayed by Maya may not have convinced. However, the casting of Chastain (her Pre-Raphaelite looks, bone china complexion and watery gaze) and her understated performance (in which these physical attributes are shown to belie a ferocious sense of purpose) create a more complex image, which permits a convergence of seemingly incompatible points of view. In the film's final scene Maya boards a cargo plane and is asked: 'Where do you want to go?' The question remains unanswered, and the final shot has her in tears. Dargis calls the ending 'non-triumphant', with the viewer left to 'decide if the death of bin Laden was worth the price we paid' (2012). Similarly, John Powers observes that the shot connotes 'exhaustion, melancholy and uncertainty' (2013). The purported uncertainty and ambiguity is taken here to be a marker of the film's recognition that 9/11 has shaped a contingent, divisive and painful period of history. However, in keeping with many of the films described in this book, it would perhaps be more accurate to see Maya's suffering (she has no friends and no relationships; her heart bleeds) as the way in which the description of the CIA as a capable and just institution is achieved. Through what Steven Shaviro calls 'Maya's passion', sympathy is elicited for the traumatic experience suffered by those fighting the 'war on terror', thereby placing CIA agents in the role of victim (2013). As such, through the ambiguity of Maya's character the film renews faith in an institution subject to considerable and legitimate criticism in the preceding decade. At the film's close Bin Laden is killed in a shadowy room. This sequence eschews first-person-shooter suspense, gung-ho dialogue and action film heroics for a more prosaic account that is detailed and suspenseful, but even though it is presented in a non-glorified way, the fact remains that the mission has been successful: Bin Laden is dead. The point of view here remains with Maya, who oversees the raid, watching remotely. Here substituting for Barack Obama and Hillary Clinton watching anxiously from the White House, Maya's is a feminine, qualified viewpoint mediating a hard-nosed act of political assassination.

Described by the *New York Times* film reviewer Dargis as 'the most important American fiction film about September 11' (2012), *Zero Dark Thirty*'s reception was polarised. A number of commentators found merit in the film's unflinching depiction of torture, the acknowledgement of the personal sacrifices made by CIA investigators and a recognition of the dislocation between the killing of Bin Laden and the continued terrorist threat (see Dargis 2012; Vishnevetsky 2012; James 2013; Powers 2013). Others, aligned with the analysis presented above, felt the film endorsed torture and functioned as an apologia for the war on terror (see Maas 2012; Atkinson 2013; Chen 2013; Coll 2013; Shaviro 2013; Zizek 2013). Here *Zero Dark Thirty* demonstrates the way in which post-9/11 cinema draws, sustains and seeks to reconcile markedly different political positions. The film is, on the one hand, readable as embodying a left-liberal sensibility: as Nick James argues, *Zero Dark Thirty* 'portrays the pursuit of bin Laden as a pyrrhic victory, gained by immoral means, and ... the weight of every violent action is felt to an unusual degree' (2013: 9). On the other, these aspects of the film are overlaid with the redemptive mechanisms of a conventional structure, a curtailed version of history, a rigorously unilateral and sympathetic point of view and, ultimately, closure. Once again, an example of post-9/11 cinema indicates how seemingly irreconcilable views of 9/11 are drawn together in alignment with a hegemonic historical revision that, while acknowledging some ambiguity, restores credibility for US national identity as a whole. The image that illustrates the cover of this book actively seeks to distance Maya from the obvious connotations of the US flag; this is not a jingoistic image. And yet her image also makes of the flag a palimpsest. As Maya retains audience sympathy so too does the flag and the myriad nationalist discourses it signifies. Following Abu Ghraib and all else, the meaning of the Stars and Stripes is here acknowledged as unstable and marked by contested and complex histories but, at the same time, is made subject (via the cinema) to a process of recuperation.

****

A number of scholars have looked at the same corpus of films and similar research questions to the ones addressed in this book, and drawn different conclusions. Douglas Kellner argues that post-9/11 cinema precipitated the shift from the neoconservatism of the Bush-Cheney administration to the social liberalism of Barack Obama, a redemptive narrative arc in which 9/11 (eventually, via processes of cultural struggle) results in progressive political change (2010: 3). Stephen Prince is more sceptical, arguing that 'popular genres in film and television readily absorbed 9/11 context as background material inflecting a storyline' without ever fully addressing the complexity of the event (2009: 304). Prince claims that only the documentary films have value for those seeking to properly understand 9/11 (2009: 306). David Holloway uses the term 'allegory-lite' to describe the way post-9/11 feature films graft on elements of the experience of the attacks to give otherwise unremarkable films emotional power (2008: 158). Yet these accounts feel reductive: Kellner's bracketing of films into two distinct political groups is too simple. Neoconservative responses were actively resisted from 11 September 11 2001 onwards, while many of the seemingly left-liberal films celebrated by Kellner have been shown to err away from critique in search of consensus and hegemonic renewal. Prince's simple feature-film-bad/documentary-film-good polarisation is unsustainable in the face of the range and variety of post-9/11 nonfiction filmmaking, with *9/11* and *In Memoriam* serving as examples of documentaries that describe 9/11 via dominant discourse. Films such as *The Mist* and *The Good German* which address 9/11

Fig. 26: Convergence and hegemony: *Parallel Lines* (2004)

indirectly but do so in provocative ways and with lasting political consequences belie Holloway's claim that the use of allegory in post-9/11 cinema
is loose and opportunist.

This picture is, inevitably, more complex. Post-9/11 cinema can be grouped
according to distinct political positions, with some films echoing and amplifying the hegemonic view and others engaging in critique. Thus a number
of parallel lines can be traced: a banal 'Americans all' patriotism (*9/11, In
Memoriam*) running alongside an engagement with questions of social class
and ethnic diversity (*7 Days in September, Parallel Lines, 25th Hour*); the use
of revenge (and religious discourse) to justify a call to war (*Man on Fire*) but
also the identification of revenge as necessitating 'ethical exchange' (*Mystic
River*); the celebration of American exceptionalism (*In Memoriam, DC 9/11:
Time of Crisis, World Trade Center*) placed alongside an insistence that the
US is already and irrecoverably entangled with other nations and peoples in
often unexceptional ways (*Rendition, Iraq in Fragments, The Good German*);
a year zero approach to history and politics (*World Trade Center, United 93*)
alongside a sense of how the past informs the present in complex and contradictory ways (*Parallel Lines, The Good German, Winter Soldier*); a claim
that torture is valid and necessary (*Man on Fire, Zero Dark Thirty*) alongside
a critique of the ways in which illegal violence has been central to the 'war on

terror' (*Rendition*, *Standard Operating Procedure*). Alongside this cinema of political struggle, this book has also traced a group of films that are marked by the convergence, or coming together, of these parallel lines. *War of the Worlds*, *Extremely Loud and Incredibly Close*, *In the Valley of Elah* and *Zero Dark Thirty* seek, if not exactly consensus, at the very least a way of living with contradiction. Arguably the most influential examples of post-9/11 cinema, these films reveal how dynamic, flexible and ultimately stable the system and its related systems of representation are – and how important the cinema remains as a mechanism of hegemonic renewal. The 'parallel lines' referred to in this book's title signal both the cinema of opposing political viewpoints and the way in which certain films bring these viewpoints together, with the two versions of US national identity provoked by the crisis of 9/11 and its aftermath converging into one.

Notes

1   The deaths of the nineteen terrorists responsible for the attacks are not usually included in official figures.

2   The focus here is on US films and their relation to a US national context. This does not discount the possibility that the readings presented in this book may also serve to explain how these films shape culture and politics in different national contexts. However, wider claims of this sort would need to be treated on a case-by-case basis. Also, the avowed focus on US cinema should not be taken as a claim that this cinema has privileged status; a range of non-US film productions related to 9/11 are ably examined by other scholars (see Cilano 2009).

3   Cynthia Weber challenges the ways in which initiatives like the Bradley Project seek to neatly bracket American national identity; Weber has set up an archive of testimonies which evidence the difficulty of settling national identity (see Weber 2011).

4   Bill Maher, host of the show *Politically Incorrect* on US network/cable channel ABC, suggested that the terrorists' willingness to die for a cause they believed in meant that they did not merit the widely used descriptor 'coward'. Maher has claimed that as a result of this statement, and under pressure from advertisers including FedEx and Sears Roebuck, his contract was not renewed.

5   Suaret has made a number of films related to 9/11, including *Loss* (2002), *Billy Green 9/11* (2003) and *Collateral Damages* (2003).

6   To my knowledge, the only other filmmaker adding references to 9/11 to a film in the immediate aftermath of the attacks was Martin Scorsese, who placed the Twin Towers in the closing montage sequence of *Gangs of New York* (2002).

7   Intriguingly, the monologue (which appears in amended form in the novel) was taken out of the script at the request of Touchstone who felt it would make

Monty unsympathetic, only to be reinstated at Lee's insistence (see Massood 2003: 9).

8　In the photographs collected in *Aftermath* (Meyerowitz 2006) Ground Zero is subject to a strongly materialist scrutiny alive to the ways in which a symbolic register might be used to convey a critical and complex sense of what has happened. Here the process of making the site safe and clearing up the rubble is shown as laborious hard work, not heroism, and photographs such as the one showing a batch of retrieved weapons, including World War II machine guns, are thought-provoking and complex.

9　The only person to vote against the resolution was Congresswoman Barbara Lee. In 2012, the *Guardian* newspaper website published an interview in which Lee explained the reasons behind her decision.

10　At the time of the film's release this was claimed to be the only film footage of the first plane strike. It is undoubtedly the best-quality footage, but a video shot by Pavel Hlava and a sequence of still frames taken by Wolfgang Staehle also recorded the event. Conspiracy theories related to 9/11 often question the provenance of this piece of footage, especially how Naudet was able to react so quickly to the plane's approach and the way some formal elements of the photograph such as the shadows don't correspond to the position of the sun.

11　McNally's photographs were published in two *Time/Life* books (Sullivan 2001; Editors of *Life* 2002) and appear in other commemorative collections that celebrate the role of the emergency services (Sweet 2002; Smith 2002).

12　To better fit this prevailing ideological discourse, plans for a statue modelled on the *Ground Zero Spirit* photograph proposed to show the flag being raised by a Hispanic-American, an African-American and an Anglo-American firefighter.

13　*Man on Fire*'s director, Tony Scott, also made *Déjà Vu* (2006), which describes a terrorist bombing and the use of sophisticated surveillance technology in order to shift time so that the attack can be prevented. The film's themes were deemed by many to be informed by the events of 9/11.

14　With hindsight, it became clear that many details surrounding Lynch's capture and rescue (including accusations that she had been sexually assaulted) were intentionally manipulated to conform to the captivity narrative; indeed, Lynch herself has been vocal in disputing some of the facts in her 'authorised' biography (see Martyn 2008: 124–64).

15　The Dakota Fanning character is the daughter of a white American woman who is married to a Mexican man. No explanation is given to indicate how this mixed-race relationship resulted in a child with such light colouring.

16　An irony here is that Brian Helgeland, who wrote the script for *Man on Fire*, also adapted the screenplay for *Mystic River*. Helgeland's *Man on Fire* script retained the Italian setting of the source novel, but Tony Scott insisted the action be moved to Mexico (where the film was shot on location) in order to avoid the film feeling like a 'period piece', a decision that clearly 'raced' the final film and

Notes

brought it in line with the framework of the captivity narrative.

17   *The Brave One*, which depicts a female vigilante figure, might be considered a partial exception.

18   The full reach of the agencies empowered by this legislation – as well as the widespread abuse of surveillance technology – would not be fully known until some years later. See, for example, 'The NSA Files' on the website of the British newspaper, the *Guardian*.

19   Mark Wheeler offers snapshots of the political commitments of a number of Hollywood politicos, including Lionel Chetwynd, who is co-chair of the Wednesday Morning Club, a regular informal gathering where Hollywood's conservatives meet with Republican leaders (2006: 154).

20   *9/11: Press for Truth* (2006) is a film based on Paul Thompson's detailed timeline compiled from mainstream news sources. Like *Fahrenheit 9/11*, the film often appears on lists of conspiracy films, though Stephen Prince objects to such classification and argues that the film 'does not proffer a conspiracy theory of the attacks; instead, it argues that much has been covered up, denied, or obfuscated' (2009: 150). The film is also notable for the appearance of the 'Jersey Girls', four women from New Jersey whose husbands were killed on 9/11, and who were instrumental in pressing for the 9/11 Commission to be formed, as well as subjecting the investigation to intense scrutiny (protesting the appointment of Henry Kissinger as chair, for example) (see Olmsted 2009: 214–17).

21   Another conspiracy theory has it that no Jewish people were killed in the attack and that the attacks were the work of Mossad, though racist scapegoating of this sort rarely appears in the popular web films/documentaries.

22   In his book *Counterknowledge*, Damian Thompson (2008) argues that the wider political culture has failed to maintain adequate standards of empirical, rational, logical reasoning, which have been degraded under exposure to 'non-empirical, non-rational, illogical reasoning or counter-knowledge'; (see debates over intelligent design, the MMR vaccine, and so on).

23   *The Complete 911 Timeline* is available on the History Commons website.

24   The different versions of *Loose Change* do pull away from the more outlandish conspiracy theories, and this trajectory towards more plausible accounts can also be seen in the different iterations of the three web films *Zeitgeist: The Movie* (2007), *Zeitgeist: Addendum* (2008) and *Zeitgeist: Moving Forward* (2011).

25   There is a range of post-9/11 conspiracy films whose titles refer to the feature film *V for Vendetta* (2005), including *Vendetta 9/11*; *Vendetta: Past, Present and Future*; *Remember, Remember, the 11th of September*; and *V for Vendetta Goes to Washington*. These films, which have disparate release dates and exist in numerous versions, and the wearing of the masks worn by the central character at political demonstrations, indicate how a political anger related to 9/11 has been extended to a wide range of political issues, from anti-globalisation to the Arab Spring.

26 I am grateful to Sebastian Horn, who gave a paper on *Syriana* at the 'Screens of Terror' conference at Southbank University in 2010. Horn's elegant plot summary provided a basis for my more prosaic account here.

27 The released version ends with the more sober 'dedicated to the memory of all those who lost their lives on September 11th, 2001'.

28 The exploitation film *Stairwell: Trapped in the World Trade Center* (2002) was not given a theatrical release, indicating the difficulty of directly depicting events. The film used footage shot for the film *Hellevator* (1999) about the 1993 World Trade Center bombing.

29 *In Memoriam*, which includes shots of falling people and an image of a dead body on the ground, is an exception here. In *DC 9/11: Time of Crisis*, a key scene shows George W. Bush visiting a hospital containing burn victims and amputees. Here serious injury is seen to justify retributive political policymaking in the lead-up to the wars in Afghanistan and Iraq. Brottman (2004) notes that there was an appetite for these images, with the website Ogrish.com (no longer accessible) showing film of people falling from the towers and body parts.

30 David Holloway argues that the same tendencies can be found in collections of photographs related to 9/11 (see 2008: 131–2).

31 Other cycles of post-9/11 films have been read allegorically, including the superhero film (see Faludi 2007; Pollard 2011) and the horror film (see Maddrey 2004; Magistrale 2005; Blake 2008; Briefel and Miller 2011; Wetmore 2012).

32 Here the film is ostensibly faithful to the source novel. Iain Johnstone, for example, observes that Wells considered *War of the Worlds* to be a critical comment on British foreign policy, especially the wholesale extermination of the people of Tasmania (see 2007: 307).

33 A child abduction/child abuse cycle, including *Keane* (2004), *Flightplan* (2005), *Freedomland* (2006), *The Changeling* (2008) and *Gone Baby Gone* (2007), can be read as a similar, and connected, allegorical response to 9/11.

34 This highly religious worldview also gives rise to what has been called a New Atheism that is associated with the work of Richard Dawkins (2006) and Christopher Hitchens (2007), among others.

35 A number of therapists were concerned about funding being diverted from projects helping poor people and/or children with mental health issues (see Seeley 2008: 156).

36 It is said that the images of a falling man (which appear as pictures in Foer's novel) are modelled on photographer Lyle Owerko's photographs, but they are also very similar to the better-known photographs by Richard Drew that came to public prominence after the book's publication.

37 On IMDb it is claimed that an early draft of the script had Oskar's grandfather regaining his ability to speak at the end of the film, something that would have made the film's redemptive arc even more pronounced. The hesitation indicated by the decision not to use this version recognises that such clear-cut resolution

Notes

requires further ideological work.

38　The television series *Rescue Me* (2004–11) undertakes an extended examination of PTSD resulting from the experience of 9/11 – the central character is haunted by those killed on 9/11, literally so – and in seasons 1 and 2 any therapeutic solutions are treated with considerable scepticism. In the difficult-to-categorise *Live from Shiva's Dancefloor* (2003), directed by Richard Linklater, avant-garde New York tour guide Timothy 'Speed' Levitch is shown responding to 9/11 via a New Age therapeutic philosophy. His suggestion that Ground Zero be made into a nature reserve for buffalo is indicative of the film's irreverent and distinctive take.

39　The bear-trap scene appears in flashback in *Saw* to provide backstory for a female protagonist, and the scenario was used to make a short film, subsequently titled *Saw 0.5*, which is available on YouTube.

40　Though, as with *Syriana*, there is a danger here of relying on the over-simplifying left-liberal presumption that poverty is the crucible of terrorism when, in fact, the majority of 9/11 terrorists were not from socially deprived backgrounds.

41　Philip Gourevitch and Errol Morris produced a book to accompany *Standard Operating Procedure* (Gourevitch and Morris 2008), as well as writing an extensive blog for the *New York Times*.

42　The television series *Battlestar Galactica* (2004–09) is often contrasted with *24* as offering a nuanced exploration of the torture debate (see Goulart and Wesley 2008).

43　The 2008 *Report of the Senate Armed Services Committee, Inquiry into the Treatment of Detainees in U.S. Custody*, is 232 pages long with 1,800 footnotes. *The Torture Papers* (2005) contains 1,249 pages of documents (Greenberg and Dratel 2005). The Torture Archive, which sponsored the film *Torturing Democracy* (2008), has a website that includes a searchable database of more than 7,000 original documents, running to over 100,000 pages.

44　The war in Afghanistan has not been so widely covered by US documentary filmmakers, though *Restrepo* (2010) is worthy of note.

45　The perceived left-liberal bias of this first wave of documentaries in this cycle prompted the production of the avowedly right-wing documentary *Buried in the Sand: The Deception of America* (2004), which claims that the war in Iraq is a positive and moral intervention.

46　*Control Room* (2004), a documentary that shows al-Jazeera's reporting of the Iraq War, contains a scene in which a US military press officer realises, to his shame, that his shocked response to seeing images of dead American soldiers being broadcast is completely different from his less troubled response to seeing dead Iraqi children on screen.

47　Two US television series – *Over There* (2005) and *Generation Kill* (2008) – and two British films – *Battle for Haditha* (2007) and *The Mark of Cain* (2007) – are also set in Iraq and provide useful points of comparison. Fewer films represent the war in Afghanistan, examples including *Lions for Lambs* (2007), *The Objective* (2009) and *Brothers* (2009).

48 The political expediency of the PTSD paradigm can be seen in the decision not to extend such diagnosis (and attendant resources) to those caught in war zones in Afghanistan, Iraq and elsewhere (see Fassin and Rechtman 2009: 282). PTSD is a resolutely American condition, something confirmed by the depiction of US UAV/drone operators as the latest group to suffer PTSD (in *5000 Feet Is the Best* (2011), for example).

49 David Holloway provides an excellent and succinct summary of the main frameworks used by historians to understand 9/11 (see 2008: 7–31).

50 Micah Ian Wright's 'remixed' World War II propaganda encourages its viewers to be similarly sceptical of the way World War II was used to encourage support for the 'war on terror'.

51 The opening sequence of the HBO television series *John Adams* (2008) shows slaves tending the fields around the White House, and it is difficult to recall a corollary for this in pre-9/11 representation of US political history.

52 When in 2008 Iraq Veterans Against the War (IVAW) held their own 'Winter Soldier' hearings and over two hundred US soldiers, alongside numerous Iraqi and Afghan civilians, testified to their experiences of the war, the mainstream media did not cover the event. The hearings are available on YouTube and are transcribed in a single-volume book (Glantz 2008).

53 Morell's views are somewhat surprising considering that the CIA supported the film in numerous ways during its production (see Chen 2013).

Filmography

9/11 (Jules Naudet and Gedeon Naudet, 2002, US)

9/11: In Plane Sight (William Lewis, 2004, US)

9/11: Press for Truth (Ray Nowosielski, 2006, US)

11'09"01 September 11 (Alain Brigand, 2002, UK, France, Egypt, Japan, Mexico, US, Iran)

21 Grams (Alejandro González Iñárritu, 2003, US)

25th Hour (Spike Lee, 2002, US)

28 Weeks Later (Juan Carlos Fresnadillo, 2007, US)

102 Minutes That Changed the World (Nicole Rittenmeyer and Seth Skundrick, 2008, US)

2012: Doomsday (Nick Everhart, 2008, US)

All the President's Men (Alan J. Pakula, 1976, US)

Apocalypse Now (Francis Ford Coppola, 1979, US)

Appaloosa (Ed Harris, 2008, US)

The Assassination of Jesse James by the Coward Robert Ford (Andrew Dominik, 2007, US)

The Assassination of Richard Nixon (Niels Mueller, 2004, US)

The Avengers (Joss Whedon, 2012, US)

Badland (Francesco Lucente, 2007, US, Germany)

Battle for Haditha (Nick Broomfield, 2007, UK)

Behind Enemy Lines (John Moore, 2001, US)

Bereft (Timothy Daly and Clark Mathis, 2004, US)

Billy Green 9/11 (Etienne Sauret, 2003, US)

Black Hawk Down (Ridley Scott, 2002, US)

The Blood of My Brother (Andrew Berend, 2005, US, Iraq)

Bloody Sunday (Paul Greengrass, 2001, UK)

Parallel Lines

Blue Velvet (David Lynch, 1986, US)

Body of War (Phil Donahue and Ellen Spiro, 2007, US)

The Book of Eli (Albert Hughes and Allen Hughes, 2010, US)

The Bourne Identity (Doug Liman, 2002, US)

The Bourne Supremacy (Paul Greengrass, 2004, US)

The Bourne Ultimatum (Paul Greengrass, 2007, US)

The Brave One (Neil Jordan, 2007, US)

Broken Blossoms (D. W. Griffith, 1919, US)

Brothers (Jim Sheridan, 2009, US)

Buffalo Soldiers (Gregor Jordan, 2003, US)

Buried in the Sand: The Deception of America (David Wald, 2004, US)

Casablanca (Michael Curtiz, 1942, US)

Celsius 41.11: The Temperature at Which the Brain... Begins to Die (Kevin Knoblock, 2004, US)

The Changeling (Clint Eastwood, 2008, US)

Children of Men (Alfonso Cuarón, 2006, US)

Cloverfield (Matt Reeves, 2008, US)

Collateral Damage (Andrew Davis, 2002, US)

Collateral Damages (Etienne Sauret, 2003, US)

Coming Home (Hal Ashby, 1978, US)

Conspiracy (Adam Marcus, 2008, US)

The Constant Gardener (Fernando Meirelles, 2005, UK, Germany, US, China)

Control Room (Jehane Noujaim, 2004, US)

The Count of Monte Cristo (Kevin Reynolds, 2002, US)

DC 9/11: Time of Crisis (Brian Trenchard-Smith, 2003, US)

Death of a President (Gabriel Range, 2006, UK)

Death Sentence (James Wan, 2007, US)

Death Wish (Michael Winner, 2004, US)

Death Wish 2 (Michael Winner, 1982, US)

The Deer Hunter (Michael Cimino, 1978, US)

Deja Vu (Tony Scott, 2006, US)

Dirty Harry (Don Siegel, 1971, US)

The Elephant in the Room (Dean Puckett, 2008, UK, US, Netherlands, France)

The Exterminator (James Glickenhaus, 1980, US)

Extremely Loud and Incredibly Close (Stephen Daldry, 2011, US)

Fahrenheit 9/11 (Michael Moore, 2004, US)

Fair Game (Doug Liman, 2010, US)

Fear X (Nicolas Winding Refn, 2003, US)

Five Fingers (Laurence Malkin, 2006, US)

Flags of Our Fathers (Clint Eastwood, 2006, US)

Flight 93 (Peter Markle, 2006, US)

Flight 93: The Flight That Fought Back (Bruce Goodison, 2005, US)

Filmography

Flightplan (Robert Schwentke, 2005, US)

The Fog of War (Errol Morris, 2003)

Freedomland (Joe Roth, 2006, US)

Gangs of New York (Martin Scorsese, 2002, US)

Ghosts of Abu Ghraib (Rory Kennedy, 2007, US)

Gone Baby Gone (Ben Affleck, 2007, US)

The Good German (Steven Soderbergh, 2006, US)

Good Night and Good Luck (George Clooney, 2005, US)

Grace Is Gone (James C. Strauss, 2007, US)

Gran Torino (Clint Eastwood, 2008, US)

Green Zone (Paul Greengrass, 2010, US)

The Guys (Jim Simpson, 2002, US)

The Hills Have Eyes (Wes Craven, 1972, US)

Home of the Brave (Irvin Winkler, 2007, US)

Hostel (Eli Roth, 2005, US)

The Hurt Locker (Kathryn Bigelow, 2008, US)

I Am Legend (Frances Lawrence, 2007, US)

Imaginary Heroes (Dan Harris, 2004, US)

In Memoriam: New York City, 9/11/01 (Brad Grey, 2002, US)

In the Bedroom (Todd Field, 2001, US)

In the Cut (Jane Campion, 2003, US)

In the Valley of Elah (Paul Haggis, 2007, US)

The Interpreter (Sydney Pollack, 2005, US)

The Invasion (Oliver Hirschbiegel, 2007, US)

Iraq in Fragments (James Longley, 2006, US)

Iron Man (Jon Favreau, 2008, US)

Keane (Lodge Kerrigan, 2004, US)

The Kingdom (Peter Berg, 2007, US)

Kingdom of Heaven (Ridley Scott, 2005, US)

Knowing (Alex Proyas, 2009, US)

Last Hour of Flight 11 (David Hickman, 2004, US)

The Last House on the Left (Wes Craven, 1972, US)

Law Abiding Citizen (F. Gary Gray, 2009, US)

Left Behind (Vic Sarin, 2000, US)

Left Behind II: Tribulation Force (Bill Corcoran, 2002, US)

Left Behind: World at War (Craig R. Baxley, 2005, US)

Legion (Scott Stewart, 2010, US)

Let's Roll: The Story of Flight 93 (Chris Oxley, 2002, US)

Letters from Iwo Jima (Clint Eastwood, 2006, US)

Lions for Lambs (Robert Redford, 2007, US)

Live from Shiva's Dance Floor (Richard Linklater, 2003, US)

Loose Change: Final Cut (Dylan Avery, 2007, US)

Parallel Lines

Loose Change 9/11: An American Coup (Dylan Avery, 2009, US)

Loss (Etienne Sauret, 2002, US)

The Lucky Ones (Neil Burger, 2008, US)

The Magnificent Seven (John Sturges, 1960, US)

Man on Fire (Tony Scott, 2004, US)

Margaret (Kenneth Lonergan, 2011, US)

Memento (Christopher Nolan, 2000, US)

Men in Black 2 (Barry Sonnenfeld, 2002, US)

Michael Clayton (Tony Gilroy, 2007, US)

A Mighty Heart (Michael Winterbottom, 2007, US, UK)

The Mist (Frank Darabont, 2007, US)

Munich (Steven Spielberg, 2005, US)

The Murder of Steven Lawrence (Paul Greengrass, 1999, US)

My Country, My Country (Laura Poitras, 2006, US)

Mystic River (Clint Eastwood, 2003, US)

Night of the Living Dead (George A. Romero, 1968, US)

No Country for Old Men (Joel Cohen and Ethan Cohen, 2007, US)

No End in Sight (Charles Ferguson, 2007, US)

Painful Deceptions (Eric Hufschmid, 2005, US)

Paisà (Roberto Rossellini, 1946, Italy)

The Parallax View (Alan J. Pakula, 1974, US)

Parallel Lines (Nina Davenport, 2004, US)

The Path to 9/11 (David L. Cunningham, 2006, US)

Pearl Harbor (Michael Bay, 2001, US)

People I Know (Dan Algrant, 2002, US)

The Punisher (Jonathan Hensleigh, 2004, US)

The Quiet American (Philip Noyce, 2002, US)

Rambo (Sylvester Stallone, 2008, US)

Rambo: First Blood (Ted Kotcheff, 1982, US)

Rambo: First Blood Part II (George P. Cosmatos, 1985, US)

Rambo III (Peter MacDonald, 1988, US)

The Reaping (Stephen Hopkins, 2007, US)

Redacted (Brian De Palma, 2007, US)

Reign over Me (Mike Binder, 2007, US)

Remember Me (Allen Coulter, 2010, US)

Rendition (Gavin Hood, 2007, US)

Restrepo (Sebastian Junger and Tim Hetherington, 2010, US)

Right at Your Door (Chris Gorak, 2006, US)

The Road (John Hillcoat, 2009, US)

Roger and Me (Michael Moore, 1989, US)

Roma, Città Aperta/Rome Open City (Roberto Rossellini, 1945, Italy)

Saving Jessica Lynch (Peter Markle, 2003, US)

Filmography

Saving Private Ryan (Steven Spielberg, 1998, US)

Saw (James Wan, 2004, US)

Saw 4 (Darren Lynn Bousman, 2007, US)

The Searchers (John Ford, 1956, US)

Serendipity (Peter Chelsom, 2002, US)

Seven Days in September (Steve Rosenbaum, 2002, US)

Shut Up and Sing (Barbara Kopple, 2006, US)

Sin City (Frank Miller and Robert Rodriguez, 2005, US)

Sir! No Sir! (David Zeiger, 2005, US)

The Situation (Philip Haas, 2007, US)

Slumdog Millionaire (Danny Boyle, 2008, UK)

Spider-Man (Sam Raimi, 2001, US)

Stairwell: Trapped in the World Trade Center (Jonathan M. Parisien, 2002, US)

Standard Operating Procedure (Errol Morris, 2008, US)

Stop-Loss (Kimberley Peirce, 2008, US)

Sudden Impact (Clint Eastwood, 1983, US)

The Sum of All Our Fears (Phil Alden Robinson, 2002, US)

Sweeney Todd (Tim Burton, 2007, US)

Syriana (Stephen Gaghan, 2005, US)

Taken (Pierre Morel, 2008, US)

Taking Chance (Ross Katz, 2009, US)

Taxi to the Dark Side (Ryan Gibney, 2007, US)

The Terminal (Steven Spielberg, 2004, US)

There Will Be Blood (Paul Thomas Anderson, 2007, US)

Three Days of the Condor (Sydney Pollack, 1975, US)

The Torture Question (Michael Kirk, 2005, US)

Torturing Democracy (Sherry Jones, 2008, US)

Traitor (Jeffrey Nachmanoff, 2008, US)

Uncovered: The War on Iraq (Robert Greenwald, 2004, US)

Underground Zero (Jay Rosenblatt and Caveh Zahedi, 2002, US)

United 93 (Paul Greengrass, 2006, US)

Unthinkable (Gregor Jordan, 2010, US)

The Upside of Anger (Mike Binder, 2005, US)

V for Vendetta (James McTeigue, 2005, US)

Voices of Iraq ('The people of Iraq', 2004, US)

War of the Worlds (Steven Spielberg, 2005, US)

The War Tapes (Deborah Scranton, 2006, US)

The War Within (Joseph Castelo, 2005, US)

We Were Soldiers (Randall Wallace, 2002, US)

Windtalkers (John Woo, 2002, US)

Winter Soldier (1972, US)

Winter Solstice (Josh Sternfeld, 2004, US)

Parallel Lines

World Trade Center (Oliver Stone, 2006, US)
WTC: The First 24 Hours (Etienne Sauret, 2001, US)
Zeitgeist: Addendum (Peter Joseph, 2008, US)
Zeitgeist: Moving Forward (Peter Joseph, 2011, US)
Zeitgeist: The Movie (Peter Joseph, 2007, US)
Zero Dark Thirty (Kathyrn Bigelow, 2012, US)

Bibliography

Abramowitz, Rachel (2005) 'Scared Silly', *The Los Angeles Times*. Available at: http://articles.latimes.com/2005/may/08/entertainment/ca-war8 (accessed 24 January 2014).

Alsultany, Evelyn (2007) 'Selling American Diversity and Muslim American Identity through Nonprofit Advertising Post-9/11', *American Quarterly*, 59, 3, 593–622.

Anderson, Benedict (1983) *Imagined Communities: Reflections on the Origin and Spread of Nationalism*. London: Verso.

Anon. (2001) 'The Return of Teach-ins'. *The New York Times*. Available at: http://www.nytimes.com/2001/10/21/opinion/the-return-of-teach-ins.html (accessed 24 January 2014).

Anon. (2003) 'Monty's Wake: A Spiky American Poet Sings for His Country'. *The Economist*. Available at: http://www.economist.com/node/1632168 (accessed 24 January 2014).

Anon. (2006) 'Bush "Inspires" Political Films', *BBC News*. Available at: http://news.bbc.co.uk/1/hi/entertainment/4661298.stm (accessed 24 January 2014).

Appelo, Tim (2012) '*Extremely Loud & Incredibly Close* Child Actor Discovered on Teen "Jeopardy!"'. Available at: http://www.hollywoodreporter.com/news/extremely-loud-incredibly-close-jeopardy-279802 (accessed 24 January 2014).

Aston, James (2008) 'Terrorist Attack!: The Spectacle of Evil in the Blended Horror of *Cloverfield*', *Scope*, 16, 1–21.

Atkinson, Michael (2005) 'Armageddon It', *Village Voice*. Available at: http://www.villagevoice.com/2005-06-21/film/armageddon-it/ (accessed 24 January 2014).

____ (2013) 'Duty Calls: *Zero Dark Thirty*', *Sight and Sound*. Available at: http://www.bfi.org.uk/news-opinion/sight-sound-magazine/features/duty-calls-zero-dark-thirty (accessed 24 January 2014).

Aufderheide, Patricia (2001) 'Therapeutic Patriotism and Beyond', *Television Archive*.

Available at: http://web.archive.org/web/20030417152041/http://www.televi-sionarchive.org/html/article_pa1.html (accessed 24 January 2013).

____ (2007) 'Your Country, My Country: How Films about the Iraq War Construct Publics', *Framework: The Journal of Cinema and Media*, 48, 2, 56–65.

____ (2008) 'Iraq in Fragments', *Visual Anthropology*, 21, 1, 92–3.

Austin, Thomas (2011) '*Standard Operating Procedure*, "the Mystery of Photography" and the Politics of Pity', *Screen*, 52, 3, 342–57.

Azcona, María del Mar (2010) *The Multi-Protagonist Film*. New York, NY: Wiley-Blackwell.

Bacevich, Andrew J. (2005) *The New American Militarism: How Americans Are Seduced by War*. Oxford: Oxford University Press.

Barker, Martin (2011) *A Toxic Genre: The Iraq War Films*. London: Pluto Press.

Barkun, Michael (2003) *A Culture of Conspiracy: Apocalyptic Visions in Contemporary America*. Berkeley, CA: University of California Press.

Barthes, Roland (1986) 'The Reality Effect', *The Rustle of Language*. Oxford: Blackwell, 141–8.

Beattie, Keith (1998) *The Scar That Binds: American Culture and the Vietnam War*. New York, NY: New York University Press.

Benjamin, Walter (1969) 'Theses on the Philosophy of History', *Illuminations*. London: Pimlico.

Benson-Allott, Caetlin (2009) '*Standard Operating Procedure*: Mediating Torture', *Film Quarterly*, 62, 4, 39–44.

Berman, Marshall (2002) 'When Bad Buildings Happen to Good People', Michael Sorkin and Sharon Zukin (eds.) *After the World Trade Center: Rethinking New York City*. New York, NY: Routledge, 1–12.

Bigsby, Christoper (ed.) (2006) *The Cambridge Companion to Modern American Culture*. Cambridge: Cambridge University Press.

Billig, Michael (1995) *Banal Nationalism*. London: Sage.

Birkenstein, Jeff, Anna Froula and Karen Randell (2010) *Reframing 9/11: Film, Popular Culture and the 'War on Terror'*. London: Continuum.

Blake, Linnie (2008) *The Wounds of Nations: Horror Cinema, Historical Trauma and National Identity*. Manchester: Manchester University Press.

Boal, Mark (2005) 'The Man in the Bomb Suit', *Playboy*, March.

____ (2007) 'The Real Cost of War', *Playboy*, March.

Bocock, Robert (1986) *Hegemony*. London: Tavistock.

Boggs, Carl and Tom Pollard (2007) *The Hollywood War Machine: US Militarism and Popular Culture*. Boulder, CO: Paradigm.

Bonevardi, Gustavo (2002) '"Tribute in Light" Explained'. *Slate*. Available at: http://slate.msn.com/?id=2063051 (accessed 24 January 2014).

Bordwell, David (2002) 'Intensified Continuity: Visual Style in Contemporary American Film', *Film Quarterly*, 55, 3, 16–28.

Brady, Jacqueline (2004) 'Cultivating Critical Eyes: Teaching 9/11 through Video and

Bibliography

Cinema', *Cinema Journal*, 43, 2, 96–9.

Braiker, Harriet B. (2002) *The September 11 Syndrome: Anxious Days and Sleepless Nights*. New York, NY: McGraw-Hill.

Brassett, James (2010) 'Cosmopolitan Sentiments after 9/11: Trauma and the Politics of Vulnerability', *Journal of Critical Globalisation Studies*, 2, 12–29.

Briefel, Aviva and Sam J. Miller (2011) *Horror After 9/11: World of Fear, Cinema of Terror*. Austin, TX: University of Texas Press.

Briley, Ron (2005) '*Fahrenheit 9/11*: Michael Moore Heats It Up', *Film and History*, 35, 2, 11–12.

Brottman, Mikita (2004) 'The Fascination of the Abomination: The Censored Images of 9/11', in Wheeler Winston Dixon (ed.) *Film and Television after 9/11*. Carbondale, IL: Southern Illinois University Press, 163–78.

Bruns, John (2008) 'The Polyphonic Film', *New Review of Film and Television Studies*, 6, 2, 189–212.

Burbach, Roger and Ben Clarke (2002) *September 11 and the US War: Beyond the Curtain of Smoke*. San Francisco: City Lights Books.

Burgoyne, Robert (2010) 'The Topical Historical Film: *United 93* and *World Trade Center*', *Film Nation: Hollywood Looks at US History*. Minneapolis, MN: University of Minnesota Press, 148–69.

Burrows, Edwin G. (2002) 'Manhattan at War', in Michael Sorkin and Sharon Zukin (eds) *After the World Trade Center: Rethinking New York City*. New York, NY: Routledge, 22–32.

Bush, George W. (2001) 'Address to a Joint Session of Congress and the American People'. *The White House Archives*. Available at: http://georgewbush-whitehouse.archives.gov/news/releases/2001/09/20010920-8.html (accessed 24 January 2014).

Butler, Judith (2004) *Precarious Life: The Powers of Mourning and Violence*. London: Verso.

____ (2009) *Frames of War: When Is Life Grievable?*. London: Verso.

Chen, Adrian (2013) 'Newly Declassified Memo Shows CIA Shaped *Zero Dark Thirty*'s Narrative', *Gawker*. Available at: http://gawker.com/declassified-memo-showshow-cia-shaped-zero-dark-thirty-493174407 (accessed 24 January 2014).

Cherry, Brigid (2009) *Horror*. London: Routledge.

Chiarella, Tom (2009) '*The Road* is the Most Important Movie of the Year', *Esquire*. Available at: http://www.esquire.com/features/movies/the-road-movie-review-0609 (accessed 24 January 2014).

Chomsky, Noam (2011) *9/11: Was There an Alternative?*. New York, NY: Seven Stories Press.

Chopra-Gant, Mike (2008) *Cinema and History: The Telling of Stories*. London and New York: Wallflower Press.

Cilano, Cara (2009) *From Solidarity to Schisms: 9/11 and After in Fiction and Film from Outside the US*. Amsterdam: Rodopi.

Clarke, Richard A. (2004) *Against All Enemies: Inside America's War on Terror*. New York, NY: Free.

Coll, Steve (2013) '"Disturbing" and "Misleading"', *New York Review of Books*. Available at: http://www.nybooks.com/articles/archives/2013/feb/07/disturbing-misleading-zero-dark-thirty/?pagination=false (accessed 24 January 2014).

Conrad, Peter (2002) 'The Presumption of Art'. *The Observer*. Available at: http://www.theguardian.com/world/2002/sep/08/september11.georgebush (accessed 24 January 2014).

Cooper, Mark (2001) 'Lights! Cameras! Attack! Hollywood Enlists'. *The Nation*. Available at: http://www.thenation.com/article/lights-cameras-attack-hollywood-enlists (accessed 24 January 2014).

Cousins, Mark (2006) 'Cinema Gets Real', *Prospect*. Available at: http://www.prospectmagazine.co.uk/magazine/cinemagetsreal/-.UuKF9PbFly4 (accessed 24 January 2014).

Craps, Stef (2007) 'Conjuring Trauma: The Naudet Brothers' 9/11 Documentary', *Canadian Review of American Studies*, 37, 2, 183–204.

Croft, Stuart (2006) *Culture, Crisis and America's War on Terror*. Cambridge: Cambridge University Press.

Dargis, Manohla (2012) 'By Any Means Necessary', *The New York Times*. Available at: http://www.nytimes.com/2012/12/18/movies/jessica-chastain-in-zero-dark-thirty.html (accessed 24 January 2014).

Davis, Darren and Brian Silver (2004) 'Americans' Perceptions of the Causes of Terrorism: Why Do They Hate Us?', paper presented at the Midwest Political Science Association Conference, Chicago, IL. Available at: https://www.msu.edu/~bsilver/RootsMarch25-Final.pdf (accessed 24 January 2014).

Dawkins, Richard (2006) *The God Delusion*. Leicester: W. F. Howes.

Dixon, Wheeler Winston (ed.) (2004) *Film and Television after 9/11*. Carbondale, IL: Southern Illinois University Press.

Doherty, Thomas (2007) 'Michael Moore's *Fahrenheit 9/11*: How One Film Divided a Nation', *Historical Journal of Film, Television and Radio*, 27, 3, 413–15.

Dower, John W. (2010) *Cultures of War: Pearl Harbor*. New York, NY: W. W. Norton.

Dwyer, Jim and Kevin Flynn (2005) *102 Minutes: The Untold Story of the Fight to Survive inside the Twin Towers*. London: Arrow.

Dyer, Richard (1993) 'A White Star', *Sight and Sound*, 3, 8, 22–4.

Eagleton, Terry (1991) *Ideology: An Introduction*. London: Verso.

Edelstein, David (2006) 'Now Playing at Your Local Multiplex: Torture Porn', *New York Magazine*. Available at: http://nymag.com/movies/features/15622/ (accessed 24 January 2014).

Editors (1972) 'John Ford's *Young Mr. Lincoln*: A Collective Text by the Editors of *Cahiers du cinema*', *Screen*, 13, 3, 5–44.

Editors (2005) 'Debunking the 9/11 Myths: Special Report – The World Trade

Bibliography

Center'. *Popular Mechanics*. Available at: http://www.popularmechanics.com/technology/military/news/debunking-911-myths-world-trade-center (accessed 24 January 2014).

Editors of *Life* (2002) *One Nation, America Remembers September 11*. New York, NY: Little, Brown.

Etzioni, Amitai (2004) *How Patriotic is the Patriot Act?: Freedom Versus Security in the Age of Terrorism*. London: Routledge.

Evans, Gareth (2002) 'Review: *Underground Zero*', *Sight and Sound*, 12, 8, 5.

Faludi, Susan (2007) *The Terror Dream: What 9/11 Revealed about America*. New York, NY: Atlantic Books.

Farber, Stephen (2005) '9/11 Is Sneaking on to a Screen Near You', *The New York Times*. Available at: http://www.nytimes.com/2005/03/13/movies/13farb.html (accessed 24 January 2014).

Fassin, Didier and Richard Rechtman (2009) *The Empire of Trauma: An Inquiry into the Condition of Victimhood*. Princeton, NJ: Princeton University Press.

Felperin, Leslie (2003) 'Interview: Spike Lee', *Sight and Sound*, 13, 4, 15.

Fetzer, James H. (ed.) (2007) *The 9/11 Conspiracy: The Scamming of America*. Chicago, IL: Catfeet Press.

Filkins, Dexter (2008) *The Forever War: Dispatches from the War on Terror*. New York, NY: Alfred A. Knopf.

Finn, Robin (2006) 'One to Watch: Playwright Ann Nelson', *New York Times*. Available at: http://www.nytimes.com/2006/02/26/theater/newsandfeatures/26finn.html?_r=0 (accessed 24 January 2014).

Friedman, Lester D. (2006) *Citizen Spielberg*. Chicago, IL: University of Illinois Press.

Froomkin, Dan (2005) 'Cheney's "Dark Side" is Showing', *Washington Post*. Available at: http://www.washingtonpost.com/wp-dyn/content/blog/2005/11/07/BL2005110700793.html (accessed 24 January 2014).

Gaine, Vincent M. (2011) 'Remember Everything, Absolve Nothing: Working through Trauma in the Bourne Trilogy', *Cinema Journal*, 51, 1, 159–63.

Gilbey, Ryan (2003) 'Review: *25th Hour*', *Sight and Sound*, 13, 3, 58.

____ (2006) 'Review: *Syriana*', *Sight and Sound*. Web. Available at: http://old.bfi.org.uk/sightandsound/review/3197 (accessed 24 January 2014).

Gitlin, Todd (1995) *The Twilight of Common Dreams: Why America is Wracked by Culture Wars*. New York, NY: Owl Books.

Glantz, Aaron (2008) *Winter Soldier, Iraq and Afghanistan: Eyewitness Accounts of the Occupation*. London: Haymarket.

Godard, François (2002) 'Canal Plus 9/11 Pic Courts Controversy'. *Variety*. Available at: http://variety.com/2002/film/news/canal-plus-9-11-pic-courts-controversy-1117871633/ (accessed 24 January 2014).

Goulart, Woody and Joe Y. Wesley (2008) 'Inverted Perspectives on Politics and Morality in *Battlestar Galactica*', in Donald M. Hassler and Clyde Wilcox (eds)

New Boundaries in Political Science Fiction. Columbia, SC: University of South Carolina Press, 179–97.

Gourevitch, Philip and Errol Morris (2008) *Standard Operating Procedure: A War Story*. London: Picador.

Grant, A. J. (2005) 'Ground Zero as Holy Ground and Prelude to Holy War', *Journal of American Culture*, 28, 1, 49–61.

Gray, Richard (2009) 'Open Doors, Closed Minds: American Prose Writing at a Time of Crisis', *American Literary History*, 21, 1, 128–48.

Gray, Richard J. (2011) *After the Fall: American Literature Since 9/11*. Oxford: Wiley-Blackwell.

Greenberg, Karen J. and Joshua L. Dratel (eds) (2005) *The Torture Papers: The Road to Abu Ghraib*. Cambridge: Cambridge University Press.

Griffin, David Ray (2008) *The New Pearl Harbor Revisited: 9/11, the Cover-Up, and the Exposé*. Moreton-in-Marsh: Arris.

Habermas, Jurgen, Jacques Derrida and Giovanna Borradori (2003) *Philosophy in a Time of Terror: Dialogues with Jurgen Habermas and Jacques Derrida*. Chicago, IL: University of Chicago Press.

Harvey, David (2002) 'Cracks in the Edifice of the Empire State', in Michael Sorkin and Sharon Zukin (eds) *After the World Trade Center: Rethinking New York City*. New York, NY: Routledge, 57–67.

Hersh, Seymour (2004a) 'Torture at Abu Ghraib', *The New Yorker*. Available at: http://www.newyorker.com/archive/2004/05/10/040510fa_fact (accessed 24 January 2014).

____ (2004b) *Chain of Command: The Road from 9/11 to Abu Ghraib*. New York, NY: HarperCollins.

Heyen, William (2002) *September 11, 2001: American Writers Respond*. Silver Springs, MD: Etruscan Press.

Hitchens, Christopher (2007) *The Portable Atheist: Essential Readings for the Nonbeliever*. Philadelphia, PA: Da Capo.

Hjort, Mette and MacKenzie, Scott (2000) *Cinema and Nation*. London: Routledge.

Hoberman, J. (2002) 'The Art of War: How Hollywood Learned to Stop Worrying and Love the Bomb'. *Village Voice*. Available at: http://www.villagevoice.com/2002-06-18/news/the-art-of-war/ (accessed 24 January 2014).

____ (2006) 'Unquiet Americans', *Sight and Sound*, 16, 10, 20–4.

Hofstadter, Richard (2008) *The Paranoid Style in American Politics, and Other Essays*. New York, NY: Vintage Books.

Holloway, David (2008) *9/11 and the War on Terror*. Edinburgh: Edinburgh University Press.

Hollyfield, Jerod Ra'Del (2009) 'Torture Porn and Bodies Politic: Post-Cold War American Perspectives in Eli Roth's *Hostel* and *Hostel: Part II*', *CineAction*, 78, 22–31.

Hufschmid, Eric (2002) *Painful Questions: An Analysis of the September 11th Attack*.

Bibliography

California, CA: Self-published.

Huntington, Samuel P. (2004) *Who Are We?: The Challenges to America's National Identity*. New York, NY: Simon & Schuster.

Hyman, Jonathan (2007) 'The Public Face of 9/11: Memory and Portraiture in the Landscape', *Journal of American History*, 94, 1, 183–92.

Ip, John (2009) 'Two Narratives of Torture', *Northwestern Journal of International Human Rights*, 7, 1, 35–77.

Jaafar, Ali (2006) 'Review: *United 93*', *Sight and Sound*, 16, 7, 80–1.

Jackson, Kathy Merlock (2005) 'Psychological First Aid: The Hallmark Company, Greeting Cards and the Response to September 11', *Journal of American Culture*, 28, 1, 11–28.

James, Nick (2006) 'Editorial: *United 93*', *Sight and Sound*, 39, 5, 3.

____ (2013) 'Editorial: Zero Tolerance', *Sight and Sound*, 23, 2, 9.

Johnson, Chalmers (2002) *Blowback: The Costs and Consequences of American Empire*. London: Time Warner.

Johnstone, Iain (2007) *Tom Cruise, All the World's a Stage*. London: Hodder and Staunton.

Jones, Alex (2002) *9-11: Descent into Tyranny*. California, CA: Progressive Press.

Junod, Tom (2006) 'The Falling Man', *Esquire*. Available at: http://www.esquire.com/features/esq0903-sep_fallingman (accessed 24 January 2014).

Kaplan, Amy (2008) 'In the Name of Security', *Review of International American Studies*, 3, 3, 15–25.

Kaplan, E. Ann (2005) *Trauma Culture: The Politics of Terror and Loss in Media and Literature*. New Brunswick, NJ: Rutgers University Press.

Kara, Selmin (2009) 'Reassembling the Nation: Iraq in Fragments and the Acoustics of Occupation', *Documentary Film*, 3, 3, 259–74.

Kean, Thomas H. and Lee H. Hamilton (2004) *The 9/11 Commission Report: Final Report of the National Commission on Terrorist Attacks upon the United States*. New York, NY: W. W. Norton.

Kellner, Douglas (2003) *9/11 and Terror War: The Dangers of the Bush Legacy*. Lanham, MD: Rowman & Littlefield.

____ (2010) *Cinema Wars: Hollywood Film and Politics in the Bush-Cheney Era*. Malden, MA: Wiley-Blackwell.

Kenisberg, Ben (2011) 'For Your Consideration: *Margaret*', *Time Out*. Available at: http://www.timeoutchicago.com/arts-culture/film/15016655/for-your-consideration-margaret (accessed 24 January 2014).

Kerrigan, John (1996) *Revenge Tragedy: Aeschylus to Armageddon*. Oxford: Clarendon Press.

King, Geoff (2005) '"Just Like a Movie"?: 9/11 and Hollywood Spectacle', Geoff King (ed.) *The Spectacle of the Real: From Hollywood to 'Reality' TV and Beyond*. Bristol: Intellect, 47–59.

Kitch, Carolyn (2003) '"Mourning in America": Ritual, Redemption and Recovery in

News Narrative after September 11', *Journalism Studies*, 4, 2, 213–24.

Knight, Peter (2000) *Conspiracy Culture: American Paranoia from the Kennedy Assassination to The X-Files*. London: Routledge.

____ (2008) 'Outrageous Conspiracy Theories: Popular and Official Responses to 9/11 in Germany and the United States', *New German Critique*, 35, 1, 165–93.

Kolko, Gabriel (2002) *Another Century of War?*. New York, NY: New Press.

Kozaryn, Linda D. (2002) 'Army Declares Black Hawk Down "Authentic"'. *American Forces Press Service*. Available at: http://www.defense.gov/News/NewsArticle. aspx?ID=43855 (accessed 24 January 2014).

Krakau, Knud (1997) *The American Nation, National Identity, Nationalism*. Munster: LIT Verlag.

Landy, Marcia (2004) '"America under Attack": Pearl Harbour, 9/11 and History in the Media', in Wheeler Winston Dixon (ed.) *Film and Television after 9/11*. Carbondale, IL: Southern Illinois University Press, 79–101.

Langewiesche, William (2003) *American Ground: Unbuilding the World Trade Center*. London: Scribner.

Lawrence, John Shelton (2005) 'Rituals of Mourning and National Innocence', *Journal of American Culture*, 28, 1, 35–48.

Lesage, Julia (2009) 'Torture Documentaries', *Jump Cut*. Available at: http://www. ejumpcut.org/archive/jc51.2009/TortureDocumentaries/ (accessed 24 January 2014).

Longley, James (2006) '*Iraq in Fragments* Press Kit', *Iraq in Fragments Official Website*. Available at: http://www.iraqinfragments.com/press/index.html (accessed 24 January 2014).

Luckhurst, Roger (2008) *The Trauma Question*. London: Routledge.

Maas, Peter (2012) 'Don't Trust "Zero Dark Thirty"', *The Atlantic*. Available at: http:// www.theatlantic.com/entertainment/archive/2012/12/dont-trust-zero-dark-thirty/266253/ (accessed 24 January 2014).

Maddrey, Joseph (2004) *Nightmares in Red, White and Blue: The Evolution of the American Horror Film*. Jefferson, NC: McFarland.

Magistrale, Tony (2005) *Abject Terrors: Surveying the Modern and Postmodern Horror Film*. New York, NY: Peter Lang.

Maltby, Richard (1982) *Harmless Entertainment: Hollywood and the Ideology of Consensus*. Metuchen, NJ: Scarecrow.

____ (2003) *Hollywood Cinema*. London: Blackwell.

Marrs, Jim (2003) *The War on Freedom*. Chicago, IL: Ares Publishing.

Martin, Geoff and Steuter, Erin (2010) *Pop Culture Goes to War: Enlisting and Resisting Militarism in the War on Terror*. Lanham, MD: Rowman & Littlefield.

Martyn, Peter H. (2008) 'Lynch Mob: Pack Journalism and How the Jessica Lynch Story Became Propaganda', *Canadian Journal of Media Studies*, 4, 1, 124–64.

Massood, Paula J. (2003) 'Interview with Spike Lee and David Benioff', *Cinéaste*, 28, 3, 4–10.

Bibliography

Mayer, Jane (2004) 'Contract Sport: What Did the Vice-President do for Halliburton?', *New Yorker*. Available at: http://www.newyorker.com/archive/2004/02/16/040216fa_fact (accessed 24 January 2014).

____ (2007) 'Whatever It Takes: The Politics of the Man behind 24'. *New Yorker*. Web. Available at: http://www.newyorker.com/reporting/2007/02/19/070219fa_fact_mayer (accessed 19 February 2014).

____ (2008) *Dark Side: The Inside Story of How the War on Terror Turned into a War on American Ideals*. New York, NY: Doubleday.

McEwan, Ian (2008) 'The Day of Judgment', *The Guardian*. Available at: http://www.theguardian.com/books/2008/may/31/fiction.philosophy (accessed 24 January 2014).

Mellen, Joan (2008) 'Spiraling Downward: America in *Days of Heaven*, *In the Valley of Elah* and *No Country for Old Men*', *Film Quarterly*, 61, 3, 24–31.

Melley, Timothy (2000) *Empire of Conspiracy: The Culture of Paranoia in Postwar America*. Ithaca, NY: Cornell University Press.

Melnick, Jeffrey (2009) *9/11 Culture: America Under Construction*. Malden, MA: Wiley-Blackwell.

Meyerowitz, Joel (2006) *Aftermath*: London: Phaidon.

Miller, David (1995) *On Nationality*. Oxford: Clarendon Press.

Miller, Nancy K. (2003) '"Portraits of Grief": Telling Details and the Testimony of Trauma', *differences: A Journal of Feminist Cultural Studies*, 14, 3, 112–35.

Montgomery, Martin (2005) 'The Discourse of War after 9/11', *Language and Literature*, 14, 2, 149–80.

Morris, Errol (2008) 'Play It Again, Sam (Re-enactments, Part One)', *The New York Times*. Available at: http://opinionator.blogs.nytimes.com/2008/04/03/play-it-again-sam-re-enactments-part-one/?_php=true&_type=blogs&_r=0 (accessed 24 January 2014).

Murphy, John M. (2003) '"Our Mission and Our Moment": George W. Bush and September 11th', *Rhetoric & Public Affairs*, 6, 4, 607–32.

Newman, Kim (2005) 'Review: *War of the Worlds*', *Sight and Sound*, 15, 9, 83–4.

____ (2006) 'Torture Garden', *Sight and Sound*, 16, 6, 28–31.

Olmsted, Kathryn S. (2009) *Real Enemies: Conspiracy Theories and American Democracy, World War I to 9/11*. Oxford: Oxford University Press.

O'Neill, Patricia (2004) 'Where Globalization and Localization Meet: Spike Lee's *25th Hour*', *Cineaction!*, 64, 2–7.

Philpott, Simon (2010) 'Is Anyone Watching? War, Cinema and Bearing Witness', *Cambridge Review of International Affairs*, 23, 2, 325–48.

Pisters, Patricia (2011) 'The Mosaic Film: Nomadic Style and Politics in Transnational Media Culture', in Mieke Bal and Miguel Á. Hernández-Navarro (eds.) *Art and Visibility in Migratory Culture: Conflict, Resistance, and Agency*. Amsterdam: Rodopi, 175–90.

Pollard, Tom (2011) *Hollywood 9/11: Superheroes, Supervillains and Super Disasters*.

Boulder, CO: Paradigm.

Porton, R. (2004) 'Weapon of Mass Instruction: Michael Moore's *Fahrenheit 9/11*', *Cinéaste*, 29, 4, 3–7.

Powers, John (2013) '*Zero Dark Thirty* and the Search for a Best Actress', *Vogue*, December.

Prince, Stephen (2009) *Firestorm: American Film in the Age of Terrorism*. New York, NY: Columbia University Press.

____ (2012) 'American Film after 9/11', in Cynthia A. Barto Lucia, Roy Grundmann and Art Simon (eds) *The Wiley-Blackwell History of American Film*. Oxford: Wiley-Blackwell, 495–513.

Randall, Martin (2010) *9/11 and the Literature of Terror*. Edinburgh: Edinburgh University Press.

Randell, Karen (2010) '"It Was Like a Movie": The Impossibility of Representation in Oliver Stone's *World Trade Center*', Jeff Birkenstein, Anna Froula and Karen Randell (eds) *Reframing 9/11: Film, Popular Culture and the 'War on Terror'*. London: Continuum, 141–53.

Read, Jacinda (2000) *The New Avengers: Feminism, Femininity and the Rape-Revenge Cycle*. Manchester: Manchester University Press.

Redfield, Marc (2009) *The Rhetoric of Terror: Reflections on 9/11 and the War on Terror*. New York, NY: Fordham University Press.

Rejali, Darius M. (2007) *Torture and Democracy*. Princeton, NJ: Princeton University Press.

Renshon, Stanley Allen (2005) *The 50% American: Immigration and National Identity in an Age of Terror*. Washington, DC: Georgetown University Press.

Rich, B. Ruby (2003) 'Revengers Tragedy'. *The Guardian*. Available at: http://www.theguardian.com/film/2003/nov/21/2 (accessed 24 January 2014).

____ (2006) 'Out of the Rubble', *Sight and Sound*, 16, 10, 14–18.

Riegler, Thomas (2011) 'Giving Memory and Meaning to All That "Howling Space" at Ground Zero', *Radical History Review*, 111, 155–65.

Robb, David L. (2004) *Operation Hollywood: How the Pentagon Shapes and Censors the Movies*. Amherst, NY: Prometheus Books.

Robertson, Robert (2009) *Eisenstein on the Audiovisual: The Montage of Music, Image and Sound in Cinema*. London: IB Tauris.

Robson, Daniel (2012) 'Ultimate Spin: *Spider-Man*', *Film Matters*, 3, 4, 50–5.

Rodrigue, Christine M. (2003) 'Representation of the September 11th Terrorist Attacks in the Online Edition of the *Los Angeles Times*', in Jacquelyn L. Monday (ed.) *Beyond September 11th: An Account of Post-Disaster Research*. Colorado: University of Colorado Natural Hazards Research and Applications Information Center Special Publication 39, 521–88.

Rothberg, Michael (2009) 'A Failure of the Imagination: Diagnosing the Post-9/11 Novel: A Response to Richard Gray', *American Literary History*, 21, 1, 151–8.

Rozario, Kevin (2007) *The Culture of Calamity: Disaster and the Making of Modern*

Bibliography

America. Chicago, IL: University of Chicago Press.

Ryan, Michael and Douglas Kellner (1990) *Camera Politica: The Politics and Ideology of Contemporary American Film*. Bloomington, IN: Indiana University Press.

Sales, Nancy Jo (2006) 'Click Here for Conspiracy', *Vanity Fair*. Available at: http://www.vanityfair.com/ontheweb/features/2006/08/loosechange200608 (accessed 24 January 2014).

Sands, Philippe (2008) *Torture Team: Deception, Cruelty and the Compromise of Law*. London: Allen Lane.

Sardar, Ziauddin and Merryl Wyn Davies (2002) *Why Do People Hate America?*. Cambridge: Icon.

Schatz, Thomas (2002) 'Old War/New War: *Band of Brothers* and the Revival of the World War II War Film', *Film and History*, 32, 1, 74–7.

Schneider, Steven Jay (2004) 'Architectural Nostalgia and the New York City Skyline on Film', in Wheeler Winston Dixon (ed.) *Film and Television after 9/11*. Carbondale, IL: Southern Illinois University Press, 29–42.

Scott, A. O. (2010) 'Apolitics and the War Film', *The New York Times*. Available at: http://www.nytimes.com/2010/02/07/weekinreview/07aoscott.html (accessed 24 January 2014).

Seeley, Karen M. (2008) *Therapy After Terror: 9/11, Psychotherapists and Mental Health*. Cambridge: Cambridge University Press.

Shapiro, Michael J. (2011) 'The Presence of War: "Here and Elsewhere"', *International Political Sociology*, 5, 2, 109–25.

Sharrett, Christopher (2009) 'The Problem of *Saw*: "Torture Porn" and the Conservatism of Contemporary Horror Films', *Cinéaste*, 35, 1, 32–7.

Shaviro, Steven (2013) 'A Brief Remark on *Zero Dark Thirty*', *The Pinocchio Theory*. Available at: http://www.shaviro.com/Blog/?p=1114 (accessed 24 January 2014).

Simpson, David (2006) *9/11: The Culture of Commemoration*. Chicago, IL: University of Chicago Press.

Slocum, David (2011) '9/11 Film and Media Scholarship', *Cinema Journal*, 51, 1, 181–93.

Slotkin, Richard (2000) *Regeneration Through Violence: The Mythology of the American Frontier, 1600–1860*. Norman, OK: University of Oklahoma Press.

Smith, Dennis (2002) *Report from Ground Zero: The Heroic Story of the Rescuers at the World Trade Center*. London: Doubleday.

Sontag, Susan (2001) 'Talk of the Town', *The New Yorker*. Available at: http://www.newyorker.com/archive/2001/09/24/010924ta_talk_wtc (accessed 24 January 2014).

____ (2003) *Regarding the Pain of Others*. London: Hamish Hamilton.

Sorkin, Michael and Zukin, Sharon (2002) *After the World Trade Center: Rethinking New York City*. New York, NY: Routledge.

Sprengler, Christine (2009) *Screening Nostalgia: Populuxe Props and Technicolor*

Aesthetics in Contemporary American Film. New York, NY: Berghahn Books.

Stearnes, Peter (2006) *American Fear: The Causes and Consequences of High Anxiety*. London: Routledge.

Stiglitz, Joseph E. and Linda Bilmes (2008) *The Three Trillion Dollar War: The True Cost of the Iraq Conflict*. New York, NY: W. W. Norton.

Stuckey, M. E. (2007) 'Michael Moore's *Fahrenheit 9/11*: How One Film Divided a Nation', *Journal of American History*, 93, 4, 1327–8.

Sturken, Marita (1997) *Tangled Memories: The Vietnam War, the AIDS Epidemic, and the Politics of Remembering*. Berkeley, CA: University of California Press.

Sullivan, Robert (2001) *In the Land of the Free: September 11 and After*. New York, NY: Time Inc.

Swartz, Anne K. (2006) 'American Art after September 11: A Consideration of the Twin Towers', *Symploke*, 14, 1–2, 81–97.

Sweet, Christopher (2002) *Above Hallowed Ground: A Photographic Record of September 11, 2001 by Photographers of the New York City Police Department*. New York, NY: Viking Studio.

Thompson, Anne (2002) 'Films with War Themes Are Victims of Bad Timing'. *New York Times*. Available at: http://www.nytimes.com/2002/10/17/movies/films-with-war-themes-are-victims-of-bad-timing.html (accessed 24 January 2014).

Thompson, Damian (2008) *Counterknowledge: How We Surrendered to Conspiracy Theories, Quack Medicine, Bogus Science and Fake History*. London: Atlantic.

Thompson, Kirsten Moana (2007) *Apocalyptic Dread: American Film at the Turn of the Millennium*. Albany, NY: State University of New York Press.

Thorburn, Nicholas (2007) 'Post-Hegemony: I Don't Think So', *Theory, Culture and Society*, 24, 3, 95–110.

Toplin, Robert Brent (2005) 'The Long Battle over *Fahrenheit 9/11*: A Matter of Politics, Not Aesthetics', *Film and History*, 35, 2, 8–10.

Torgovnick, Marianna (2005) *The War Complex: World War II in Our Time*. Chicago, IL: Chicago University Press.

Trifonova, Temenuga (2012) 'Agency in the Cinematic Conspiracy Thriller', *SubStance*, 41, 3, 109–26.

Valantin, Jean-Michel (2005) *Hollywood, the Pentagon and Washington*. London: Anthem.

Versluys, Kristiaan (2009) *Out of the Blue: September 11 and the Novel*. New York, NY: Columbia University Press.

Vest, Jason (2006) 'Future's End: Steven Spielberg's *War of the Worlds* (2005)', *Film and History*, 36, 1, 67–70.

Vincent, Jonathan (2010) 'Left Behind in America: The Army of One at the End of History', Jeff Birkenstein, Anna Froula and Karen Randell (eds.) *Reframing 9/11: Film, Popular Culture and the 'War on Terror'*. London: Continuum, 45–57.

Vishnevetsky, Ignatiy (2012) 'The Monitor Mentality, or a Means to an End Becomes an End in Itself: Kathryn Bigelow's *Zero Dark Thirty*', *MUBI*. Available at: https://

Bibliography

mubi.com/notebook/posts/the-monitor-mentality-or-a-means-to-an-end-be-comes-an-end-in-itself-kathryn-bigelows-zero-dark-thirty (accessed 24 January 2014).

Weber, Cynthia (2005) *Imagining America at War: Morality, Politics and Film*. London: Routledge.

____ (2006) '*Fahrenheit 9/11*: The Temperature Where Morality Burns', *Journal of American Studies*, 40, 1, 113–31.

____ (2011) '*I am an American*': *Filming the Fear of Difference*. Bristol: Intellect.

Wegner, Phillip E. (2009) *Life Between Two Deaths, 1989–2001: US Culture in the Long Nineties*. Durham, NC: Duke University Press.

Westwell, Guy (2006) *War Cinema: Hollywood on the Front Line*. London and New York: Wallflower Press.

____ (2008) 'One Image Begets Another: A Comparative Analysis of "Flag-Raising on Iwo Jima" and "Ground Zero Spirit"', *Journal of War and Culture Studies*, 1, 3, 325–40.

____ (2013) 'In Country: Narrating the Iraq War in Contemporary US Cinema', Robert A. Rosenstone and Constantin Parvulescu (eds.) *A Companion to the Historical Film*. Wiley-Blackwell, 384–407.

Wetmore, Kevin J. (2012) *Post-9/11 Horror in American Cinema*. New York, NY: Continuum.

Wheeler, Mark (2006) *Hollywood: Politics and Society*. London: British Film Institute.

Williams, Linda (2010) 'Cluster Fuck: The Forcible Frame in Errol Morris's *Standard Operating Procedure*', *Camera Obscura*, 25, 173, 29–67.

Williams, Linda Ruth and Michael Hammond (2006) *Contemporary American Cinema*. Maidenhead: Open University Press.

Willis, Susan (2005) *Portents of the Real: A Primer for Post-9/11 America*. London: Verso.

Winter, Jessica (2006) 'Roll Call of the Dead', *Sight and Sound*, 16, 6, 15.

Wood, Robin (1986) *Hollywood from Vietnam to Reagan*. New York, NY: Columbia University Press.

Wootton, Adrian (2003) 'Play Madigan for Me', *Sight and Sound*, 13, 11, 12–14.

Young, Marilyn B. (2003) 'In the Combat Zone', *Radical History Review*, 85, 253–64.

Zimbardo, Philip G. (2007) *The Lucifer Effect: Understanding How Good People Turn Evil*. New York, NY: Random House.

Zizek, Slavoj (2013) '*Zero Dark Thirty*: Hollywood's Gift to American Power'. *The Guardian*. Web. Available at: http://www.theguardian.com/commentisfree/2013/jan/25/zero-dark-thirty-normalises-torture-unjustifiable (accessed 24 January 2014).

Zuber, Devin (2006) 'Flânerie at Ground Zero: Aesthetic Countermemories in Lower Manhattan', *American Quarterly*, 58, 2, 269–99.

Index

Index